The
Book
of
Origins

The
Book
of
Origins

TREVOR HOMER

PORTRAIT

Visit the Portrait website!

Copyright © 2006 by Trevor Homer

First published in 2006 by **Portrait**, an imprint of
Piatkus Books Limited
5 Windmill Street
London W1T 2JA
e-mail: info@piatkus.co.uk

The moral right of the author has been asserted

A catalogue record for this book is available from the British Library

ISBN 0 7499 5110 9

Design and typesetting by Paul Saunders
Additional illustrations by Alison Sturgeon

This book has been printed on paper manufactured with respect for the environment using wood from managed sustainable resources

Printed and bound in Great Britain by MPG Books Ltd, Bodmin, Cornwall

CONTENTS

Acknowledgements

My thanks are due to the many hundreds of specialists who compile reference works. The *Encyclopaedia Britannica* has been my Bible and Google is God. The British Library has been a second home for two years and the library of the Wellcome Trust, the greatest depository of medical knowledge in the world, has provided me with all I could ever need about the origins of medicine.

I thank John Connolly (in memoriam) who first said I should, Bill Taylor who said it second and Keith Ward who said it third.

I have been fortunate to have Andrew Lownie as my agent. He gave me the unfailing encouragement and support that all writers need, and indeed crave, and found my publisher, Portrait.

My thanks also to Stephanie Hale, David Haviland and Carl Cutler who edited my manuscript with sympathy and consummate skill. They corrected mistakes and improved my English. Any errors remaining are entirely my own. Among the many who responded to my emails, special thanks to April Ashley and Herbert Deutsch who helped me with dates.

I am particularly indebted to Alan Brooke at Portrait who kept me on track if I began to deviate.

I would like to thank my dear sister Dianne who did the early reading. It couldn't have been easy.

I have been lucky that Susan, to whom I have been married for thirty years, never lost faith, allowed me to work late and came up with the chicken and egg cover concept. I am aware of the sacrifices, and you were always there.

I dedicate this book to my two
exceptional sons, Max and James.
This is for you.

INTRODUCTION

E VERYTHING HAS AN ORIGIN. This book is for people who want to know how and when things began, where they came from, and why they started. It celebrates the work of explorers, scientists and inventors, pioneers who wanted to go further than anyone had gone before them – people who wanted to know what was over the next hill or beyond the ocean – people who wanted to know how the world works and ended up discovering or inventing something that no one had ever seen before.

Some things have an entirely unsuspected origin, for example the Hollywood 'tough guy' career of James Cagney (*see* Famous People p. 106), and other origins have been wrongly attributed to famous people. Hedy Lamarr, the great beauty and Hollywood star of the 1930s, invented something that affects almost all our everyday lives, which could have brought her a major fortune. She earned not a penny from it (*see* Communication p. 33 and War p. 302).

Ancient cave painters began something that led to the sublime work of Michelangelo and Leonard da Vinci. Everyday items such as the clothes we wear, the food we eat, the phones we use, the televisions we watch, the medicines that cure us, the sports we play, the languages we use, as well as capitalism, began somewhere.

From the simple hunting and gathering activities of the earliest ape-like creatures, through to the advances made by today's sophisticated human beings, the pace of development has been astonishing, and it all had an origin. We human beings, alone among the animals, changed cosmic dust into axes, motorcars, palaces, films, computers, perfumes and sausages (*see* Food and Drink p. 119).

We even started religions, wars and political parties. We human beings, without any innate ability to take to the air, have developed machines to fly to the other side of the world in the same time it used to take our grandparents to cross a couple of shires (*see* Transport). Human beings invented a device that enables a person, at the touch of just a few buttons, to speak to another person in the furthest places of the world. Human beings watched on live television as men walked on the surface of the moon; and, most importantly, human beings routinely cure diseases that once killed millions (*see* Health p. 135).

We invented abstract thought, such as philosophy or budgeting. The signs for add, subtract, multiply and divide, which are so much a part of our existence that we most likely never even think about them, began somewhere. We also invented question marks, poison gas and money. None of it, not even the Beatles (originally the Quarrymen), came to us fully formed. Some of the things we look at, such as frozen peas or the second New Zealand – that is the New Zealand that disappeared off the map in 1792 (*see* Countries and Empires p. 50) – have little to do with human creativity.

So, where has it all come from? What are the origins? The Chinese have an elegant proverb: 'With time and patience, a mulberry leaf becomes a silk gown.'

Looking at a silk gown, and knowing nothing about the digestive systems of silk worms or their diet, who could imagine such a beautiful object could owe its origin to a simple mulberry leaf?

From Art to War, via Sport, Language and Buildings with some Crime and Sex thrown in, let's take a look at their origins.

ART

COVERING: Painting, Sculpture, Music, Opera, Poetry and Literature, Dance.

All art has this characteristic – it unites people.
LEO TOLSTOY (1828–1910)

PAINTING

Most people associate painting and art so closely that they are almost interchangeable, so it is appropriate that painting is the first of the art forms.

Cave Painting

The earliest of all art forms, cave painting dates from approximately 40000 BC. An explosion of creativity started around 35000 BC, lasting to about 14000 BC until it ceased completely in 10000 BC. This is known as the Upper Palaeolithic period.

The Western European cave artists are unknown by name, but are referred to generally as the Magdalenians, after one of the sites, La Madelaine, in the Dordogne region of France. They mainly painted animals to a large scale, including now extinct species such as the woolly mammoth and the woolly rhinoceros. They also painted human hands and used signs and geometric shapes, but they did not depict ceremonial or sacrificial events. The main colours used were black and red, with some white, brown and yellow.

The sheer scale of some of the paintings and the fact that they appear on inaccessible surfaces high up in the roofs of caves suggest that it is entirely possible the artists were professionals, who were rewarded for their efforts, rather than undertaking the work for personal pleasure.

There is evidence from socket holes in the cave walls that some of the painting required scaffolding and platforms to execute the work. It is now believed that the artists could have been part of an organised studio system, which provided the decorations for the occupants.

The first discovery of cave painting was made at Alta Mira, near Santander, in northern Spain in 1879 by Maria de Sautuola, a nine-year-old girl who was helping her father, a local archaeologist, to explore a cave system in search of ancient bones. Walking ahead of her father she became the first person for more than 30,000 years to see what is regarded by experts as some of the finest cave art so far discovered. The roof of the main cave is covered with paintings of wild boar, bison, a deer and some horses, executed in vivid red, violet and black. The artist also left hand-prints and hand outlines, as if signing the work.

Australian cave art Cave paintings have also been discovered on the Arnhem Land Peninsula in Australia, and these may be older than the European examples. Some sources speculate that Australian cave art may span the whole period of human habitation on Australia, some 60,000 years. Traditional subject matters are still painted today by Aboriginal men.

British cave art Until recently it was thought that Britain had no cave art. However, in 2003, bas-reliefs and paintings were discovered at Church Hole Cave on the Nottinghamshire–Derbyshire border. They were dated at 15,000 years old and are now regarded as being among the best examples in existence.

Ancient Greek Painting

Despite their fondness for sculpture, the ancient Greeks regarded painting as the highest of the art forms. The main painting surface was the wooden panel. These deteriorated over time and unfortunately no examples have survived.

The first painter to indicate perspective in his works was Polygnotus of Thasos (fifth century BC). His paintings were still being admired 600 years after his death, but none of his works has survived.

Oil Painting

From the time of the ancient Greeks the chemistries of art and medicine were closely related and were often discussed in the same books.

Oil paint developed from 'drying oils', which were originally used for dressing wounds. The oils were also used to form a protective cover or varnish on paintings. Experimentation with pigments enabled colour to be added.

The Van Eyck brothers (Hubert 1370–1426, Jan 1390–1441), who came from Maseyck near Liege in Flanders (present-day Belgium), are credited by some authorities with refining the process, until oil paint provided a flexible medium suitable for painting whole pictures.

Chinese Painting

The Chinese method of drawing or painting, with an unbroken tradition of more than 2,000 years, is to use ink or watercolour on silk or paper.

The earliest known example of Chinese painting was excavated from a tomb dating from the time of the Western Han Dynasty, which ruled China from 206 BC to AD 9. The painting is known as the *Mawangdui Banner* and is presently in the Hunan Museum.

Oil painting was introduced to China during the early Qing Dynasty (AD 1644–1911) by Jesuit priests employed in the Court of the Emperor, but it never became more than a novelty.

Frescoes

The term fresco refers to the application of paint to fresh plaster or mortar. As the plaster dries, it absorbs the pigment of the paint, which then becomes part of the plaster. As a result, frescoes are far more durable than ordinary paintings.

The earliest frescoes discovered so far date from 1700–1400 BC. They were found in King Minos's palace on the island of Crete.

The ceiling of the Sistine Chapel, painted by Michelangelo (AD 1475–1546), is an example of Italian Renaissance fresco work.

Mosaic

The first known mosaics were terracotta cones which were embedded into the outer walls of buildings during the third millennium BC in Uruk (present-day Warka in Iraq). The cones were placed with the blunt end outermost providing additional protection for the sun-dried bricks, which were the main building material. The red, white and black cones were arranged to form geometric patterns.

Pebble mosaic was developed during the eighth century BC around Ankara (in present-day Turkey). It was laid on the floor to provide a hard-wearing surface.

Greek mosaic The ancient Greeks refined the use of mosaics, and during the fifth century BC began to produce floor mosaic as we would recognise it today. The best-preserved examples are in Motya Morgantine in Sicily.

Roman mosaic began in the second century BC. The Romans largely copied the Greeks and began the process of turning mosaic from an exclusively upper-class art to a commonplace floor decoration.

SCULPTURE

The earliest known of all sculptures or carvings is the Willendorf Venus, found close to the town of Willendorf in Austria in 1908. Dated at between 10,000 and 25,000 years old, the figure is carved from limestone and stands only a few inches high, representing a Stone Age woman, and is understood to be a fertility symbol. The face is obscured but the buttocks, breasts and genitalia are exaggerated out of all proportion.

There are several other carvings of the same period, Venus of Kostienski, Venus of Maina, Venus of Malta, Venus of Avdeevo and other Venuses, all of which exhibit the same exaggerated features.

Ivory carvings were produced in ancient Egypt between 4000 and 3200 BC. Civilisation in ancient Egypt was highly religious and this was reflected in the subject matters of their carvings, which generally depicted gods and goddesses.

Gigantic monolithic (massive stone) sculptures with a mainly ritual significance rather than having aesthetic merit began to appear in ancient Egypt between 3200 and 2780 BC. The Great Sphinx of Giza has been variously dated between 3000 and 2500 BC.

Greek Sculpture

By the fifth century BC the ancient Greeks were creating sophisticated sculptures of the human form. The statues were shown in sporting and heroic poses, and the leading Greek sculptors were the first to display emotions in their figures. Before the Greeks, the faces of all sculptures were left frozen and without displaying any feeling.

For the first time, the names of sculptors became known. Phidias (*c.*490–*c.*430 BC), who designed many of the works surrounding the Parthenon in Athens, is generally regarded as the greatest of the Classical Period Greek sculptors.

Praxiteles, probably the greatest of the fourth-century BC Greek sculptors, introduced the concepts of grace and sensuous charm into his sculpt-ures. His statue of the naked goddess, Aphrodite of Cnidus, was a bold innovation, and was thought by the Roman historian Pliny the Elder (AD 23–79) to be the greatest statue in the world.

Roman Sculpture

Around 1000 BC the Villanovan civilisation, living in the region of present-day Bologna, began to produce small bronze and terracotta statues for symbolic purposes. Regular changes in style occurred until fine Roman sculptures in bronze and clay, such as the *Reclining Couple*, presently in the National Museum of Rome, emerged in the sixth century BC.

The Romans closely followed the Greeks in their sculpture of the human form. These sculptures, usually in stern heroic poses, gave the people an opportunity to see what their leaders and heroes looked like, as there was little opportunity to see them in the flesh.

Chinese Sculpture

In ancient Chinese culture, any creative activity that involved physical labour was not considered one of the fine arts; sculptors were regarded as mere craftsmen, and few of their names are known. The earliest carved jade figures date from 3400 BC and there are stone figurines from the eighteenth century BC, the Shang Dynasty. They were intended for use as funerary objects, and generally the subject matters were small animals and birds.

China's most famous statues – the serried ranks of 8,000 life-size statues of soldiers, known as the Terracotta Army – were begun in 240 BC. The first Chinese Emperor, Qin Shi Huangdi (259–210 BC), commissioned the sculptures. He died at the age of 50 and the statues of the soldiers in battle-ready formation, all with individually moulded facial features and hairstyles, were buried with him to protect him in the afterlife. Work on the statues by 700,000 conscripts took 30 years to complete. Also known as the Terracotta Warriors, the statues were chanced upon in 1974 near to the city of Xi'an in central China, by villagers digging in a field to sink a well.

MUSIC

Music is the shorthand of emotion.
LEO TOLSTOY (1828–1910)

Musical Notation

The earliest song to have been written down is a Syrian cult hymn, the Hymn to Creation, written in cuneiform (*see* Communication p. 33) and has been dated at between 3,400 and 4,000 years old.

The ancient Greeks were the first to develop a system of symbols to make a record of musical sounds. Music was annotated by the use of two different systems of letters for instrumental and vocal music. Boethius

(AD 470–525) wrote five textbooks on music theory, developing a system of annotation using the first 15 letters of the alphabet.

Gregorian chant was developed by Pope Gregory I (the Great) (AD 540–604) during his papacy from AD 590 to 604. The original annotation of Gregorian chant used neumes, which are small marks above the text to indicate the shape of a piece of music. Neumes are thought to have derived from symbols in the Greek language, and modern musical notation is derived from them.

The first published musical score was written in 1581 by Vincenzo Galilei, the father of Galileo, who was a famous performer on the lute and a singer–songwriter.

Scales were invented in the eleventh century by Guido d'Arrezzo (c.991–c.1033). His system of naming scale degrees used the initial syllables of the lines of a Latin hymn (*ut, re, mi, fa, sol, la*). This was the origin of the eight-note scale (the octave) now used in Western music (the tonic sol–fa) and made world famous by the film *The Sound of Music* – doh, ray, me, fah, soh, lah, te, doh.

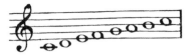

Arabian Music

Nothing is known of Arabian music before AD 622, but it flourished under various caliphs (Islamic rulers claiming descent from the Prophet Muhammad) from 661 to 750, using complex tonal colours and constantly changing rhythms.

Chinese Music

Chinese music dates back to the dawn of civilisation in China, and by 1100 BC there was a well-established culture of stylised musical theatre, in which the music was only one of the elements, not the principal one. The Chinese Imperial Music Bureau was established between 221 and 207 BC, during the Qin Dynasty.

Musical Instruments

The first known musical instrument is the flute played by Neanderthal Man. The earliest examples have been dated at between 43,000 and 82,000 years old, and one ancient bone flute has been discovered with holes spaced for half tones. The Egyptians, Etruscans and ancient Greeks all played flutes, sometimes with the nose.

The earliest known drums were excavated in Moravia (eastern part of the Czech Republic) and date from 6000 BC. These examples are hollowed-out tree trunks, having a membrane of fish or reptile skin stretched across the open ends.

The earliest Chinese musical instrument is a globular clay ocarina (a simple wind instrument) from 5000 BC.

Pan pipes that date from 2500 BC have been found on the Cyclades in the Greek islands.

The first string instrument was the lyre which dates from 2000 BC in Mesopotamia and ancient Greece. Homer describes Achilles making and playing a lyre, which was used to accompany popular songs in the way the modern guitar is used.

According to the myth, Nero was 'fiddling' while Rome burned. In fact he was plucking a lyre, as there were no violins (fiddles) in those days. All string instruments were struck or plucked, until the bow was developed in the Middle Ages.

The organ was invented in 246 BC. We actually know the inventor's name: Ctesibius of Alexandria (*c*.285–222 BC). The organ, known as a hydraulis, used the pressure of water to maintain a continuous sound. An example of a Ctesibius organ dating from 228 BC has been discovered close to Budapest, having survived a recent house fire there. The bellows had been destroyed in the fire, but the rest was in good condition. Ctesibius also invented the keyboard, the bellows, compressed air, moving statues, automatic doors and the clepsydra (a water clock, which was not surpassed in accuracy for more than a thousand years).

The **piano** was invented in Italy in 1700 by Bartolomeo Cristofori (1655–1732).

The origin of the violin cannot be established with any certainty. The closest dating is the first half of the sixteenth century, when Andrea Amati (*c*.1511–*c*.1580) of Cremona, Italy, was asked to produce a stringed instrument for the Medici family. He was also asked to design an instrument that could be played by street musicians, and came up with the violin. It became an instant success, and some Amati violins from 1564 survive today.

The saxophone was invented in 1846 by Adolphe Sax (1814–94), a Belgian musical instrument maker.

The first electrical musical instrument was the Telharmonium (also known as the Dynamophone), which was patented in 1897 by lawyer Thaddeus Cahil (1867–1934) of the United States. The Telharmonium weighed in at over two hundred tons, and Cahil demonstrated it for the first time in public at Holyoke, Massachusetts, in 1906. He went on to build a further two instruments.

The music was created electro-mechanically, not electronically.

Performance

Singers

Primitive man sang to invoke his gods and to celebrate rites of passage.

Orchestras

Large groups of instruments making up orchestras were a seventeenth-century development. Until that time, music had been played in small ensembles with no need to specify what instrument was to play which notes. As the numbers of musicians grew, orchestration became vital to prevent a complete shambles of sound.

The first example of large-scale orchestration was employed for performances in 1615 of Giovanni Gabrieli's (1555–1612) *Sacrae Symphoniae*, which he composed in 1597. Orchestras as we would recognise them today became fully developed in the late eighteenth century.

Early orchestras that survive today:

Orchestra	Date of Inception
Mannheim	1741
Leipzig Gewandhaus	1742
London Philharmonic	1813
Paris Conservatoire	1828
Vienna Philharmonic	1842
New York Philharmonic	1842
St Louis Philharmonic	1880
Boston Philharmonic	1881
Berlin Philharmonic	1882
Chicago Philharmonic	1891

Conductors

Conducting developed in the Middle Ages and was known as cheironomy, which was the use of hand gestures to indicate melodic shape.

The first well-known conductor was Johann Stamitz of the Mannheim Orchestra in the eighteenth century.

Conductors began to use batons to beat time in the early nineteenth century. Before that, they used a variety of devices including rolled-up papers or a conducting staff, which they would beat rhythmically on the floor. In 1687, Jean-Baptiste Lully (1632–87) of the Paris Opera hit himself in the foot with his conducting staff and died when the wound turned gangrenous.

OPERA

Developing out of Italian music, opera has a long history dating back to St Ambrose (AD 340–97), the Bishop of Milan and adviser to the Emperor Gratian (AD 359–83). Ambrose imported Syrian musical practices and wrote hymns. He also developed plainsong, now known as Ambrosian Chant, out of the Coptic, Byzantine, Jewish and Hindu chanting traditions.

The Play of Daniel (also known as Ludus Danieli) was a twelfth-century musical drama by an unknown composer, and is very close to being an opera. It originated at Beauvais Cathedral in northern France, and presented familiar episodes from the Book of Daniel.

The oldest surviving opera is *Euridici* by Jacopo Peri (1561–1633) and Octavio Rinuccini (1562–1621). It was performed in Florence in 1600 and had developed from carnival songs and madrigals, which emerged in the fifteenth and sixteenth centuries. Peri and Rinuccini had previously co-operated with Jacopo Corsi (1561–1602) to produce an earlier opera, *Dafne*, but this has not survived.

In the same year another opera, *Rappresentatzione di Anima e di Corpo*, by Emelio de Cavalieri was performed in Rome.

The world's first purpose-built opera house was the Teatro Farnese in Parma, Italy. It opened to the public in 1628 after taking ten years to be built.

The first English opera was *The Siege of Rhodes* by Sir William d'Avenant (1606–1668) in 1656. England's first professional actress, Mrs Coleman, took part.

The D'Oyly Carte Opera Company was set up to manage the first Gilbert & Sullivan operettas in the 1880s. In 1887 Richard D'Oyly Carte built the Royal English Opera House, which is now the Palace Theatre, London.

POETRY AND LITERATURE

'If poetry comes not as naturally as leaves to a tree,
it had better not come at all.
JOHN KEATS (1795–1821)

The five main influences from the ancient civilisations were Babylon, Egypt, Greece, Rome and the Israelites. The Babylonians produced the oldest written narrative, the epic *Gilgamesh*, which dates from 2000 BC and is recorded in verse. The Egyptians had a view of a supernatural world, which they recorded in the earliest known books: the Egyptian papyrus rolls and clay tablets of Mesopotamia.

The earliest poetry in the form of epic poems, such as *Gilgamesh*, seems to have developed out of oral history and storytelling, which began long before man could write. Storytellers would rely on stock phrases, fixed rhythms and rhyme as an aid to memory.

Jewish (Hebrew) Literature

With a history going back more than 3,000 years the earliest texts in Jewish literature date from 1200 BC. Twenty of the Bible's Old Testament books were written between 1200 and 587 BC. The literature was mostly written in Hebrew, although Greek, Aramaic and Arabian languages were also used.

The earliest examples of Jewish literature are some of the books of the Old Testament in the Bible and the Apocrypha, the hidden stories, which were handed down as teachings for future generations. The main influence of ancient Hebrew literature, which dates from 1200 BC, came from the writings in the Old Testament of the Christian Bible, and some of the conversations seem to be attempts to reproduce in writing the style of everyday speech.

The Talmud, one of Judaism's sacred books, was compiled between the first and sixth centuries AD as the written record of the oral traditions. The Talmud remains the principal authority on Jewish ethics, law and customs.

Greek Literature

Modern Western literature derives from the Greek model. Although only a small amount survives, few doubt that the Greeks invented the literary genres of the epic, drama, history (as opposed to chronicling), poetry and oratory. The first prose writer was Pherecydes of Syros, whose work dates from *c.* 550 BC.

Greek literature had few influences from other sources.

The oldest of all surviving poems are works in ancient Greek by Homer and Hesiod (*c.*700 BC). The *Iliad* and *Odyssey*, attributed to Homer, were probably written down in the mid-eighth century BC. They were the principal Greek records of the Trojan War and arose out of a long oral storytelling tradition.

There is not a great deal known about Homer, although he is generally thought to have been a blind poet who made his home on the Greek island of Chios and may well have dictated the poems to others to write down. Around the same period Hesiod wrote two epics: the *Theogony*, designed to instruct readers in the ways of the gods, and the *Works and Days*, describing peasant life.

The first great writer of tragedy was Sophocles (496–405 BC) who won the dramatic competition in Athens 24 times. He wrote 130 plays of which only seven survive, the greatest of which is considered to be *Oedipus Tyrannus.*

The first great woman poet was Sappho (610–580 BC), who was born on the island of Lesbos. In her work, she expressed feelings of tenderness and passionate love for other women, from which the term 'lesbian' has derived. Historians have speculated that Sappho may have written her work not for herself but to help others, particularly less articulate men, who may have been seeking ways to express themselves poetically to an admired woman. (*see also* Homosexual Sex p. 234)

Latin (Roman) Literature

Lucius Livius Andronicus (284–204 BC), the first great Latin writer, was actually a Greek. He translated Homer's *Odyssey* into Latin and, inspired by Homer's massive vocabulary, wrote many other works of his own coining new Latin words and phrases. He was an immense influence on writers who followed, such as Plautus (254–184 BC) who wrote comic plays, and Naevius (264–291 BC), who was an influential dramatic poet.

Chinese Literature

Chinese literature began around 3,000 years ago and has the longest continuous history of any literature in the world. The earliest known texts are records of divinations of the future, carried out for imperial rulers. In contrast to other great literary cultures, Chinese literature did not make use of mythology or great epics. The main subject matters were religious and philosophical thought.

The first anthology of Chinese poetry is the *Shih Ching* containing religious and folk songs. It was produced between *c.*550 BC and *c.*480 BC, during the Chou Dynasty (1111–255 BC).

The five classics of Chinese literature are:

Shih Ching	poetry
I Ching	changes (fortune telling)
Shu Ching	history
Li Ching	rites
Ch'un-Ch'iu	spring and autumn

Japanese Literature

Chinese writing heavily influenced Japanese literature, and, in fact, the earliest Japanese texts were written in Chinese. The first examples date from AD 440 and are inscribed on ceremonial swords.

Arabian Literature

The earliest known form of Arabian literature is the heroic poetry of the so-called 'noble tribes' of pre-Islamic Arabia (before AD 622). It is known to Muslims as the *Jahiliyyah* or the Period of Ignorance and the literature was recorded only two centuries later, in the *Mu'allaqat*, a group of seven long poems, and the *Mufaddaliyat*, a collection of 126 poems dating from AD 500.

Often considered as the greatest of the poets of the *Jahiliyyah* was Zuhayr (AD 520–609), who wrote in minute detail about the everyday life of the Bedouin. The standard Arabic verse is the *Qasidah*, a long poem, often reciting incidents from the poet's life or that of his tribe.

Pre-Islamic poetry was preserved orally until the late seventh century when Arab scholars undertook the mammoth task of collecting and recording verses that had survived only in the memories of the reciters. The Golden Age of Arabian literature began after the rise of Islam in 622.

English Literature

The origins of English literature are found in the Old English alliterative verse written by Caedmon, who wrote *The Hymn of Creation* in the seventh century AD. Caedmon was mentioned in *The Ecclesiastical History of the English People* written by the Venerable Bede (AD 673–735) in the eighth century. According to Bede, Caedmon was an uneducated herdsman who received a divine call in later life, became a monk, and began to write poetry in vernacular language.

The oldest surviving Anglo-Saxon epic poem is *Beowulf*. It was written sometime around the tenth century AD, and describes the adventures of a Scandinavian warrior of the sixth century. Beowulf is the earliest poem in what could be described as early English and the only surviving text was almost destroyed when the Cotton Library at Ashburnam House caught fire on 23 October 1731.

The first novel written in English is said to be *The Unfortunate Traveller or The Life of Jacke Wilton*, a picaresque story written by Thomas Nashe (1567–1601) that was published in 1594.

The first detective novel is widely regarded to be *The Woman in White*, written in 1860 by Wilkie Collins (1824–89). Collins was famous for his formula for writing a best-selling novel – not giving the end away until the very last moment. The principal reason for this was the Victorian publishers' requirement for novels to be published in three volumes. No hint of a resolution could be given until the third volume had been produced. Collins summed up the principle when he said: 'You make 'em laugh, you make 'em cry, but most of all … you make 'em wait.'

Irish Literature

The earliest surviving examples of Irish literature are the Ogham inscriptions of AD 300 to AD 500. These inscriptions were carved into tombstones and other funerary items in Celtic, which had been introduced to Ireland in the third century BC.

Ogham script is a unique writing system that uses sets of one to five dots for vowels, and combinations of parallel lines for consonants. The origin of Ogham is uncertain, but according to Irish legend it was created by the Irish god Ogma.

The earliest known Irish poem is a eulogy to St Columba (AD 512–97) thought to have been written by Dallan Forgaill, the chief poet of Ireland, in the eighth century.

The famous illustrated manuscript known as *The Book of Kells* was begun around AD 750 in the monastery of Iona. The manuscript contains the four gospels and some Hebrew names. It is thought the book was most likely captured by the Vikings and transferred to Kells in County Meath and completed in the ninth century.

Korean Literature

The earliest known examples of Korean literature are the religious songs that were performed in Korea before 57 BC. The Golden Age of Korean literature dates from 57 BC to AD 668 during the period of the Three Kingdoms.

DANCE

Dance is the only art of which we ourselves are the stuff of which it is made.
TED SHAWN (1891–1972)

The earliest dance is shown in the cave paintings that date from BC 40,000–10,000 BC at Les Trois Frères in southern France. Half-human figures wearing animal costumes are shown in dancing poses.

From as early as 5000 BC there are clay figurines shown with their hands raised above their heads that indicate dance formed part of religious activity in ancient Egypt. Tomb carvings of around 3500 BC depict masked dancers with the priest or king dancing to represent a god.

The oldest surviving European dance is the Austrian–Bavarian Schuh-plattler (the shoe-slapping dance), which is thought by historians to date from Neolithic times around 3000 BC. In the Schuhplattler, the man lifts his feet to knee height to slap his shoes, and the woman spins round on the spot.

Ballet

Although the Romans had a form of ballet called *Fabulae Atellanae,* it was not until the sixteenth century that ballet began to emerge out of lavish masquerades, which were balls where everyone wore a mask, and mum-meries – festivals during which people went about the streets in disguise.

The first ballet combining all the elements of movement, music, decor and special effects was *Le Ballet Comique de La Reine,* which was per-formed in 1581 for Catherine de Medici (1519–87), Queen of France. The ballet was performed at the Valois court, and is the first known work to have combined dance, verse and music into a coherent whole.

The first set of principles governing ballet was *Orchesographie,* written by Thoinot Arbeau in 1588.

The first ballet school was the Academy of the Art of Dancing, started in Paris in 1661 by Louis XIV, King of France.

The first time women were allowed to dance ballet in public was in 1681 at the Paris Opera (strangely, this is the name of the Paris ballet company).

The artistic positions of ballet were set out in *Letters on Dancing and Ballet,* published in 1760 by Jean-Georges Noverre (1727–1810). Noverre was the major modern reformer of ballet, and by 1773 it had developed into the form of dance spectacle performed nowadays.

Buildings

We shape our buildings. Thereafter, they shape us.
Sir Winston Churchill (1874–1965)

Construction of the first buildings marks the change from prehistoric man's dependence on caves for his dwellings to his ability to create a controlled environment for himself. Man began to experiment with building shelters 80,000 years ago.

The first human shelters were very simple, and excavations at several sites in Europe have revealed rings of stones that are believed to have formed part of temporary shelters dating from around 12,000 BC. In the late Stone Age, the hunter-gatherers moved across a wide area and built these shelters, which are the earliest buildings so far discovered by archaeologists. It is thought the stones acted as supports for wooden poles for these basic huts, which were roofed with animal skins.

Britain's (probable) earliest house dated at 10,000 years old has been discovered near the village of Howick in Northumberland. Archaeologists have discovered post-holes and hearths filled with the remains of baked hazel nuts.

Until the Howick discoveries, Skara Brae in the Orkneys, dated between 2000 BC and 1500 BC was the oldest evidence of human habitation in a built environment in the British Isles. At the time of its abandonment, Skara Brae had seven stone huts with interconnecting alleyways in the form of narrow lanes.

BUILDING MATERIALS

There is a trend since the earliest buildings for construction materials to have increasing durability. The earliest materials were leaves, branches and animal hides, which were supplanted, firstly by timber, stone and clay, and then by synthetic materials such as bricks, concrete, steel and plastic.

Bricks

Architecture begins when you place two bricks carefully together.
MILES VAN DER ROHE (1886–1969)

The humble brick is probably the most ancient man-made building product still in common daily use. Approximately 6,000 years ago, the Babylonians began the practice of using bricks for construction. The bricks were produced from clay that was deposited by the overflowing rivers Tigris and Euphrates. As the region lacked timber for fuel, the Babylonians were forced to rely on drying the bricks in the sun, which is effective in areas of low humidity.

Kiln-dried bricks were first used in Mesopotamia by the Babylonians 5,000 years ago. Because of their greater cost in labour and imported timber for fuel, kiln-fired bricks were only used sparingly, and mainly for the harder wearing surfaces such as pavements. By then bricks had evolved, making it possible to build elaborate temples and ziggurats (a tower built in several stages, similar to an elaborate stepped pyramid).

Babylon was the capital of southern Mesopotamia from the early second millennium to the early first millennium BC, and capital of the Chaldean empire in the seventh century BC. Alexander the Great conquered Babylon in 331 BC.

Concrete

Modern cement, used for building purposes, is a lime-based powder which, when mixed with water, sets into a hard mass. When it is mixed with sand, cement forms into mortar, and when aggregates such as gravel or small stones are added to the mortar, it forms concrete.

In 2500 BC the Egyptians used gypsum and lime mortar to bond, level and align the stone blocks when building the pyramids. Large quantities of gypsum had to be shipped in from the lime-rich Nile Delta to the Giza plateau, and mixed with smaller quantities of lime to produce the mortar for the pyramids. As there was little timber in the region for firing the mortar, the low temperature requirement for the manufacture of gypsum mortar made it an ideal material for bonding the building. Only desert conditions are suitable for this kind of mortar, as it is unstable when it comes into contact with water.

The mortar also acted as a kind of lubricant, enabling the blocks to be moved into place more easily during the building phase. Only 50 per cent of the force is required to move blocks set on mortar than for unmortared blocks, which are set against each other in a dry condition.

The Romans used concrete (*opus caementicium*). The main constituents were lime, volcanic ash and aggregate. According to Vitruvius, a Roman architect writing in 20 BC, the long-lasting quality of Roman concrete, which is substantially greater than the modern equivalent, is thought to be due to the technique of tamping the concrete into place in the almost dry condition. This technique avoids excess water, which is a source of weakness in concrete.

Roman concrete construction reached its peak with the building of the 2,000-year-old dome of the Pantheon in Rome, which is made entirely of concrete.

Stucco is a fine cement or plaster for the covering or decoration of external walls. It was patented in 1779 by Bry Higgins of the USA, although many previous civilisations had used stuccowork to decorate their buildings.

Reinforced Concrete

A Parisian gardener, Joseph Monier (1823–1906), invented reinforced concrete in 1849. He inserted steel rods into still-wet concrete before it had begun to set. As the concrete hardened, the rods, which were fixed at each end of the concrete block, were bound permanently within the concrete, under high tension, thereby increasing the tensile strength of the concrete. Monier's invention was exhibited at the Paris exhibition of 1867 and he was awarded a patent.

The first concrete street in the USA was built in 1891 in Bellefontaine, Ohio. It remains in use today.

The first time concrete was used in the construction of dams was in the two major dams that were built in the USA in 1936: the Hoover Dam over the Colorado River by the Nevada/Arizona border, and the Grand Coulee Dam over the Columbia River in Washington State.

Asbestos

Magnesium silicate, asbestos, has been used for more than 2,000 years. The ancient Egyptians used it for burial cloths, and the ancient Greeks recognised its fire-proofing qualities and used it for lamp wicks, naming it *asbestos* (inextinguishable). The ancient Romans made table napkins out of asbestos and when the meal was over they would throw them into a fire for cleaning.

As early as AD 70, the Roman naturalist and historian, Pliny the Elder (AD 23–79), was the first to note that slaves working with asbestos were contracting 'sickness of the lungs'.

Asbestos was re-established as a building and roofing material during the Industrial Revolution in the late 1800s.

Despite several studies during 1917 and 1918, noting that asbestos workers were dying young, asbestosis was not recognised as a lung disease until 1924.

Glass

Although Stone Age man used obsidian, which is a naturally occurring glass, it was for decoration and not as a building material. According to Pliny the Elder (AD 23–79), Phoenician merchants had discovered a way to manufacture glass in Syria as early as 5000 BC, although the first written instructions for glass making are dated 650 BC, contained in the tablets from the library of the Assyrian King Ashurbanipal (669–626 BC).

The first glass windows were used by the Romans. The glass they produced was cast only in small quantities and possessed poor optical qualities as there were no effective means in Roman times of achieving perfectly flat surfaces. Despite its poor quality, glass remained the most effective means of admitting light to important buildings and the villas of prominent people. It was the Roman writer Lactantius (AD 240–320) who first mentions the existence of stained glass in Christian churches, although evidence of coloured glass, in the form of a green glass rod, has now been discovered at Eshunna, Babylonia, dated around 2600 BC.

The use of glass in larger windows was made possible by the production of sheet glass for the first time in eleventh-century Germany. Small glass panes were joined together using lead strips, to create windows. Glass remained a luxury, for use only in palaces and churches until around the end of the thirteenth century.

The Fourcault process was first developed in Belgium in 1905. Although laborious it enabled larger sheets of glass to be produced. A continuous sheet is drawn from the melting tank, cooled and cut to size, and then each sheet is individually polished to achieve a flat surface. Commercial production began in 1914.

Float glass was pioneered in 1959 by Pilkington Brothers of St Helens, Lancashire. It enables very large windows to be glazed with a single sheet of unpolished glass. In the process, molten glass is floated on a bed of liquid tin and progressively cooled, to achieve a perfectly flat surface.

Glass in its cooled state, despite its solid appearance, is not a solid, but a super-cooled liquid. (The molecular structures of solids and super-cooled liquids are markedly different). Evidence of this can be seen in ancient windows, in which the thickness of a pane of glass is much less at the top than at the bottom. The glass, looking like a solid, but behaving like a liquid, has been microscopically flowing downwards over the course of the centuries.

STONE BUILDINGS

The earliest stone structures were little more than piles of uncut stones that were used to form walls, with simple roofs made of wooden branches covered with animal skins and furs or leaves.

Megalith (massive stone) structures were built all across Europe, including the recently discovered Calabrian structure in southern Italy. Dating from 4000 BC, archaeologists believe this may be the oldest stone structure of all.

Stonehenge

The first of the three building phases of Stonehenge was begun around 3100 BC, and formed a circle of timbers with a ditch and bank. It was altered in 2500 BC by the addition of massive stones, dragged and floated on rafts up the River Avon, from the Prescelli Mountains in Pembroke, South Wales, about 250 miles away. This second phase was abandoned until 2300 BC, when the third and most impressive stage was begun. Giant Sarsen stones (sandstones) were hauled 20 miles from Marlborough Downs and set upright in a circle; the drag marks from hauling the Sarsen stones can still be seen. A stone lintel then linked each pair of upright stones.

The Pyramids

Cut stone was strictly controlled by the state in ancient Egypt, and stone was reserved for use on the most important buildings only. No building would have been more important to a ruling pharaoh than his tomb, the pyramid.

The first Egyptian pyramid was built in 2630 BC at Saqqara for the Pharaoh Djoser (aka Zoser) (2687–2668 BC). It is always known as the Step Pyramid, because of its stepped walls.

We even know the architect, Imhotep (2667–2648 BC), who was one of the greats of the ancient world. He was born a commoner, but rose to great prominence as a result of his intellect and drive. Two thousand years after his death, when the Persians conquered Egypt in 550 BC, Imhotep was made into the god of healing and medicine, at Memphis, becoming one of only two Egyptian commoners to be afforded this honour.

TYPES OF BUILDING

Palaces

The word 'palace' is derived from the Palatine Hill in Rome, where Roman Emperors had their homes. Subsequently, they were generally built as royal residences or seats of government, as distinct from castles, which were merely fortified buildings.

The earliest known royal palace was built in Thebes by King Thutmose III who reigned from 1504–1450 BC. Ancient Thebes was where modern Luxor lies, approximately 400 miles south of Cairo.

Castles

Generally castles were built for the purpose of defence, usually having a garrison of troops housed within high curtain walls of enormous thickness. Castles were also sited in strategic locations as symbols of power to control the local populace, and evolved to serve as residences for royalty or local lords.

The earliest castle wall is that of the ancient city of Babylon, which was protected by a high curtain wall from about 1600 BC.

From the ninth century AD castles proliferated rapidly across the whole of Europe.

Tunnels

The first tunnel under a river was built under the Euphrates, and completed in 2180 BC. The Euphrates rises in present-day Turkey, passes through Iraq and Syria and empties into the Persian Gulf after merging with the Tigris. To construct the tunnel, first the river was diverted, next a deep channel was cut across the riverbed, and finally a brick tube was built into the channel. The river was then allowed to take its original course through the channel.

The next major tunnel under a river came with Sir Marc Brunel's (1769–1849) Thames Tunnel in London built between 1825 and 1843, which connects Rotherhithe with Wapping. The tunnel remains in use by London Underground. French born Sir Marc Brunel was the father of the great Isambard Kingdom Brunel (1806–59).

The first water-carrying tunnel was built on the Aegean island of Samos off the coast of present-day Turkey between 550 and 530 BC, with Eupalinos, an engineer from Megara, in charge of construction. It passes right through the middle of Mount Kastro and was in use for more than a thousand years.

The most astonishing feature of the construction was that tunnelling was started simultaneously at both ends, and met in the middle of the one-kilometre-long (half mile) tunnel, with an error of only 60 centimetres (2 feet). This feat of engineering pre-dated the invention of the theodolite, and was way before laser-guided surveying equipment. All the surveying was achieved by using geometry and the dioptra, an instrument with sighting tubes, which was originally used for measuring the angles of celestial bodies.

The first canal tunnel was the Malpas tunnel in France, which was built in 1681. The Malpas tunnel was also the first tunnel to be excavated using gunpowder.

The first tunnel in the USA was the 213-metre-long (700 feet) Union Canal tunnel in Lebanon, Pennsylvania. Construction was completed in two years, ready for the opening of the canal in June 1827.

The Channel Tunnel excavation was completed in 1991. It stretches 58 kilometres (36 miles) from terminal to terminal with 37 kilometres (23 miles) of those under the Channel. The two sides met under the English Channel in 1990, linking Britain and Europe for the first time since the end of the last Ice Age more than 8,500 years ago. The 'Chunnel' opened for passenger traffic in May 1994.

Dams

The first great water dam, the Sadd El-Kafara Dam (dam of the pagans), was built near modern-day Cairo in 2900 BC.

The first dam in England, the Arlesford Dam, was built in 1189 at the suggestion of Geoffry de Lucy, the Bishop of Winchester. The reason for building the dam is uncertain but it was most likely to supply the Bishop's palace with fish. Several downstream mills were able to operate from the force of the head of water behind Alresford Dam.

The first water-generated electricity was produced by damming the Fox River in the USA. The electricity went on stream in 1882 and was used to power two paper mills and a house.

Bridges

The first bridges were simple beams of flat stones or tree trunks across streams. These were followed by 'step stone' bridges, which consisted of flat stones placed between existing stepping stones.

The earliest 'designed' bridges were clapper bridges (derived from Latin *claperius*, which means 'pile of stones', and Anglo-Saxon *cleaca*, meaning 'bridging the stepping stones'), which date from the second millenium BC.

A clapper bridge is formed by using large flat slabs of suitable stone to make a beam-like deck extending between stone bases or piers on either side. Clapper bridges are often found on Dartmoor and Exmoor and, although extremely difficult to date, are believed to be the oldest standing bridges in existence.

The first long bridge was the two-mile-long floating bridge built for King Xerxes (520–465 BC) across the Hellespont in 481 BC. Herodotus, the ancient Greek historian, recorded that Xerxes had 800 boats lashed together to create a bridge, but it was destroyed by a storm. The bridge was rebuilt and, this time, the sea stayed calm and Xerxes' vast army was able to march over it to attack Greece. Herodotus claimed 5,000,000 soldiers crossed over the bridge.

The first bridge across the river Tiber in Rome was the Pons Fabricus, constructed in 62 BC. It was a multiple arch stone bridge. Arched structures had been used in the Middle East before Roman times, but the Romans were the first to discover the load-bearing properties of the arch. They used these load-bearing properties to create bridges and aqueducts that would occupy less land and require less material to construct than the existing clapper bridges. The most important surviving arch bridge, the Ponte di Augusto in Rome, was built during the reign of Augustus Caesar (63BC–AD14).

The first bridge in the USA was built in 1697 in Philadelphia, and still carries modern traffic on Route 13.

The first iron bridge was built in 1779 by Abraham Darby (1750–91) over the river Severn at Coalbrookdale in Shropshire. The bridge was finally closed to vehicles in 1934.

The first concrete bridge was built by Francois Coignet (1842–1921) in 1865 to span the river Vanne in France.

The first steel bridge was the St Louis Bridge, which was completed in 1874 and spans the Mississippi. It was the first bridge constructed exclusively from steel.

The first major suspension bridge was the Menai Bridge built for carrying vehicles and pedestrians across the Menai Strait to the island of Anglesey from the North Wales mainland. It was built between 1819 and 1826 by Thomas Telford (1757–1834) using a truss girder deck and wrought iron chains which were made with iron bars joined together. The bridge is 176 metres (580 feet) long and remains the only road bridge to Anglesey.

The first wire suspension bridge was built in France in 1825, by engineer Marc Seguin (1786–1875), the nephew of Joseph Montgolfier, the ballooning pioneer. Seguin's bridge spanned the river Rhone at Tournon, France.

The first important wire suspension bridge in the USA was the Wheeling Bridge in Ohio built in 1849 by Charles Ellet Jnr (1810–62), who was known as the Brunel of America. He had been dismissed from his other bridge project, across Niagara Falls, after a series of publicity stunts. These included riding a horse across the seven-foot-wide bridge platform, which had no handrails at the sides.

The bridge was damaged by a massive storm in 1854 but reopened in 1860, just in time to play a crucial role in the American Civil War.

Bridges over the river Thames

The earliest known bridge across the river Thames was built around 1500 BC at Vauxhall. Large oak posts, which have been radiocarbon dated as early as 1750 BC, lead into the river. They were discovered during excavations in 1999.

The first Roman bridge across the river Thames in London was built in AD 50. The bridge was sited at an old ford, close to what is now the London Financial District, known as the Square Mile.

The first brick bridge across the river in London was built by Peter de Colechurch in AD 1176. Construction was completed in 1209 with shops and houses contained in a tunnel-like structure. The bridge stood for more than 600 years on the site of the present London Bridge, between the City of London and Southwark. The next bridge was built in 1749 at Westminster.

Walls

The earliest city walls were those built encircling the city of Jericho around 8000 BC. Jericho is 250 metres (820 feet) below sea level and as each set of walls collapsed from fire, flood or earthquake a new set was built on top. In 1400 BC Joshua led the Israelites to capture Jericho and, according to the ancient myth, blew his trumpet so hard that it brought down the walls.

The Great Wall of China is more than 6,000 kilometres (3,720 miles) long, which makes it the largest man-made object on earth. It was built between 221 BC (the Qin Dynasty) and AD 1644 (the Ming Dynasty).

Skyscrapers

The first skyscraper was the ten-storey Home Insurance Company building in Chicago built by Major William Le Baron Jenney in 1885. It was the first building to use steel girder construction. The term 'skyscraper' first came into use in the 1880s in the USA and was originally applied to buildings which were ten to 20 storeys high. Nowadays the term is applied only to buildings above 40 storeys high.

There were two technological developments that made higher buildings possible: improvements in steel technology that gave it greater tensile strength through refinement of the Bessemer steel smelting process (invented by Sir Henry Bessemer 1813–98) and the development of safe passenger lifts (also known as elevators in the USA).

The safety lift (elevator) was invented by Elisha Graves Otis (1811–61) and in 1853 at P.T. Barnum's Crystal Palace Exposition in New York, he successfully demonstrated the mechanism that halted the elevator's fall if the hoisting cable was severed. The first commercial passenger lift had a steam-driven lifting mechanism, and was installed in the E.V. Haugwout and Company Department Store in New York in 1857.

The Otis design was improved by Werner von Siemens when he fitted an electric motor to the underside of the elevator car. Siemens demonstrated his improved design at the Mannheim Exposition in 1880. Seven years were to pass before the first electric-powered elevator was installed for passenger use, in Baltimore, Maryland.

Although primitive hoisting devices using animal power had been in use from the third century BC, the first passenger lift was not installed until 1743. It was for the exclusive use of King Louis XV of France, and was known as the 'Flying Chair'. The lift was counterbalanced by an arrangement of weights and pulleys, but lifted only one person at a time from the ground to the first floor, and was installed on the outside of the palace. The King entered the lift from his balcony, and was hoisted or lowered by men stationed inside a chimney.

Staircases

The precise origin of staircases is uncertain, but the Cretan palaces at Knossos and Phaistos, built around 1500 BC, both have staircases, and on the Tai Shan road in China there are 6,000 ancient granite steps, which were built around 3,000 years ago.

The moving staircase was invented by Jesse W. Reno (1861–1947) in 1891. It was the forerunner of the modern escalator and took the form of a moving conveyor belt. It had a stationary handrail and inclined at an angle of 25 degrees. It was not until 1896 that the first example was installed on Coney Island, New York.

The first escalator in the form of a moving staircase was produced and installed by the Otis Company at its factory in 1899. Otis registered the word 'escalator' as a trademark, but it quickly passed into common use and the registration was dropped. The first escalator installed for public use was at the Paris Exposition of 1900.

COMMUNICATION

COVERING: Person to Person, Broadcast Communication.

Since messages were first left on tablets of stone man has used every means at his disposal to communicate private, public and secret messages to others. Immense fortunes have been made and countries conquered, by the controllers of communication.

PERSON TO PERSON

Writing

As with all ancient technologies, it is impossible to date the origins of writing precisely. Leaving scratches on rocks with the use of flint hand tools was almost certainly primitive man's first attempt at a form of coded communication.

The first written language was cuneiform, which was developed by the Sumerians of southern Mesopotamia more than 5,000 years ago (*see also* Language).

The earliest hieroglyphs were discovered carved into burial stones in Egypt and date from 3200 BC to 2950 BC (the pre-dynastic period). In 1894, two English archaeologists, James Quibell (1867–1935) and Frederick Green (1869–1949), working at Nekhen in Upper Egypt, discovered the Narmer Palette, a type of shield. For many years the Narmer Palette was the earliest evidence of hieroglyphic writing, but recent archaeological discoveries have revealed hieroglyphic symbols on earlier Gerzean pottery that have been dated provisionally at c.4000 BC. The Gerzean people were the prehistoric dwellers along the west bank of the Nile.

Until AD 1799 hieroglyphs were impossible to translate, but in that year Napoleonic soldiers stationed close to the town of Rosetta discovered a large black basalt stone. Frenchman Jean-Francois Champollion (1790–1832) examined the stone and realised that it bore the same inscriptions written in Greek, hieroglyphs and demotic (the language of the common Egyptian people). As Greek was a known language, it then became possible to translate the hieroglyphs.

The earliest known alphabet was devised in Ugarit in present-day Syria around 1500 BC. Discoveries at Ras Shamra in 1929 unearthed the Ugarit alphabet.

The earliest Chinese writing dates from 1500 BC and is inscribed on pieces of bone and tortoiseshell. The system of writing the Chinese language has changed little since then, as it still relies on pictograms and characters.

Pens

The first pens were developed around 1000 BC from the brushes normally used by the Chinese for writing.

In 300 BC the Egyptians used thick reeds as pens. The reed had to be continuously dipped into the writing material (a form of ink), which dried quickly in use.

A bronze pen was found in the ruins of Pompeii.

Quill pens were used in the seventh century AD by St Isodore of Seville (c.560–c.636), although feathers were probably used at an earlier unknown date.

The first machine-made pen nib was produced by John Mitchell of Birmingham in 1828.

The earliest known example of a fountain pen was produced by Monsieur Bion of Paris in 1702.

The fountain pen was patented in 1884 by Lewis E. Waterman (1837–1901) in the USA, although he did not actually invent it. Robert Thomson (1822–73), the inventor of the pneumatic tyre, obtained a British patent for the principle of the fountain pen in 1849.

The ballpoint pen was patented by John J. Loud on 30 October 1888, but he failed to exploit his invention, using it only for marking leather. Loud's patent was ignored in later battles over the rights to claim the invention.

The first successful mass-produced ballpoint pen was developed and patented in the 1930s by Lazlo Biro of Hungary (1899–1985), who also invented the automatic gearbox for cars (*see also* Transport p. 273). The pen became universally known as the Biro.

Baron Marcel Biche introduced another mass-produced ballpoint pen, the Bic, in 1950.

Soft-tip pens using porous material for the nib were introduced in the 1960s.

Ink

The Chinese developed a type of ink around 3000 BC. It was made from a mixture of soot from pine smoke, lamp oil and gelatin from animal skins, and was applied by brush.

Pencils

The modern lead pencil only became possible after the discovery of a deposit of pure graphite in Borrowdale, Cumberland, in 1564, and was first described by Conrad Gesner (a Swiss–German) in 1565. Early versions were made by wrapping graphite in string, but by 1662, wood pencils were being mass produced in Nuremberg, Germany. William Monroe of Concord Massachusetts made the first American wood pencils in 1812.

The lead pencil is misnamed as it contains no lead. The name originated from the lead wheels that were used to produce straight lines on paper or parchment. The result looked remarkably like that from the pencil and hence the pencil became the 'lead' pencil.

The pencil eraser, also known as a rubber, was invented by Edward Naime of England in 1770.

The pencil sharpener was invented by Therry des Estwaux of France in 1847.

Paper and parchment

Papyrus The ancient Egyptians first used a form of writing material called papyrus from about 2400 BC. Although the word paper is derived from papyrus, the two products are fundamentally different. Papyrus is made from sheets of thinly cut strips from the stalks of the *Cyperus papyrus* plant, whereas paper is made of the matted fibres of several different plants, which are soaked, sieved and rolled flat.

Parchment derives its name from the ancient Greek city of Pergamum (Bergama in present-day Turkey), where it is supposed to have been invented in the second century BC. Between 197 and 159 BC, the skin of specially bred cattle was used for the production of parchment.

The earliest paper was invented by Ts'ai Lun in China in AD 105. By AD 750 paper was being used in Samarkand, and by AD 794 it had spread to Baghdad and then on to the rest of the world.

The first papermaking machine was produced by Nicholas-Louis Robert of France in 1798.

Writing Systems

Around 600 BC there was general consensus among Mediterranean cultures to adopt left-to-right, top-to-bottom writing and reading. Before that, there had been a mixture of right-to-left and bottom-to-top, and even 'boustroph edonic', which involved writing backwards and forwards on alternate lines.

Shorthand

The earliest known shorthand was used during the fourth century BC by the ancient Greeks. They used a system of symbols in which a single stroke could represent complete words. This system was referred to as stenography (narrow writing).

In Rome, in 63 BC, Cicero's secretary, Tiro, devised a system of simplified letters and symbols to help him record Cicero's speeches in the earliest organised system of shorthand. It was known as *notae tironianae* and was still being used in Europe into the Middle Ages.

The first modern shorthand was devised by Sir Isaac Pitman (1813–97). Called the Pitman Shorthand system it was published it in 1837. Before the use of dictation machines, this system enabled notes to be taken at talking speed.

The speed record for taking shorthand was set in 1922 when Nathan Behrin succeeded in taking 350 words per minute for a sustained two-minute period. The record still stands.

Printing

The first printing process had been developed by the Chinese by the second century AD. It was a simple form of fixed-type printing in which the type was permanently fixed to the printing head. Between AD 1041 and 1048 the Chinese alchemist Pi Sheng also developed moveable type in which the letters were changeable, but the complexity of the language discouraged further development.

The modern printing press as we know it today was invented by Johannes Gensfleisch Gutenberg (AD 1400–68) in Germany.

The first printed book in English was the *Recuyell of the Historyes of Troye* printed by William Caxton (AD 1422–91) on a printing press in Bruges, Belgium in 1474/75.

The first book known to have been printed in England was the *Dictes or Sayengis of Philosophres* printed by William Caxton after he had set up a printing press in Westminster, London, in 1476.

Mail Delivery

Pigeon post was used first by the Sumerians in 776 BC.

The first royal mail in the United Kingdom was introduced by Henry VIII (1491–1547) in 1516 when he appointed Sir Brian Tuke as his Master of the Posts. In theory the service was for everyone, but the general public was discouraged from using what was effectively the King's private mail service. The Royal Mail as we know it today was established in 1635 and the Royal Charter was granted on 26 September 1839. Postcoding of all addresses in the United Kingdom was completed in 1974.

The earliest reference to a continuous message relay system that employed a horse and rider is from ancient Egypt around 2000 BC. Cyrus the Great, in sixth century BC Persia, had permanent post-houses set up at intervals along mail routes to service both horses and riders.

The Pony Express began operating on 3 April 1860, between Missouri and Sacramento, California, and ran its last mail in 1861, shortly after the overland telegraph had been completed in October of that year. During its short, romantic existence, the Pony Express was the fastest means of delivering messages across the USA.

Airmail

The world's first airmail service began in 1911, when 'aerial post' was flown from Hendon to Windsor in England.

The first overseas airmail was established in 1919 between London and Paris.

The first transatlantic airmail link was established only six weeks after Charles Lindbergh had made his historic first solo crossing of the Atlantic. On 29 June 1927, US airmen Richard E Byrd, Bert Acosta, Bernt Balchen and George Noville took off from Roosevelt Field, New York, to fly to France. The aircraft was a Fokker C-2. Thick fog in Paris forced them to change course and they had to ditch in the sea 275 metres

(300 yards) off the beach at Ver-sur-Mer. The mail got damp but was still delivered.

Semaphore

A system of signalling by holding flags or lights in a particular pattern, semaphore was originally developed in 1794 by the Frenchman Claude Chappe (1763–1805) to transmit messages quickly across long distances on land or sea. On land, observers were sited 8 to 16 kilometres (5 to 10 miles) apart to receive and send messages and the system became the standard form of ship-to-ship communication before radio.

Telegraph and Telegrams

The first electromagnetic telegraph was invented in 1837 by two English physicists, Sir Charles Wheatstone (1802–75) and William Cooke (1806–79).

Morse code was invented in 1838 (together with the Morse Telegraph) by Samuel Finley Breese Morse (1791–1872). On 6 January 1838, Morse succeeded in sending the first private telegraphic message along a 5-kilometer-long (3-mile) wire stretched around a room. The message was 'A patient waiter is no loser.'

International Morse Code (a modified, simpler version) was developed in 1851.

The first public telegraph line was erected in 1843 between Washington DC and Baltimore, a distance of 64 kilometres (40 miles). Samuel Morse sent the first message on 24 May 1844 over an experimental line. It said, 'What hath God wrought?'

The first telegram was transmitted on 8 April 1851 when a group of businessmen formed the New York and Mississippi Valley Printing Telegraph Company. It started immediately with 880 kilometres (550 miles) of wire and a licence to use a printer invented by Royal E. House. The device was the first to print letters and numbers instead of the dots and dashes of Morse code, thus enabling the transmission of the first telegram.

Later the New York and Mississippi Valley Printing Telegraph Company changed its name to Western Union.

The first undersea telegraph cable was laid between France and England in 1850. The cable was cut by the anchor of a French fishing boat after three days, and not replaced until the following year, when a more substantial cable was laid. A previous 1.6-kilometre-long (1-mile) experimental cable had been laid between HMS *Blake* and HMS *Pique* under the waters of Portsmouth Harbour.

The first transatlantic cable was laid in 1858 by Massachusetts-born Cyrus Field (1819–92) but it only lasted a month. The cable ran between Newfoundland and Ireland, and Queen Victoria sent President Buchanan a telegram of congratulation on its opening on 16 August 1858.

Telex

Connected by the telephone lines, telex is a system of linked teleprinters (electro-mechanical typewriters), which allows trained operators to transmit and receive typed words simultaneously. Twenty-five messages could be transmitted simultaneously on a single telephone connection, which made telex the cheapest form of long-distance communication.

The global telex network was put in place in the 1920s and although it was mostly superseded by fax in the 1980s more than 3,000,000 telex lines remain in use worldwide.

The predecessor of the telex system was the 'stock ticker' of 1870, which printed share prices and other financial information on to a continuous strip, direct to the offices of stockbrokers, banks and similar institutions. It was called the 'stock ticker' because of the continuous ticking sound it made as the information was printed.

Fax

The fax was invented by Scottish philosopher and clockmaker Alexander Bain (1811–77) and patented as long ago as 1843. Bain produced a line-by-line scanning mechanism, using his knowledge of pendulums. The idea behind the patent was for the message to be scanned and transmitted line by line along the telegraph wires.

The first commercial fax machine, the Pantelegraph, was sold by Giovanni Casselli in 1861, before the telephone was in common use, and messages could actually be carried over public telephone wires. The Pan-telegraph entered service in 1863 between Paris and Marseilles, and in the first year of operation over 5,000 faxes were transmitted.

Email

The first use of email was in 1971 on ARPAnet (*see also* Internet p. 48). It had been developed by Ray Tomlinson (b. 1941). The first email message was 'qwertyuiop' (symbols on the top line of a keyboard) and Tomlinson chose the @ symbol to denote which user was 'at' which computer. Asked how he had come to invent such a thing as emails when there was no known demand for it Tomlinson said, 'Because it seemed like a neat idea.'

Telephone

The telephone was invented in 1876 by Scotsman Alexander Graham Bell (1847–1922) at the age of 29 after he had emigrated to Boston in the USA. He had succeeded in transmitting speech sounds the year before.

Elisha Gray (1835–1901) also claimed to have invented the telephone in 1876, but Bell beat him to the Patent Office by just a few hours. A major court battle followed that went in favour of Bell. Gray had produced a working prototype in 1874, but neglected to patent it.

The first microphone was part of the telephone transmitter, which was invented in 1876 by Emile Berliner (1851–1929) while he was working for Bell.

Mobile Phone

The use of a form of mobile telephone (two-way radio) was pioneered by the Chicago police in the 1930s to stay ahead of Prohibition gangsters. The Untouchables led by Eliot Ness (1903–57) were the first users.

The mobile phone (also known as the cell or cellular phone) as we know it was invented by Dr Martin Cooper of Motorola. It was first used in 1973 in a demonstration call, which was made by Cooper to his rival, Joel Engel, the Head of Research at Bell Laboratories.

Hedy Lamarr, the 1930s Hollywood beauty, invented the frequency switching system that allows cell phones to work. The device works by rapidly switching the signal between the frequency channels, which are recognised by both the transmitter and receiver. Her patent ran out before it was developed commercially, but if she had lived long enough, and not lost the patent rights, she could have been one of the wealthiest women on earth. (*see* Sex on Screen p. 233 and Torpedoes p. 311)

By 1977, Bell Laboratories built a prototype cell system, which was trialled by 2,000 selected customers. In 1979 the Japanese trialled mobile phones in Tokyo.

BROADCAST COMMUNICATION

Newspapers

The first official publication was the *Acta Diurna* (Daily Acts), which were instituted in 59 BC by Julius Caesar in Rome. They were a record of the daily goings-on such as births, marriages, divorces and deaths, engraved on metal or stone and displayed in public places for the general population to read. They continued to be displayed for the next 300 years.

A form of *Acta Diurna* had previously appeared in 131 BC merely as a record of the outcome of trials and legal proceedings.

The first Chinese newspapers were posted in public places in the eighth century AD.

The Anglo Saxon Chronicle was published in 890 AD at the request of Alfred the Great (AD 849–99) to keep a year-by-year record of events rather than publish news. The Chronicle actually starts at year AD 1 and was maintained until the middle of the twelfth century at ecclesiastical centres such as Peterborough Abbey.

The *Nottizie Scrittie* was published in 1556 in Venice, which was then a city-state. The public paid a small coin: a *gazetta*. Hence the common newspaper title 'gazette'.

The *Gazette* was first published in France in 1731.

The first and oldest magazine still being published anywhere is the *London Gazette*, which was first published in 1665 in Oxford. In its present form the *London Gazette* is a court magazine, and no longer publishes general news.

The first American/US newspaper was *Public Occurrences, Both Forreign and Domestick*, which was published in 1691 in Boston. Only a single issue was printed before the paper was suppressed by the Colonial Governor.

In 1719 Benjamin Franklin's brother James published the *Boston News-Letter*, which was the first United States newspaper to have a regular circulation.

The first British daily newspaper was the *Daily Courant*, which was published from 1702 to 1735.

The Times was first published in 1785 by John Walter.

The *Observer* was first published in 1791.

Le Figaro was first published in 1826 in Paris.

The *Financial Times* was first published on 13 February 1888 and sold for one penny. It was the first daily financial paper and incorporated an earlier publication, the *London Financial Guide*, which had been published weekly. The businesses covered on the title page of the first FT included:

- Welsh Gold Mining (reporting the discovery of 2,500 tons of gold ore).

- The American Machine-made Bottle Company (raising £600,000).

- The Freshwater, Yarmouth and Newport Railway Company (Isle of Wight), which was inviting subscriptions for debentures.

- Swan United Electric Light Company (reporting annual profits – *see also* Inventions – Electric Light Bulbs p. 168).

The first tabloid newspaper was the *Daily Mirror*, which was published in 1905 by Alfred Harmsworth, later Lord Northcliffe.

The word 'tabloid' was coined by medical benefactor Sir Henry Wellcome (1853–1936), and registered as a trade mark in 1884. It denotes paper size, not the type or style of content.

The first American tabloid newspaper was the *New York Daily News*, published in 1919. It was devoted to sex and sensationalism.

Japan's first daily newspaper the *Yokohama Mainichi* was published in 1870.

The first linotype set newspaper was the *New York Herald Tribune* in 1886. Until then the printing type had to set by hand but the startling development in the printing process of the linotype machine, by Ottmar Mergenthaler (1854–99), increased the speed of typesetting by a factor of six.

The *Newcastle Chronicle* was the first British newspaper to install a linotype machine in 1889.

The first computer-based printed newspaper was *Today* published in 1986 by Eddie Shah (b. 1944). It was also the first newspaper to be printed in colour. The new computer-based print technology developed rapidly in the 1970s and 1980s, enabling journalists to input articles directly into the print room, and editors to move stories about on a computer screen to fit the page. Shah's breakthrough in the use of print technology led to the breaking of the power of the printworkers' union. *Today* ceased publication in 1995.

The first successful daily comic strip in newspapers emerged in 1907 in the *San Francisco Chronicle* with Mutt and Jeff. The cartoon was syndicated worldwide and ran uninterrupted until 1982.

The Yellow Kid was included in a comic section in William Randolph Hearst's (1863–1951) *New York Journal American* in 1897. The cartoon lasted only until 1899, having been trialled for a few occasions in *Truth*

Magazine in 1894. Richard Outcault, the artist of The Yellow Kid, pioneered speech bubbles.

The *New Statesman* was first published in 1913 by Sidney (1859–1947) and Beatrice Webb (née Potter) (1858–1943).

The *New Yorker* was first published in February 1925 by Harold Ross (1892–1951). Ross edited every edition until his death – a total of 1,399 issues.

The *Sun* was first published in 1963 as the successor to the defunct *News Chronicle*.

The *Independent* was first published in 1984 as the most recent of the current national daily newspapers to be launched.

Newsreels

The first newsreels were shown by Frenchman Charles Pathé (1863–1957). He began showing short films (a reel of news) of current events in the music halls of France in 1909. He expanded the idea into Britain and the USA in 1910. Pathe News still exists as Associated British Pathé.

Radio

Michael Faraday (1791–1867) demonstrated the theoretical possibility of radio communications when he proved that an electric current could produce a magnetic field, and as early as 1864, James Clerk Maxwell (1831–79) proved mathematically that electrical disturbances could be detected over considerable distances.

Radio waves were first detected in 1884 by the German physicist Heinrich Hertz (1857–94) who proved Maxwell's theory over a short distance at Bonn University. Hertz originally named the waves he had identified as Hertzian waves but they were soon to be renamed radio waves.

The father of radio is widely regarded to be Guglielmo Marconi (1874–1937) and by 1901 Marconi had perfected a radio system, which was tested by transmitting Morse Code across the Atlantic.

However, he had in fact infringed 17 patents previously registered by Serbian born Nikola Tesla (1856–1943). Marconi's US patent applications were initially turned down due to Tesla's previous work in 1893, but in a major about-turn, Marconi was granted a patent for the invention of radio in 1904. Despite the award of the Nobel physics prize to Marconi in 1909, the patent for radio was reversed in favour of Tesla in 1943 a few months after Tesla's death.

Nikola Tesla was born in Serbia in 1856 and granted American citizenship in 1891. He was a prolific inventor who worked with Thomas Edison and George Westinghouse, and held more than 700 patents.

The first voice broadcast on radio was a message sent from Brant Rock, Massachusetts, on Christmas Eve in 1906 to shipping in the Atlantic. The speaker, Reginald Fessenden (1866–1932), had previously transmitted from station to station (as opposed to broadcast) across the Potomac River in 1900.

The first live broadcast of opera on radio was in 1920 from Marconi's Chelmsford factory. The Australian soprano Dame Nellie Melba (1861–1931) performed in the opera.

The first transmission from the British Broadcasting Company Limited, which was set up as a commercial company, was on 14 November 1922 from Marconi House in London. By the end of 1922 there were four employees, including John Reith (later Lord Reith 1889–1971), the first managing director. By the end of 1925 there were more than 600 staff. In 1926 the name was changed under a non-commercial Crown Charter to the British Broadcasting Corporation (BBC).

The first transmission from the BBC's World Service was in 1932, the same year as the first broadcast of King George V's Christmas Day message, which was written by Rudyard Kipling (1865–1936).

The first broadcast of the BBC 'pips' for the time signal, more properly known as the Greenwich Time Signal, began in 1924, and they have been broadcast ever since.

There are five pips of a tenth of a second each and a final pip of half a second long. The hour changes at the start of the final pip. Every few years there is a 'leap second', when a seventh pip is added to take account of the slowing down of the earth's rotation.

The first commercial radio station was KDKA in Pittsburgh, USA, which began broadcasting in 1920.

Television

In 1884, the Prussian Paul Gottlieb Nipkow (1860–1940) invented a means of transmitting pictures by wire, using rotating metal discs. Nipkow was granted a patent at the Imperial Patent Office in Berlin, but was never able to demonstrate his system.

Television was first demonstrated by John Logie Baird (1888–1946) in 1926 at Selfridges in London using a mechanical system of rotating discs, which had been successfully patented in 1924. Baird's system was adopted by the BBC in 1929, although the wholly electronic American system, invented by Philo T. Farnsworth (1906–1971) of the USA, replaced it in 1937.

The first televised broadcast by the BBC was in 1932 from Alexandra Palace using Baird's mechanical system.

The first outside broadcast by the BBC was the coronation of George VI in 1937.

Wimbledon was also broadcast for the first time in 1937, followed by the FA Cup Final in 1938.

The first successful colour television system designed by the Radio Corporation of America (RCA) began broadcasting on 17 December 1953.

The first programme broadcast in colour was an episode of *Dragnet*, a hard-boiled detective series.

The first coast-to-coast colour television broadcast in the USA was on 1 January 1954. It showed the annual Tournament of Roses Parade in Pasadena, California.

The first BBC colour television broadcast was a four-hour-long tennis match at Wimbledon on 1 July 1967. This followed a number of test colour transmissions in 1967, of which the first was *Late Night Line-Up*.

Microphones
The first carbon microphone was invented in 1878 by David Edward Hughes (1831–1900), but it was Sir Charles Wheatstone (1802–1875) who coined the word 'microphone' in 1827.

An earlier version of the microphone was invented by Emile Berliner while working for Alexander Graham Bell (*see also* Telephone p. 41).

Video
The first videotape recorder was the AMPEX VRX-1000. It was introduced for use in the broadcasting industry in 1956 in Chicago at the National Association of Radio and Television Broadcasters.

The first domestic video cassette recorder was developed by JVC of Japan.

The Internet
The forerunner of the Internet was the ARPAnet. ARPA stands for Advanced Research Projects Agency, a division of the US Defence Department that possessed linked computers across North America, and wanted them to exchange information.

ARPAnet was planned in 1966, started working in 1969 and ceased operations in 1990.

The World Wide Web was invented in 1989 by Tim (now Sir Tim) Berners-Lee and his colleagues at CERN, an international scientific establishment based in Switzerland. They developed HTML (Hyper Text Mark-up Language), the format that tells a computer how to display a web page, HTTP (Hyper Text Transfer Protocol) that allows clients and servers to communicate and URLs (Universal Resource Locators) that identify resources in the web such as documents, images, downloadable files, services and electronic mailboxes, and reduce a range of complex instructions to a single mouse click. Vannevar Bush (1890–1974) of the USA, as Director of the Office of Scientific Research Committee, and an adviser to President Harry Truman, had proposed the basics of hypertext as early as 1945.

The World Wide Web provides the facility for all the world's computers to be linked, making it easy to send documentation electronically via the Internet. Tim Berners-Lee deliberately withheld from patenting his work on HTTP, HTML and URLs, as he wanted to encourage as many people as possible to use the web.

COUNTRIES AND EMPIRES

COVERING: Countries, Old Empires, New Empires.

*Men may be linked in friendship. Nations are linked
only by interests.*
ROLF HOCHHUTH (b. 1931)

COUNTRIES

United States of America (USA)

The first inhabitants of what is now the USA were the Native Americans, who crossed the land bridge that then existed between Asia and Alaska, and spread through Canada into the USA. There is very little archaeological evidence, but what there is suggests that this migration occurred between 35,000 and 15,000 years ago. DNA analysis links Asians and Native Americans, supporting the view that it was Asians who were the first to migrate to the New World.

Analysis of the three main Native American language groupings, Amerind, Nadene and Eskaleut, led researchers initially to believe that there were three main migration waves. However, recent language analysis, using a Cray supercomputer, suggests that many more migration waves took place.

It is widely believed that the Genoese Christopher Columbus (1451–1506) was the first European to sail to America in 1492, although he most likely landed on theCaribbean island of San Salvador (*see also* Questionable Origins p. 210).

The first permanent European settlement in America was at St Augustine, Florida, set up by Don Pedro Menendez (1519–74) on 8 September 1565.

According to legend the whole of America was named after an Italian explorer and map maker Amerigo Vespucci (1454–1512). There is also disputed evidence that America was named after Richard Amerike (1455–1503), a Welshman also known as Richard ap Merykem. Amerike sponsored John Cabot's 1497 voyage, which led to the discovery of Newfoundland. Amerike had specifically requested that any new found lands were to be named after him. It is thought possible that John Cabot (1425–c.1500), knowing of Columbus's discovery in 1492, crossed the short distance to the east coast of America from Newfoundland, and returned to Britain with the new land named after his sponsor. Interestingly, Amerike's family coat of arms is made up of stars and stripes, almost identical to the US flag (*see also* Discovery of America p. 209).

The first European to sight California on the west coast of the USA was Sir Francis Drake (1540–96); he claimed the land for England in 1579.

Australia

The first inhabitants of Australia were the so-called Aborigines who arrived on the continent between 40,000 and 60,000 years ago from the Asian mainland. They most likely arrived either by a now submerged land bridge or by rafts and canoes.

The first Europeans to visit Australia were the Dutch in 1606, although there may have been earlier sightings by the Portuguese. In 1688 the English pirate and travel writer William Dampyre landed on north-western Australia as captain of the *Cygnet*.

The first European to claim possession was Captain Cook (1728–79) when he stood on Possession Island on 15 August 1770 and claimed eastern Australia for England and King George III. Cook had made his first landfall in the *Endeavour* on 29 April 1770.

The first European settlement was established in 1788 when the British First Fleet, under the command of Captain Arthur Philip (1738–1814) sailed into Botany Bay with more than 1,000 prisoners and officers. Port Jackson was considered more suitable, so they moved down the coast, and Philip became the first governor of what was then named New South Wales.

The first free settlers were Thomas and Jane Rose of Dorset, who landed in Australia on 15 January 1793 with their four children. The Roses' second home 'Rose Cottage' is still standing today.

The European settlers gradually occupied the land that had been the ancestral home of the Aborigines. Although they were grouped under the title 'Aborigine', there were up to 700 distinct groupings, with widely differing societies, languages and cultures.

New Zealand

The first inhabitants of New Zealand were the Maori who, it is estimated, migrated there at some time around AD 800, although they may have arrived much earlier. This makes New Zealand the most recent of the Pacific Islands to be occupied.

The first European to discover New Zealand was the Dutch explorer Abel Tasman (1603–59), in 1642. Earlier that year, Tasman had discovered Tasmania, the island that is now named after him, although he started by naming the island Van Diemen's Land after his sponsor. Tasman then sailed east and on 13 December discovered the west coast of South Island of New Zealand, which he named Staten Landt. The name was changed to Zelandia Nova (New Zealand) after the Dutch province of Zeelandt. It is thought a group of directors of the Dutch East India Company took the final naming decision.

Captain Cook (1728–79) charted New Zealand in 1769, on his way back from Tahiti. Cook had been visiting Tahiti to observe the transit of Venus across the sun for the Royal Observatory.

Until 1792 there were two New Zealands. The other New Zealand was an island off the coast of New Guinea (the western half is Indonesian, known as Irian Jaya, and the eastern half is British, now known as Papua New Guinea). The name of the second New Zealand fell into disuse rather than being formally changed.

Eire

On Easter Monday in April 1916, the Easter Rising took place in Dublin, in which the Irish Volunteers and the Irish Citizen Army seized key locations across the city. The revolt was a protest against British rule and an attempt to declare Ireland a republic.

In the immediate aftermath of the Easter Rising, great public sympathy was generated after the British executed several of the leaders. This led to the Irish War of Independence, which lasted from 1919 to 1921 and to the Anglo-Irish Treaty, which was signed on 6 December 1921. The treaty gave independence to 26 of the 32 counties of Ireland, which were then grouped under the name of the Irish Free State.

The Irish Free State became Eire after the Constitution was formally adopted by plebiscite in 1937.

OLD EMPIRES

The concept of empire refers to an extended territory dominated by a single person, family or group of interested persons, from the Latin *imperium*, meaning supreme or absolute power, especially of an emperor.

Sumerian

In 2300 BC Sargon (*c.*2334–*c.*2279 BC) the ruler of Akkad conquered the city states of Sumer (in present-day Iraq) along the banks of the river Euphrates. He created the first empire in history. It lasted until the fall of the last dynasty in 2000 BC.

Roman

> *Rome speaks. The case is concluded.*
> ST AUGUSTINE (AD 354–430)

The Roman Empire can trace its origins back to 753 BC after Romulus, who according to legend, killed his twin brother Remus to become king. Romulus combined two settlements, one on the Palatine Hill and the other on the Quirinal, to create Rome. The city faced considerable pressure from the Etruscans to the north, who eventually supplanted Romulus with a king of their own.

The city-state of Rome became a republic in 509 BC under the first joint leaders, Lucius Tarquinius Collatinus and Lucius Junius Brutus.

It is generally accepted that the accession to power in 27 BC of Augustus (63 BC–AD 14), the grand-nephew of Julius Caesar (100–44 BC), who had adopted him, marks the de facto beginning of the Roman Empire. Augustus (real name Gaius Octavius Thurinus – also known as Octavian) had himself proclaimed Emperor and ruled until his death in AD 14. After years of civil war and instability, Augustus ruled a stable and prosperous empire, with little opposition, even from the urban poor, until his death. The last Roman Emperor was Romulus Augustulus who abdicated in AD 476.

Persian

Much of the history of Persia (present-day Iran) is shrouded in the mythology created by successive ancient historians, but it is generally accepted that the Persian Empire began in 559 BC with the rise of Cyrus the Great (580–529 BC), who led an army to topple his grandfather, the tyrannical Hishto-waiga, the king of the Medes. This unified all of the Persian peoples under a single ruler and created the greatest empire the world had known until that time.

Cyrus then led the combined Median and Persian Empires to conquer Lydia, which was ruled by King Croesus. The expression 'rich as Croesus' originated from the fact that Croesus had coffers overflowing with gold coins. Eventually Cyrus went on to capture Babylon in 539 BC.

The Persian Empire continued to expand, firstly with the conquest of Egypt and then westward into Europe. Persian expansion was halted by the Greeks at the Battle of Marathon in 490 BC. Herodotus, the great Greek historian, records 6,400 Persians died for the loss of 192 Greeks.

The last ruler of the remnants of the Persian Empire was Mohammad Reza Shah Pahlavi (1919–80), who was toppled by Ayatollah Khomeini in 1979.

Macedonian

The Macedonian state emerged under its founder Perdiccas I in the seventh or eighth century BC. In the years between 500 and 450 BC Macedonia began to expand into neighbouring territories, and with the ascendancy of Philip II (382–336 BC), captured the Greek states of Thracia and Illyria, and the empire began to take shape.

Philip's son, known as Alexander the Great (356–323 BC), captured other Greek states and eventually the Persian Empire, which included part of Egypt. Alexander also added parts of what are modern India and Pakistan to his empire.

When he was only 33 he became ill and died at Babylon in 323 BC. The empire he had conquered was divided up between his generals.

Byzantine

The Byzantine Empire was the Greek-speaking, eastern half of the Roman Empire, ruled from Byzantium.

The Roman Emperor Diocletian (c.AD 245–c.312), who ruled from AD 284–305, had split the Roman Empire into eastern and western halves in AD 284 for administrative purposes. Constantine I (known as Constantine the Great) ruled the eastern half until he defeated Licinius, the western ruler, in AD 324, becoming sole Emperor of the Romans. He transferred the capital from Rome to the ancient Greek city of Byzantium situated on the Bosphorus (in present-day Turkey), which he renamed Constantinople (now known as Istanbul). The Byzantine Empire thus succeeded the Roman Empire. Constantine, the first Emperor, ruled from AD 306–337.

Finally conquered by the Ottoman Turks, the Byzantine Empire drew to a close in AD 1453, almost a full millennium after the fall of Rome in 476.

Ottoman

The Ottoman Empire began as a small Turkish state around AD 1281 and started to absorb other states from 1451. It was founded by Osman I (hence Ottoman) (1258–1326) and expanded at the expense of the Byzantine Empire, capturing Constantinople in 1453.

It was effectively dissolved in 1923, losing all its territories after the end of the First World War. The Treaty of Lausanne in 1923 established the boundaries of modern Greece and Turkey, which had formed the core of the Ottoman Empire.

Holy Roman

This agglomeration which was called, and still calls itself the Holy Roman Empire, was neither holy nor Roman nor an empire.
VOLTAIRE (1694–1778)

The Holy Roman Empire was the successor to Charlemagne's Christian Empire, which traced its origins from AD 768, the year Charlemagne (AD 747–814) succeeded his father Pepin III to become king of the Franks. For the first three years of his reign Charlemagne shared the kingdom of France with his younger brother Carloman. When Carloman died in 771, Charlemagne became sole ruler and began his Christian imperial expansion.

The period of Charlemagne's time in power is known as the Carolingian Renaissance. According to Carolingian theory, the Roman Empire had only been suspended in 476, and had not ceased to exist. Charlemagne, as the leader of Christianity, was crowned Roman Emperor by Pope Leo III on Christmas day AD 800.

The first to be crowned as Holy Roman Emperor was Otto I (AD 912–973), who ruled from 962. The empire was partly dissolved in 1648 with the Peace of Westphalia, and the office of Holy Roman Emperor was abolished in 1806.

The Holy Roman Empire was a unique institution, not being based on a nation state. At its peak it encompassed Belgium, Germany, Austria, Switzerland, the Netherlands, Czechoslovakia and Slovenia, as well as large parts of France, Italy and Poland.

Mongol

The Mongol Empire occupied the largest contiguous geographical area in history ever to be under the control of a single person. The Mongols never numbered more than 2,000,000 people, but what they lacked in numbers, they made up for in fighting skills, savagery and determination. They came out of the fringes of the Gobi Desert and struck with ferocious speed to conquer all before them.

The founder of the Mongol Empire, Temuchin, was born in AD 1167, the son of a local tribal chieftain. Renamed Genghis Khan (Universal Ruler), he united the disparate tribes of Mongol peoples to found the Mongol Empire in 1206.

Genghis Khan used a system of hand signals to control his men, who were organised in decimal units of ten, one hundred and one thousand, moving them around the battlefield like chess pieces.

By 1214 the Mongol Empire stretched from Poland and Siberia to Vietnam, and from Moscow to the Arabian Peninsula. By 1215 Ghengis Khan controlled most of China. In 1227, he fell from his horse and died.

His grandson Kublai Khan (1219–94) established the Yuan Dynasty in China. The dynasty was overthrown in 1368 and the Mongol leaders retreated to modern Mongolia. By 1501 all remnants of the Mongolian Empire in China had been destroyed.

Spanish

In 1469, Isabella of Castile (1451–1504) and Ferdinand of Aragon (1452–1516) married and united their two kingdoms to establish Spain. They began to build an empire, partly to secure their territory against Muslim invaders, but also to protect trade. Their masterstroke was to sponsor the 1492 expedition of the Italian Christopher Columbus (1451–1506) to the Americas. Apart from the earlier acquisition of a few small territories, the Spanish Empire began with the discovery of these overseas lands in 1492 and all the riches it unearthed.

Under Charles V (1516–22), the Spanish Empire became the most diverse since the Roman, and at its greatest extent, its American territory stretched from Alaska, through western North America and Mexico, to southern Chile and Patagonia. Charles's European lands included Austria, Hungary and Spain as well as several Mediterranean islands.

The Spanish Empire came to an end in the War of the Spanish Succession, which lasted from 1701 to 1714. By the end of the hostilities in Europe, Spain had lost Belgium, Luxembourg, Milan, Naples, Sardinia,

Minorca and Gibraltar. The war was fought on several fronts including North America, where it became known as Queen Anne's War. The English effectively captured territory from Florida to Canada, including South Carolina, Massachusetts, Newfoundland, the Hudson Bay region and St Kitts.

Dutch

The Dutch Empire began, as other empires had done, by seeking trading opportunities, which were subsequently defended by force. Its origins are rooted in the success of the Dutch East India Company, which was founded in 1602. The company was granted a 21-year, tax-free monopoly of colonial activities in Asia, and the formation of the company was effectively the beginning of the Dutch Empire. By 1669 the Dutch East India Company had 50,000 employees and an army of 10,000 soldiers. It also possessed 150 merchant ships and 40 warships. It was the biggest private company the world had ever known.

The Dutch Empire continued after the Dutch East India Company ceased to trade in 1798, and by then it encompassed Indonesia, Sri Lanka, Tobago, Surinam, Belgium (1815–30), Cape Province of South Africa, parts of Malaysia, parts of Brazil, New York, and Albany and trading posts over most of the globe. Indonesia, Surinam and parts of Malaysia remained under the control of Amsterdam until the twentieth century.

In 1624 the Dutch established a colony at Albany in North America with 30 families. Peter Minuit, the Governor of the colony, bought an island from the Native Americans and named it New Amsterdam. It is now known as Manhattan.

Portuguese

The Portuguese Empire began in 1415 when Henry the Navigator (1394–1460) captured Ceuta in Morocco from Spain. To finance the expansion of the empire, Portugal focused its energies on the trade in gold, spices and slaves.

Portugal acquired vast colonies in Africa, the Far East, China and India.

The Portuguese explorer Pedro Cabral (1467–1520) discovered Brazil in 1500 and it became a Portuguese colony in 1530, until its Declaration of Independence in 1822.

In 1999 Portugal relinquished its final overseas territory, when Macau was ceded to China.

French

In the early sixteenth century the French looked covetously at Portuguese and Spanish empire building.

The earliest French overseas territory, the area around the mouth of the St Lawrence River in present-day Canada, was discovered by Jacques Cartier (1491–1557) in 1534. He claimed the land for France, named the region New France and named the high point on an island in the bay Mont Real (Mount Royal), now Montreal.

The French Empire grew to include the whole of Canada and extended through the Great Lakes, south through Ohio and down as far as the Mississippi. In 1682, after the French had pushed on and located the mouth of the Mississippi, the whole of Louisiana was claimed for France, and named after the French King Louis XIV.

By 1763 all French territory in America except Louisiana had been ceded to the British, and in 1769 the French East India Company, which had been formed in 1664, was dissolved amid massive financial scandals.

A vast area in the centre of the continent was sold to the new USA in 1803, in what came to be known as the Louisiana Purchase. The agreed price was US$11,250,000, which valued the land at 3 cents per acre. Louisiana in those days included what would now be one quarter of the continental USA.

There were two French Empires. The First Empire, commonly known as the Napoleonic, lasted for a decade from 1804, when the French

Senate elected Napoleon Bonaparte (1769–1821) as Emperor. He abdicated on 30 March 1814 at Fontainebleau, after losing all the territory gained by France since 1792.

The Second Empire covers the period 1852–70. Napoleon III (1808–73) was elected the first Emperor, almost unanimously, by plebiscite. During this period, France won territory in Italy, Austria, Syria, Vietnam and China.

The final remaining French colonies in Africa, among them Algeria, were relinquished amidst great bloodshed in the 1950s and 1960s.

German

The German Empire (also known as the Second Reich) was one of the shortest-lived empires in history. Otto von Bismarck (1815–98) was appointed Prime Minister of Prussia from 1862–73, and then the first Chancellor of Germany from 1871–90. Bismarck allied with Austria to defeat Denmark in 1864, and formed the North German Confederation in 1866.

The German Empire was proclaimed on 18 January 1871 in Versailles after the defeat of the French in the Franco-Prussian War, and King William I of Prussia was proclaimed Emperor. As well as its European territories, Germany held Togo, the Cameroons, East Africa and Southwest Africa (present-day Namibia).

Bismarck resigned in 1890 and Germany lost the whole empire in 1918 after defeat in the Great War (the First World War) of 1914–18.

Habsburg

The origin of the Habsburg Empire (also known as Hapsburg) can be traced to the Union of the Alpine hereditary lands in Switzerland, with the crowns of Hungary, Bohemia and Croatia in 1526–27. It was dissolved in 1918 at the close of the First World War.

British

The first reference to a British 'Empire' was made in 1603 by James I of England (James VI of Scotland) (1566–1625) after he had become monarch of England, Ireland, Scotland and Wales. The Act of Union of 1707 (which united England and Scotland) is generally recognised as the formal beginning of the British Empire.

There have been two distinct periods of British Empire, followed by a Commonwealth. The first empire was fuelled by the commercial aspirations of individuals and organisations, which set out to conquer and exploit overseas lands. The origins of this first empire can be traced to the licensing of Chartered Companies such as the Muscovy Company, which was formed in 1555. This first empire effectively came to an end with defeat in the American War of Independence that lasted from 1775–83.

The second empire emerged in the late 1760s and 1770s with Captain Cook's (1728–79) voyages to Australia and New Zealand, and the conquest of most of India under Robert Clive (1725–74) in 1763. At its height, Britain controlled 25 per cent of the world's population, and due to its vast geographical extent, it was said that 'the sun never sets on the British Empire'.

The British Commonwealth of Nations was formed in 1931 to bring together all former dominions and to recognise them as equal and independent nations. This began the demise of the British Empire, which ceded independence to India, Pakistan and its African territories over the following 40 years.

New Empires

European Union

The origins of the European Union (EU) can be traced to a speech given by Winston Churchill on 19 September 1946, advocating a form of 'United States of Europe'. He stated, 'We need to put the horrors of the past behind us.'

Unlike most empires, which formed through conquest, secession or marriage, the EU, which has been renamed on a number of occasions, has emerged with the full co-operation of the participating countries. This process has been ongoing for more than half a century, and continues to the present day.

Main Events

The European Recovery Programme (also known as the Marshall Plan) was put into effect on 5 June 1947, to stimulate the European economies shattered after the Second World War. Over four years, a sum of US$13 billion was given in help, which would amount to £100 billion at the 2005 exchange rate.

The Council of Europe was formed on 5 May 1949. The original members of the Council were Belgium, Denmark, France, Ireland, Italy, Luxembourg, Netherlands, Norway, Sweden and the UK.

The European Coal and Steel Community (ECSC) was formed on 18 April 1951. The original members were West Germany, France, Italy, Belgium, Netherlands and Luxembourg.

The European Economic Community (EEC) was formed by the same members when the Treaty of Rome was signed on 25 March 1957. The EEC was known in Britain as the Common Market.

Britain was refused membership of the EEC in 1963. The veto was applied with great relish by French President Charles de Gaulle (1890–1970), with his famous and emphatic 'Non!' It was always supposed that de Gaulle harboured an old dislike of Britain from the period of the Second World War, when he had been kept out of the planning process for the final assault on mainland Europe, known as D Day.

The European Community (EC) was formed in 1967, when the ECSC, EEC and EURATOM were merged.

Britain was finally admitted to membership of the EC in 1973 following a national referendum. The EC was renamed as the European Union (EU) following the Treaty on European Union or Maastricht Treaty in 1991. The EU now has 25 participating countries.

The Soviet Union

Following the Russian Revolutions of 1917, the Soviet Union was founded. There were two revolutions, 24 to 29 February and 24 to 25 October.

The first revolution ended with the overthrow of Tsar Nicholas II (1868–1918) and his government, and the installation of the Provisional Government. The second revolution saw the Bolshevik Party lead the Russian workers and peasants to create the Soviet Government.

Soviet territory was extended to include Armenia, Azerbaijan, Belarus, Estonia, Georgia, Kazakhstan, Kyrgyzstan, Latvia, Lithuania, Moldova, Russia, Tajikistan, Turkmenistan, Ukraine, and Uzbekistan.

In 1956 Soviet tanks rolled into Hungary to impose direct control, and in 1968 Czechoslovakia suffered the same fate. Afghanistan was occupied by the Soviets in 1980.

The disintegration of the Soviet Empire began with Mikhail Gorbachev's (b. 1931) reforms in 1985. The empire quickly unravelled with the demand for autonomy by Estonia in 1987, and, by popular demand, it ceased to exist in January 1992.

USA

Although there is not a United States Empire in a traditional sense, the USA, with its immense global political, economic and cultural influences, has considerable power over the economies of many other countries.

From the 13 territories that formed the original United States in 1776, the USA now comprises 51 states that have been acquired by a variety of means. Some have been purchased from foreign powers (Louisiana from France in 1803 and Alaska from Russia in 1867), some have been ceded to the USA (California from Mexico in 1848) and some were annexed (Texas from Mexico in 1845). Hawaii was annexed voluntarily after a coup financed by American interests.

The USA is the only remaining nation/empire that can successfully intervene as world policeman at its own choice. It is the closest thing to a contemporary empire, and according to the great American writer Gore Vidal (b. 1925), perhaps the last.

CRIME

COVERING: Prevention and Detection, Organised Crime, Punishments, Judicial Systems, Fictional Detectives.

*If this is the way Queen Victoria
treats her criminals, she doesn't deserve any.*
OSCAR WILDE (1854–1900)

PREVENTION AND DETECTION

British Police

Between AD 450 and 1066 a system of policing called Frankpledge was developed in England. This placed the responsibility for law enforcement on the nominated leader, the tytheman, of a group of ten people (a tythe). Each tythe was then responsible to a hundred, which was led by a hundredman. He was responsible for bringing suspected wrongdoers to justice at a 'view of frankpledge', a kind of assize, which was held twice a year.

The first nationally unified police force was organised by Sir Robert Peel (1788–1850) in 1829. For the first time police forces worked to a consistent set of rules across the country. Sir Robert's name inspired nicknames for the officers, who were known as 'bobbies or 'peelers'.

Fingerprinting to catch criminals was developed in Bengal in 1858 and adopted in England in 1901. Genetic fingerprinting was developed in 1984, by British scientist Alec (later Sir Alec) Jeffreys (b. 1950).

The first use of radiotelephony to apprehend a criminal was in 1910, when Dr Hawley Harvey Crippen (1862–1910) was arrested as he disembarked from the SS *Montrose* in Quebec after the ship had received a radio signal from England. He was hanged for the murder of his wife, whose dismembered head has never been found.

The first use of 999 for emergency telephone calls was in 1937. Originally the emergency number had been the single figure '1' but there had been a large number of accidental false alarms.

US Law Enforcement

Before the USA became an independent nation in 1776, and introduced federal laws, the law was enforced on a city-by-city basis, with each city adopting its own legal system. The severity of the punishments relied to a large degree on the prevailing circumstances in the city and the attitude of the city fathers.

The first Night Watch was established in Boston in 1631, and Slave Patrols, the forerunners of US police forces, were instituted in the Southern States in 1704.

US Marshalls were first appointed in 1789, under the Federal Judiciary Act, and in 1823 the Texas Rangers were formed to protect settlers from hostile Indian attacks. At the time, Texas was part of Mexico and would remain Mexican until 1836.

The first unified, prevention-oriented police force in the USA was established in New York City in 1845, but uniforms were not issued until 1853.

The Pinkerton Detective Agency was established in 1850 by Allan Pinkerton (1819–84), after success as an amateur in locating the hideout of a counterfeiting gang which had eluded capture by official forces. He was a Scottish barrel maker, who had emigrated to the USA in 1842 and settled close to Chicago.

The forerunner of the FBI (the Federal Bureau of Investigations) was a force known as the Special Agents, which was set up in 1908 under the leadership of Attorney General Charles Bonaparte (1851–1921) with just 34 agents. At the time, there were only a handful of federal crimes on the statute book, which included banking, anti-trust and land frauds.

ORGANISED CRIME

Chinese Tongs and Triads

During the 1840s and 1850s the Asian community in the USA, made up principally of Chinese immigrants, experienced racist treatment by whites. In response, the Chinese population in Chicago formed a visible community, and it was in this Chinatown that gang activity first began. Tong gangs were established as merchants' associations, organised to protect members' interests.

Contrary to popular myth, Tong gangs are virtually unheard of in China. Triads differ from Tongs in having a rigid structure that has existed for hundreds of years in China. Both groups preserve secrecy from the authorities through the concept of 'saving face'. This code prevents members of the Chinese community from reporting crime, as it would be seen a failure of the community, which would then suffer a loss of face.

Mafia

The most notorious criminal organisation in the world is the Mafia, which originated as a secret organisation in Sicily in the late Middle Ages. The Mafia was originally formed to overthrow the rule of foreign conquerors such as the Saracens, Normans, and Spanish.

The Mafia's origins were in small private armies (*mafie*), which began to hire their services to absentee landlords to protect their estates. During the eighteenth and nineteenth centuries these armies became very powerful and began to extort money from their previous employers.

It was sometimes referred to as the Black Hand Gang, after its signature of a black hand print left at the scene of a murder. This practice fell into disuse after the establishment of fingerprinting.

The Mafia survived successive foreign governments and also the efforts of the Italian dictator Mussolini, who came close to eliminating the organisation by the application of repressive methods equally as harsh as those used by the Mafia itself.

After the Second World War the Mafia transferred its powers and interests from rural to industrial areas, and subsequently came to dominate organised crime in the USA.

The first Godfather or Capo di Tutti Capi (Boss of Bosses) was 'Lucky' Luciano (1896–1962). He created the National Crime Syndicate in the USA in 1934 through alliances with Meyer Lansky (1902–83) and 'Bugsy' Siegel (1906–47), his boyhood friends and fellow gangsters.

Al (Scarface) Capone, perhaps the world's most famous gangster, was never Capo di Tutti Capi of the Mafia in USA, as he was Neapolitan by extraction, not Sicilian, and therefore not fully trusted.

Kray and Richardson Gangs

The Kray and Richardson gangs are the best known of the organised crime gangs that reigned over London during the 1950s and 1960s.

The Kray gang was led by the twin brothers Reggie (1933–2000) and Ronnie (1933–95) with their older brother Charlie (1927–2000). Their criminal activity began with a protection racket, which they ran from their snooker club in Bethnal Green, London. During the 1950s and 1960s, with a reputation for savage violence, the Krays built a major criminal organisation, which vied with the Richardson gang for control of London crime.

The Krays' criminal careers came to an end in 1969 when the twins were convicted of the 1967 murder of Jack 'The Hat' McVitie, and were given life sentences. Ronnie died in prison after 28 years and Reggie was released a few weeks before his death, after serving 32 years.

The Richardsons owned scrapyards in south London and operated a lucrative extortion racket at Heathrow car parks, which the Krays tried to take over. The Richardsons' criminal careers came to an end after the 'Battle of Mr Smith's Club' in which a cousin of the Krays, Richard Hart, was shot dead.

Ku Klux Klan

The origin of the name of the Klu Klux Klan is uncertain, but one theory maintains that the name comes from the Greek word *kuklos*, meaning wheel, and clan, meaning family.

The original Klu Klux Klan was a group of six members, who met on Christmas Eve 1865 in a law office in Pulaski, Tennessee, supposedly with the intention of forming a social group, devoted to wearing weird costumes and playing practical jokes on unsuspecting people. By the end of 1866, in the wake of the American Civil War, its activities had spread beyond Tennessee and progressed to violence. This was aimed at intimidating 'freedmen', the 4,000,000 former slaves that had been emancipated with the defeat of the Southern States.

In 1867 the Klu Klux Klan appointed its first Grand Wizard, the former Confederate General Nathan Forrest (1821–77), with the backing of former Confederate leader General Robert E. Lee (1807–70). Some of the other original ranks were Grand Dragon, Titan, Giant, Grand Cyclops and Ghoul (the lowest rank).

Up to 1,300 murders were reported during 1868, for which the Klu Klux Klan was blamed. It was disbanded in 1869.

The second Klu Klux Klan was formed in 1915 by William J. Simmons (b. 1880), who set down the prospectus of the organisation while he was recovering in hospital from a road crash injury. Simmons's thinking was strongly influenced by the film *The Birth of a Nation*. The re-formation of the Klan was marked by the burning of a cross on Stone Mountain in Atlanta, Georgia, USA, on 25 November.

The second version of the KKK was a deeply sinister organisation, bent on serious, racially motivated crime. In 2005 it still had approximately 2,500 members.

PUNISHMENTS

Until the late nineteenth century, the usual method of dealing with convicted offenders in Britain was not imprisonment, which is a fairly modern form of punishment, but the imposition of a hefty fine or the meting out of some form of institutionalised brutality. Favourites were public flogging, the ducking stool, mutilation or branding. Public humiliation was also a favourite, with the use of the stocks or pillory.

The English justice system also imposed transportation, which resulted in extensive numbers of convicted prisoners being taken to

America and Australia. Fifty thousand offenders were transported to the American colonies between 1607 and 1776. When these colonies were lost as a result of the War of Independence, Australia became Britain's new penal colony. From 1787, it is estimated that 100,000 men and women were shipped out, before transportation ceased in 1852. During those years, prisoners were held in old ships, the so-called prison hulks. The filthy conditions on board strongly influenced the work of the penal reformer John Howard.

Capital Punishment

Over the centuries, there have been many methods of capital punishment, such as burial alive, boiling alive, hurling off cliffs, drowning, burning at the stake, crucifixion, decapitation, stoning, hanging and shooting.

Around 1700 BC, Hammurabi (dates uncertain), the ruler of the Babylonian Empire, codified 25 different crimes for which execution was the punishment. Murder was not one of them.

The first recorded death sentence was handed down in Egypt in the sixteenth century BC, when a nobleman was ordered to take his own life having been found guilty of practising magic.

Lethal Injection

Originally proposed by Dr J. Mount Bleyer of New York in 1888 as means of execution, lethal injection was not used in the USA until Charles Brooks was executed in Texas on 7 December 1982.

Dr Stanley Deutsch formulated the contents of the lethal injection in 1977.

The Nazis instituted their T4 Euthanasia Programme in 1940 for the mass extermination of hereditarily deformed and mentally disturbed Germans. Phenol was injected as the lethal dose.

The Electric Chair

The original idea for the electric chair came from American dentist Albert Southwick in 1881. Southwick had witnessed the instant death of an elderly drunk, who accidentally touched the terminals of an electricity generator.

The first execution by electric chair was of the axe-murderer William Kemmler in 1890 in New York's Auburn State Prison. The alternating current electric chair invented by Dr J. Mount Bleyer was used but the whole event was a shambles, with the condemned man suffering a horrible lingering death. The public outcry over Kemmler's death agony played into the hands of Thomas Edison, who had a business manufacturing the far more lethal direct current electric chairs.

Gas Chamber

The gas chamber was invented in 1924 by Major Delos A. Turner of the US Army Medical Corps, as a humane way of executing people. It turned out to be the very opposite, as the average dying time from dropping cyanide tablets into acid to produce the poison gas turned out to be more than nine minutes, with several examples of the process lasting 20 minutes.

The first execution by gas chamber took place in Nevada on 8 February 1924. Mr Gee Jong was executed for a murder, which was linked to a Tong war. Jong's accomplice, Hughie Sing, was also sentenced to death, but this was commuted to life imprisonment.

Eaton Metal Products of Salt Lake City had almost a complete US monopoly on gas chamber manufacture.

After the prisoner is confirmed dead, by use of a long stethoscope from safely outside the chamber, the warders who enter to remove the dead man or woman are instructed to ruffle the prisoner's hair to release any trapped gas.

Hanging

It was in the fifth century AD that hanging was first adopted for capital punishment in England. Tyburn, in London, was first used as a place of hanging in 1196 when William Fitz Osbert was the first to suffer the noose. The famous 'Triple Tree' of Tyburn was built as a permanent gallows in 1571.

The first execution in America was by hanging. George Kendall, an English colonist, was hung in 1608 for plotting to betray England to the Spanish.

The first woman to be executed in America was Jane Champion; she was hanged at Jamestown, Virginia, in 1632.

Beheading/Decapitation

The Bible refers to beheading as a means of capital punishment, although stoning to death was far more common.

The Greeks and Romans used beheading as a less dishonourable method of execution than the alternatives in use at the time. The Romans reserved beheading exclusively for their own citizens, but crucified all others.

William the Conqueror (1028–87) introduced beheading as a means of capital punishment in 1076 but confined it to those of royal birth. The first victim was Waltheof, Earl of Northumberland, who had conspired against the king.

Saudi Arabia beheaded 33 men and one woman in 2004.

The Japanese used a particularly brutal form of decapitation until the late 1860s. The victim was buried in the ground and his head was sawn off with a blunt wooden saw.

The Guillotine

Widely supposed to have been invented by Joseph-Ignace Guillotin (1738–1814) of France in 1792, the guillotine was intended to provide a more merciful way of beheading people. As the executioner sometimes failed to behead his victim with the first stroke of the axe, a more reliable method was sought.

In fact Guillotin only went as far as proposing mechanical decapitation. The actual design was by Dr Antoine Louis (1723–92) of the Paris Academy of Surgery, and the first contraption was built by Tobias Schmidt, a piano maker.

The first execution by guillotine was of the highwayman Nicholas-Jacques Pelletier in April 1792. The crowd, who treated the dance of death in hanging as entertainment, voiced its disappointment and called for the return of the gallows.

Louis XVI, King of France, was guillotined in 1793 on a machine that had been named *Louisette*.

The first decapitation machine was not the guillotine but the Halifax gibbet, which had been used in Halifax, England, since 1286. John of Dalton was the first to be executed on the gibbet.

The only way to escape the gibbet was for the condemned person to withdraw his or her head before the blade fell and escape across the parish boundary a mile away. If successful, the felon was then allowed to go free providing he did not return to the town.

A man called Dinnis managed to do precisely that. As he made his escape, he encountered people who were on their way into the town to witness the execution, and he was asked if Dinnis had been executed yet. He replied, 'I trow not', an expression that is still used in the area.

The Halifax gibbet only differed from the guillotine in having a massive horizontal axe blade, whereas the guillotine had a much slimmer blade and a leading edge at forty-five degrees from horizontal. This angle added the 'scissoring' effect to the cutting stroke.

In 1564, the 4th Earl of Morton (1525–81) introduced the Halifax gibbet to Scotland, where it became known as the Scottish Maiden. On 2 June 1581, Morton himself was executed on the Maiden.

The term 'gibbet' can mean a gallows on which condemned men and women are hanged, or as in the case of Halifax, a form of beheading machine. In the USA a gibbet can also mean a device, sometimes body shaped, for displaying the remains of executed criminals to encourage good behaviour in others.

Lynching

The extra-judicial execution of lynching refers to the concept of vigilantism in which citizens, in the form of a mob, illegally assume the roles of prosecutor, judge, jury and executioner.

The term 'lynch' is derived from the name of Colonel Charles Lynch (1736–96) a Virginia landowner, who began to hold illegal trials in his backyard in 1790. The accused was normally found guilty, then immediately tied to a tree and whipped by Lynch. In some cases he administered the death penalty by hanging.

The first victim in America of this summary justice was John Billington in 1630. He had arrived in America on the *Mayflower* in 1620 as a pilgrim, and was the prime suspect when his neighbour John Newcomen was shot. He was summarily hung by a mob of other pilgrims.

The majority of lynchings in the USA took place between 1880 and 1930, in most cases the result of racial hatred in the Southern states. Of the 2,800 known victims, 2,500 were black. But according to Ida Wells (1862–1931), an African American journalist born into slavery, writing in the *Chicago Defender*, as many as 10,000 may have been lynched between 1879 and 1898.

The Anti-lynching Bill was first proposed in 1900 and was passed by the House of Representatives in 1922. Its passage to approval was delayed by a number of filibusters and the Senate finally approved the bill in June 2005 with a formal apology for its failure to approve it earlier.

Prison/Jail

In the ancient world, prisons were used for holding the accused pending trial, rather than as a punishment. In ancient Babylonia the state did not act as the prosecuting body, but held accused persons in prison, ready for private prosecutions to be made.

It was not until the late eighteenth century, in England, that imprisonment generally came to be seen as a punishment in itself. Prior to that prisons had been considered as places for holding debtors and prisoners awaiting trial and sentencing.

The first English prison was built in 1557 at St Bride's Well, London. Subsequently prisons were known as Bridewells. There were no individual cells and the whole population of inmates of a prison was housed in a single dormitory.

The first prison with cells was built by the Duke of Richmond (1735–1806), in 1775 in Sussex.

The Panopticon Prison was designed in 1791 by the English philosopher Jeremy Bentham (1748–1832). It had all the cells on the outside of a circular building, so that all the prisoners could be seen from a central viewing position. The Panopticon was never built in England, but several were built in Europe, Australia and the USA.

British Member of Parliament and social reformer Thomas Fowell Buxton (1786–1845) described a prisoner awaiting trial in 1818:

> The moment he enters prison, irons are hammered on to him; then he is cast into a compound of all that is disgusting and depraved. At night he is locked up in a narrow cell with perhaps half a dozen of the worst thieves in London whose rags are alive and in actual motion with vermin. He may spend his days deprived of free air and wholesome exercise. He may be half starved for want of food, clothing and fuel.

The first prison reformer was the Italian Cesare Marchese de Beccaria (1738–94), who campaigned against the use of corporal and capital punishments and torture. Beccaria argued that punishment should have a reforming characteristic, not to be used only as vengeance of the state.

The first English prison reformer was John Howard (1726–90). As the High Sheriff of Bedfordshire he studied the effects of prisons throughout Europe and Russia. The recommendations in his book *The State of Prisons in England and Wales*, published in 1777, were not put into effect until the nineteenth century.

Pillory and Stocks

These were common forms of punishment for more than one thousand years before imprisonment was introduced. The victim was displayed in public, either seated in the stocks, secured by the feet, or standing in the pillory, with arms, legs and head pinioned firmly so that passers-by could both view and abuse him or her. The standard procedure was to hurl rotten fruit and eggs at the prisoner, but sometimes harder objects such as stones and rocks were hurled. Serious injuries and even death resulted from this abuse. The pillory was abolished in England in 1837.

A refinement was the revolving pillory, looking rather like a four-fingered road sign, which could hold four prisoners simultaneously, secured only at the head and arms. Each fastening was mounted on a central revolving post, and the criminals were compelled to walk round in a circle, so that they could be viewed from all sides, and all could be abused at the same time.

JUDICIAL SYSTEMS

Ancient Law

The oldest laws are held to be those of Ur-Nammu, the founder of a Sumerian dynasty in the city of Ur in Mesopotamia, whose legal code dates from the twenty-first century BC. The code sets down laws governing the flight of slaves, punishments for bodily injury and witchcraft, and is written in cuneiform script, the oldest of all writing systems.

Judges

In ancient civilisations the earliest legal specialist was the judge. The chief of a society dispensed justice as part of his role of governance, but as his power spread, the chief would delegate the legal function to an official, and often the official sitting as a judge would be a religious man. If not religious himself, the judge would be advised by a religious man.

Judges were first cloaked in robes to follow the fashion of the Roman toga, which was felt to convey authority.

Trial by Ordeal

The brutal trial by ordeal pre-dates trial by jury. It involved the accused person being required to undertake a painful task, such as carrying red-hot irons. Innocence was established if the accused recovered without injury, on the premise that God would help the innocent.

Juries

The origins of the jury system are shrouded in mystery but forms of jury trial are evident in the primitive institutions of most European nations. It is a commonly held, but false, belief that the jury was a creation of Alfred the Great in AD 870 in England.

The earliest form of trial by jury is the system of 'sworn inquest', which was brought to England by the Normans after the Conquest in 1066.

The right to trial by jury in the USA was established in 1787 by the First Congress of the USA and preserved in the Constitution. The ten amendments, known as the Bill of Rights, were finally ratified by the last state to vote in 1791. The Sixth Amendment states, 'An accused person has the right to a speedy trial by an impartial jury.'

The first colonial grand jury under the jurisdiction of the British sat in America in 1635.

World's First Detective Agency

The first known private detective agency was set up in 1833 by Eugene Francois Vidocq (1775–1857), in Paris. Vidocq called his agency Le Bureau des Renseignments (Office of Intelligence).

After a long career as a criminal, Vidocq managed to persuade the police to employ his services as an informer in exchange for an amnesty on his previous crimes. In 1811, after considerable success as a police spy, Vidocq formed the Brigade de Surete, the forerunner of the French Sûreté National, and became its first Chef de Police.

FICTIONAL DETECTIVES

The earliest setting for fictional detectives is the first century BC in ancient Rome. The most prominent example is *Gordianus the Finder*, created by Steven Saylor (b. 1956). Gordianus is active during the time of well-known figures from history, such as Julius Caesar, Cleopatra and Mark Anthony, and the plots weave real historical characters with fictional. Saylor introduced Gordianus in *Roman Blood* (1991), as part of the Roma sub-Rosa series, and set the story in 80 BC. In the story, the young Cicero, a newly qualified advocate, turned to Gordianus for help.

The first modern detective in crime fiction was Dupin. He was the creation of Edgar Allan Poe (1809–49) and was introduced in *The Murders in the Rue Morgue* in 1841, and appeared twice more in: *The Mystery of Marie Roget* in 1842 and *The Purloined Letter* in 1844. Poe created Dupin as the first fictional detective to use superior powers of observation and reasoning to solve crimes and thus paved the way for later characters such as Sherlock Holmes. Poe is regarded as the creator of the modern crime fiction novel.

The most famous fictional detective in the world is probably Sherlock Holmes, introduced in *A Study in Scarlet* in 1887. His creator was Arthur Conan Doyle (1859–1930), who credited his own exceptional powers of deduction to the years he spent studying under Professor John Bell at Edinburgh University.

Conan Doyle was a founder and the first goalkeeper of Portsmouth United Football Club. He also investigated real criminal cases, a direct result of which was the setting up of the Court of Appeal.

Maigret was created by Georges Simenon (1903–89), whose first work featuring Maigret was published in 1935.

Simenon wrote very quickly, expecting to take no more than a month to write a book. Alfred Hitchcock (1899–1980) phoned him one day but was told by his secretary that Simenon couldn't be disturbed as he had just started to write a new novel. Knowing how fast Simenon wrote, Hitchcock said, 'Would you mind if I wait?'

Hercule Poirot was first featured by Agatha Christie (1890–1976), the world's most famous crime writer, in *The Mysterious Affair at Styles* in 1920. She wrote this, her first book, while working as a nurse during the First World War.

Miss Jane Marple was another creation of Agatha Christie. *Murder in the Vicarage* was her first appearance in 1930.

Philip Marlowe first appeared in the 1939 novel *The Big Sleep* by Raymond Chandler (1888–1959). In the 1946 film of the book, Humphrey Bogart (1899–1957) provided the definitive performance of Marlowe, starring with his future wife Lauren Bacall (b. 1924).

Sam Spade first featured in 1922 in stories written by Dashiel Hammett in the *Black Mask* magazine. Humphrey Bogart was perfectly cast again in this hard-bitten role in the 1941 film *The Maltese Falcon*.

In the McCarthy anti-American witch-hunt of the 1950s Hammett refused to give the names of his left-wing friends and was sentenced to six months in prison.

Inspector Morse debuted in Colin Dexter's (b. 1930) novel *The Last Bus to Woodstock* in 1975. Morse's forename – Endeavour – was not revealed until 1996 in *Death Is Now My Neighbour* and he was killed off in the final story, *The Remorseful Day*, in 2000.

DICTIONARIES AND ENCYCLOPAEDIAS

COVERING: Dictionaries, Encyclopaedias, Roget's *Thesaurus*.

DICTIONARIES

The earliest dictionary appeared in the seventh century BC. The Assyrian king Ashurbanipal (*c.*669–627 BC) had a dictionary produced on terracotta tablets, inscribed with columns of cuneiform writing. The ancient Greeks and Romans both had a form of dictionary in the first century AD. The purpose of these dictionaries was to keep a record of words that had passed out of common parlance, rather than to explain the meaning of words in current usage.

The first English dictionary was *A Table Alphabeticall of Hard Words*, published in 1604 by Robert Cawdrey (b. 1538). The word 'dictionary' came from the Latin word *dictio*, meaning 'the art of speaking'.

Dr Samuel Johnson of Lichfield (1709–84) compiled the first comprehensive English Dictionary. It was the first dictionary anywhere to attempt to standardise the pronunciation and spelling of the English language, and went by the title of *A Dictionary of the English Language in which the words are deduced from their Originals*.

He began work on his dictionary in 1747, but it was a further eight years before he completed it in 1755. Despite the dictionary's success, he did not make a significant amount of money from it. Johnson had left Oxford University without a degree, but went on to become one of the most quotable men in England.

The *Oxford English Dictionary* with 15,000 pages was begun in 1879 and finished in 1928. James A.H. Murray (1837–1915), the largely self-educated first editor, worked on the compilation for 35 years, but died in 1915 from a heart attack brought on by pleurisy. The dictionary was completed almost exactly 70 years after the Philological Society had first resolved to prepare it.

The first volume of the *OED* appeared in 1888 with the completion of the letter 'B'.

Dictionaries of Slang

> *Slang is a language that rolls up its sleeves, spits on its hands and goes to work.*
> CARL SANDBURG (1878–1967)

The detailed study of slang is recent, with most reference books being produced in the second half of the twentieth century.

The original dictionary of slang *Vocabulary of the Flash Language* was written by James Hardy Vaux, a criminal transported from Britain to Australia in 1811. It was published in 1819 and mainly featured the language of the underworld. It was also the first dictionary of any sort to be published in Australia.

An example of the slang is 'Frisk the cly and fork the rag, speak to the tattler and hunt the dummy.' Translated into normal English, this means: 'Pick the pocket and take the money, steal the watch and look hard for the wallet.'

ENCYCLOPAEDIAS

The first encyclopaedia was produced by Plato's nephew, Speusippus, (407–339 BC), who, in about 348 BC, recorded his uncle's ideas on mathematics, natural history and philosophy. Speusippus also included Aristotle's lecture notes in the encyclopaedia.

Vincent of Beauvais (*c.*1190–1264) a Dominican friar from Paris, produced *Speculum Maius* (the Great Mirror) in 1244. The book, which ran to over 50 volumes, claimed to show the whole world not only as it existed, but also how he thought it should be.

The Chinese claim that the *Yongle Canon* or *Yongle Dadian*, compiled between AD 1403 and 1407 and running to more than 11,000 books, was the world's first encyclopaedia. The work was too vast to print and only two manuscripts were made. There are now only 400 of the original books left, the majority having been destroyed.

The Chinese *Yu-Ha*i, which ran to 240 volumes, was published in 1738.

The prototype of the modern encyclopaedia was Ephraim Chambers' *Cyclopaedia*, published in 1728.

The *Encyclopédie* was published in France between 1751 and 1765.

The first English language encyclopaedia was the *Encyclopaedia Britannica*, published in 1768. It became available on the Internet in 1999.

The first multi-volume encyclopaedia was *The Encyclopedia Americana*. It was published in 13 volumes between 1829 and 1833 in the USA and by 1919 had expanded to 30 volumes.

ROGET'S THESAURUS

This reference book enables writers to find the correct word to express an idea or meaning, when that word eludes them. It does not show the meaning of the word or phrase, and it is not arranged alphabetically as in conventional dictionaries and encyclopaedias, but according to concepts and themes.

In 1805 at the age of 26, Peter Mark Roget (1778–1869), an English doctor and lecturer of Huguenot descent, began to compile what he called 'a classed catalogue of words' to help him express himself better. By 1852, when he was in his seventies, he felt the time had come to publish his great work, which was titled the *Thesaurus of English Words and Phrases*.

Before his death in 1869, there had been a further 28 editions of Roget's *Thesaurus*, and right up to the present day it has never been out of print.

Entertainment

Covering: Acting, Theatre, Dance, Humour, Circus, Music Hall, Musicals, Film, Gramophone.

Acting

Only since the end of the nineteenth century do we have any photographic, video or sound recordings of actors' performances. Before then we have to rely on the written recollections of those who witnessed a performance, and on paintings, which were created to convey how it looked.

Cave paintings in the Trois Frères caves in France dated between 40000 and 10000 BC depict men in costume, who could conceivably have been acting out a ritual.

However, acting is thought to have begun around 4000 BC, when Egyptian actor-priests worshipped the memory of the dead. It is believed that theatre evolved out of primitive rituals, which were created to symbolise natural events such as fertility or death. By acting, early man may have been reducing these events to a more human scale to make the unknown more understandable and accessible.

The earliest records of professional non-religious acting appear in the Sui Dynasty of the sixth century BC in China.

Theatre

Mime

Mime is one of the earliest forms of self-expression, which was used by primitive people to convey meaning.

Instead of fading from use, once spoken language developed, mime changed to become a form of entertainment.

The origins of mime theatre are in the fifth and fourth centuries BC at the Greek Theatre of Dionysus in Athens, when audiences of ten thousand would watch outdoor festivals in honour of Dionysus, the god of theatre.

The most elaborate form of mime was hypothesis, which was performed by troupes of actors. The main idea was to develop the character rather than the plot.

Greek Theatre

The first time theatre is known to have been freed from religious ritual, to become an art form in its own right, was in ancient Greece in the sixth century BC. Based around the Attica district of Athens, Greek theatre developed out of the recital and singing of poetic texts, and from ritual dances to honour Dionysus, the god of wine and fertility.

Aeschylus (525–456 BC) introduced the possibility of conflict between characters, by introducing a second actor into the format.

The first known actor was the ancient Greek Thespis, who in the sixth century BC introduced impersonation, or the pretence of being another person. He used masks so that he could play several different characters in the same play.

The first Festival of Drama was held in Athens in 534 BC, which Thespis is said to have won. Unfortunately no written records of the winners survive. The term 'thespian' remains in use to this day when referring to an actor.

Roman Theatre

Beginning around 240 BC, Roman theatre developed out of the Greek model, but with more emphasis on the voice than was traditional in Greek plays. The actors, who were mostly slaves, wore masks that may have been designed to amplify the actors' voices to carry to the far reaches of large outdoor theatres. After centuries of competing with the Roman Games, in which gladiators fought to the death and Christians were killed by wild animals, Roman theatre came to an abrupt end.

Pantomime

The ancient Romans, with the approval of Augustus (63 BC–AD 14), developed the *pantomimi*, which was acted out in silence, using only gestures to illustrate the drama and humour. During some early performances of *pantomime*, Roman audiences thought the actors were Greeks who couldn't speak their language.

Puppet Theatre

Xenophon (427–355 BC), a Greek soldier and historian, made the first written record of puppet theatre in the fifth century BC.

Punch and Judy

The first literary reference to Punch and Judy is in the diary of Samuel Pepys of 9 May 1662, in which he writes of having seen what he called an 'Italian Puppet Play' in Covent Garden. Pepys recorded that the character is derived from Punchinello, a brutal and vindictive character from the Italian commedia del'arte, and that Judy was originally called Joan.

Medieval Theatre

Western medieval drama emerged as an entirely new form in the church. At Easter and Christmas church services priests would act out small scenes from biblical stories and impersonate biblical figures. These playlets became more elaborate and transferred from inside the church to the church steps and then to the marketplace.

Once the action was outside church property, artisan guilds took over the responsibility for performances, and non-religious subject matter was slowly introduced.

Passion plays were first performed in thirteenth-century France and Flanders.

The world-renowned Passion play based on the life of Christ was first performed in 1634. This came about as a result of a vow taken by the residents of Oberammagau (in the Bavarian Alps) to do something for God, in which all the residents would have a part, no matter whether rich or poor. They hit upon the idea of a play and they vowed that if only God would spare the town from the spread of bubonic plague, which had already claimed the lives of 15,000 in nearby Munich, they would perform it for ever.

The Passion play is performed by the whole community with 1,700 parts. It only takes place once every ten years and is faithfully continued today.

Modern Theatre

During the early sixteenth century, modern theatre originated in Italy. Troupes of actors performed the *Commedia dell' arte* (Comedy of Art) from town to town. Performance in the *Commedia dell' arte* included improvisation and the invention of new words.

There were ten members in a troupe, and each of them would develop a particular type of character, such as the captain, the valet, the doctor, Harlequin and so on, with female parts originally being played by men but later by women. Before going on stage they would agree a basic plot and a general idea of how it would be performed, and then improvise on stage. The humour was often coarse or bawdy, and rarely subtle.

The Italian troupes travelled all over Europe, strongly influencing theatre in Spain, England, Germany and France.

Method Acting

In 1897, Konstantin Stanislavski (1863–1938) and Vladimir Danchenko (1858–1943) met in a restaurant in Moscow. Eighteen hours and a couple of bottles of vodka later, they had formed the Moscow Art Theatre. The mode of acting throughout was to be the Stanislavski system, which became known as method acting, in which the actor's role was to be believed, rather than understood or recognised.

Method acting was introduced to America in 1922 when two Russian actors, Maria Ouspenskaya (1876–1949) and Richard Boleslavski (1889–1937), defected from the visiting Moscow Art Theatre. Ouspenskaya founded the School of Dramatic Art in New York and, for the rest of her life, advocated and taught 'the method', as the Stanislavski System became known.

DANCE

(*See also* Art.)
In its earliest form, dance was not regarded as entertainment.

The ancient Egyptians in the third millennium BC had formal and ceremonial dances that were part of their religious ceremonies. Eventually the dances became so complex that only specially trained dancers could perform them.

By the fourth century BC there is evidence that dancing had been transformed into something much more personal. There are tales of couples indulging themselves in erotic and lascivious dancing performances for their own pleasure.

The ancient Greeks were strongly influenced by the earlier Egyptian dances. They held their bull dance on Crete as early as 1400 BC and, using their lively imaginations, developed over 200 different dances. Some of these were in preparation for war. They also developed the *kordax*, an uninhibited lascivious dance performed in comedies, in which the dancers wore masks.

Plato (428–348 BC) became a dance instructor and wrote texts which divided dance into two types: ugly and beautiful.

The Romans had an early dance of a military nature called the *Bellicrepa Saltatio*, which is said to have been started by Romulus when he carried off the Sabine women.

Roman dance was courtly and formal, and not universally popular.

Men who danced were considered effeminate and all dancing schools were closed in 150 BC.

Romans generally took their public displays seriously, and would not allow themselves to look undignified. The Roman statesman and orator Cicero (106–43 BC) said that only madmen danced.

Types of Dance

The Apache is a dramatic dance for a man and woman, with the woman being thrown about the floor by the man. It is said to resemble a pimp dealing with a prostitute, and ends with the woman being sent skidding across the floor in an act of violence and submission. There is no connection with the Native American Apache tribe; the dance is named after a Parisian street gang.

The barn dance originated in Scotland around 1860 and was usually held to celebrate the raising of a barn.

The black bottom was introduced in New Orleans in 1919 by songwriter Perry 'Mule' Bradford (1893–1970) and the Blues singer Alberta Hunter (1895–1984). Bradford claims that he had seen a similar dance performed in 1907 called the Jacksonville Rounders Dance, which was not a success, as a 'rounder' is another word for a pimp.

The black bottom was a solo 'challenge' dance, which featured slapping the backside while simultaneously hopping backwards and forwards and gyrating the hips. In 1926 the dance became the latest fashion on both sides of the Atlantic, and replaced the Charleston.

The cancan emerged in 1822 its present form in Paris from earlier dances such as the Triori. Risqué rather than lewd it is a display dance for the stage, which is normally danced to the same tune, the *Galop Infernal* by Jacques Offenbach. It features a troupe of high-kicking female dancers, lifting their full skirts to show their underwear and legs, and, to the final notes of the music, doing the jump splits.

Until 1866 the cancan was banned from public performance in New York.

The cha-cha, or cha-cha-cha In 1954, after complaints from audiences, Enrique Jorrin (1926–87), a Cuban violinist, slowed down the beat of the mambo dance to about a third of its original pace to make it easier to perform and so started the cha-cha.

The dance itself is sensual and sinuous and requires small steps and plenty of hip movement to make it expressive. The name is supposed to have originated from the sound of Cuban ladies' heels tapping the floor in a cha-cha-cha sound.

The Charleston was first performed in 1903 in Charleston, Virginia, USA, and transferred to the stage in Harlem, New York, in 1913. It was energetic and fun – with plenty of head-shaking and ankle-lifting.

Harper's Weekly Magazine of 13 October 1866 describes a similar dance, which was most likely a version of the twelfth-century French chain dance, the branle.

Clog dancing began in the 1520s in Lancashire in England. It is similar to tap dancing but much slower.

The fandango developed as a seventeenth-century Spanish courtship dance, in which the dancers would dance close together, but would not touch. It is said to be the forerunner of all Spanish dances. There is some evidence that a similar dance may have existed in ancient Rome, known even then as the Spanish Dance.

The foxtrot was invented by vaudeville performer Harry Fox (b. 1882) in 1914. Fox introduced the new dance steps in the Jardin de Danse on the roof of the New York Theatre. The foxtrot is unique in being named after the inventor rather than the town or style of dance.

The jive is a vigorous swing dance with plenty of partner twisting and twirling, which developed in 1940s USA.

The jitterbug was created by Cab Calloway (1907–94), the dance band leader, but it was actually coined in 1934 by Harry Alexander White. It was a popular exuberant dance in the USA in the 1930s and 1940s.

During the Second World War, 1,500,000 American servicemen arrived in Britain, and brought the jitterbug with them. Horrified dance hall proprietors not used to seeing such energetic dances and wanting to preserve their dance floors soon erected notices saying 'No Jitterbugging'. It had little effect.

Morris dancing is thought to have developed in England in the mid-fifteenth century, although some sources claim it derives from a form of Spanish–English dance current in the 1360s. The term 'Morris' is thought to be a corruption of 'Moorish', as the Arab or Muslim population of Spain were referred to in English as Moors.

The okey cokey originated in Kentucky as a nineteenth-century Shaker song. It is a group dance with silly words; participants stand in a ring during the dance and sing: 'You put your right arm in, you put your right arm out …' The craze was brought to Britain during the Second World War by American servicemen.

The polka was developed by Joseph Neruba in 1835 in Poland. He had learned the steps from watching a young girl dance and recognised there was a possibility of making money from the exciting new dance steps.

Rock and roll emerged naturally from jive and jitterbug and grew enormously in popularity throughout 1950s USA after the electrifying start given to it by Bill Haley and the Comets with 'Rock Around the Clock' in 1954. The term 'Rock and Roll' was first used in 1951 by Alan Freed, a Cleveland disc jockey, who took the words from another song, 'My Baby Rocks Me with a Steady Roll'.

'Rock Around the Clock' sold only 75,000 copies on first release. However, after it was used as the title track for the film *The Blackboard Jungle*, it sold millions. Haley (1925–81) was not the first performer to record 'Rock Around the Clock'. That honour fell to Sunny Dae in 1952.

The tango evolved in the lower-class districts of Buenos Aires in the 1880s. The dance amalgamated elements of the milonga, the mazurka and the habanera, and by 1900 it had become a worldwide sensation.

Tap dancing developed in the southern USA in the 1830s from dances introduced by African slaves. It also has close connections with clog dancing.

The twist Hank Ballard (1927–2003) wrote 'Let's Twist Again', the song that started the craze, in 1955, but the dance itself was not popularised until Chubby Checker (b. 1941) released the record in 1959 opening every performance with a dance lesson. The Twist was a worldwide sensation from 1960 through to 1970, and remains a favourite dance of middle-aged couples at weddings.

Chubby Checker's real name was Ernest Evans. His stage name was given to him by the wife of Dick Clark as a play on the name of jazz musician Fats Domino.

The waltz originated in Germany in 1520 as a more intimate development of the Westphalia, a thirteenth-century dance. The waltz was one of the first dances in which dancers touched each other, pressing against each other's bodies in public, known as a closed dance. It was at first deemed to be too lewd for women.

HUMOUR

Dictionary definition of humour: 'A form of communication in which a complex mental stimulus illuminates or amuses, or elicits the reflex of laughter.'

Ancient Humour

There are 29 'jokes' in the Old Testament, and Jesus (8–4 BC–AD 29–36), like all great public speakers, used a form of humour in his sermons.

Although our modern sense of humour may prevent us from seeing the joke, scholars suggest it is quite likely that Jesus' listeners were doubled up with laughter when they heard Jesus speak about the 'speck in your brother's eye' (Matt. 7: 3, 4), or 'pearls before swine' (Matt. 7: 6) or the one about 'a rich man having as much chance of going to Heaven as a camel passing through the eye of a needle'. The 'eye of a needle' referred to by Jesus was the common name for a small gate through the wall into Jerusalem. It was passable by pedestrians, but too small for a camel.

It is evident and strangely comforting that Jesus could also take a joke. An early example of irony at his expense came when one of His disciples asked, while looking at Him, 'How could anything good come out of Nazareth?'

Ancient humour was based on cruelty and harshness until the fifth century BC, when a softer, broader humour began to replace aggression and unpleasantness, and appear in performance art.

The earliest dramatic comedy emerged from the rowdy choruses and words of the fertility rites of the feasts of the Greek god Dionysus. 'Old Comedy', as it is known, lasted until around 450 BC, and was a collection of loosely connected scenes, which exploited coarse humour in satire, parody and fantasy, usually at the expense of public figures. Old Comedy was hard-hitting and similar, in a way, to modern satire.

It was superseded by the much milder 'New Comedy' around that time, becoming more politically correct. The subject matters in New Comedy included a collection of stock characters such as the thwarted lover, the bragging soldier and the clever slave. The most famous exponent of New Comedy was Menander (342–391 BC), writing in about 320 BC in Greece. One of his few surviving plays is *Dyscolus* (*The Grouch*) which was rediscovered on a papyrus manuscript in 1957.

Early Humour

In the Middle Ages, the Church tried to keep all the humour and joy out of drama, but it survived in folk plays and festivals.

Court jesters are mainly thought of as existing in the Middle Ages. However, the Roman philosopher and author Pliny the Elder (23–79 AD) mentions court jesters (planus regium) in his tale of a visit to King Ptolemy I (367 BC–283 BC).

The earliest entertainers were the *gleomen*, who were active in England from the fourth century AD, entertaining the Angles, a Germanic people who had settled in East Anglia and Northumbria. *Gleomen* would tell amusing stories through song and are described in the Anglo-Saxon epic *Beowulf* as court entertainers. Following the Norman Conquest in 1066 the court and noble house entertainers were known as minstrels, whereas entertainers for the lower classes were known as jongleurs.

The profession of minstrel was at its height between the twelfth and sixteenth centuries, with minstrels being fully employed servants at court as an entertainer of any kind, but usually as a musician. A Guild of Royal Minstrels was formed in 1469, but their popularity began to fade during the seventeenth century, becoming obsolete soon after, with the advent of the more sophisticated troubadour. Troubadours sang of love and chivalry and, as they moved around the kingdom, helped to transmit news from other areas and to spread trade.

Modern Humour

Cartoon Characters

Mr Magoo (first name Quincy) was introduced in 1949 in *Ragtime Bear*. In 1997, Magoo was played by Leslie Neilsen in the film Mr Magoo.

Mickey Mouse, the most famous of all cartoon characters, first appeared in the 1928 film *Steamboat Willie*.

Walt Disney was travelling back by train to his studio in California, having fallen out with his financial backers in New York. They had withdrawn financial support and taken back Oswald the Rabbit, a character that had been copyrighted to them. To fill in the time on the long journey, Disney sketched a new rabbit cartoon character, but changed it to a mouse and called it 'Mortimer'. His wife re-christened the character 'Mickey Mouse'.

Minnie Mouse, the girlfriend of Mickey, also first appeared in *Steamboat Willie*.

Pluto was introduced in 1930 in *The Chain Gang*.

Goofy first appeared in 1932 in *Mickey's Revue*.

Donald Duck put in his first appearance in 1934 in *The Wise Little Hen*.

Bambi, a character from a 1928 book by Felix Salten, scampered on to the screen in 1942.

Li'l Abner was drawn by Al Capp (Alfred Gerald Caplin) (1909–79) for the first time in 1940.

The Andy Capp cartoon strip was first published in northern editions of the *Daily Mirror* newspaper in 1957. Capp was created by Reg Smythe (1917–98), who started by submitting cartoons to Cairo magazines while he was stationed in Egypt during the Second World War. Andy Capp was syndicated to 1,400 newspapers worldwide and read by 175,000,000 people.

CIRCUS

The first building known as a circus was the Circus Maximus in Rome. It is thought to have been founded in the sixth century BC for chariot races. The track was U-shaped with a low wall running down the centre and seating on three sides. When it was developed by Julius Caesar (100–44 BC) in the first century BC it could hold 150,000 spectators. It was further extended in the fourth century AD to seat a quarter of a million people. The Circus Maximus was the largest seated stadium ever built. Nowadays, only the ruins remain.

The modern circus was founded in 1768 by an English trick-rider Philip Astley (1742–1814), who found that centrifugal force made it easy to stand on a horse's back while it galloped round in a circle. He set up a ring close to Westminster Bridge, where he operated a riding school in the mornings, and in the afternoons performed equine acrobatic displays to paying crowds. He took his idea to Paris and formed *Le Cirque*.

The name circus was coined by Charles Hughes (1748–1820), one of Astley's riders, who established his own ring in 1782 and called it the Royal Circus. Hughes took his ideas, which by then incorporated jugglers, trapeze artists, clowns and animals, to Russia, and the Moscow State Circus was born.

The first circus tent was pioneered by J. Purdy Brown in 1825, in the USA. Until the advent of the 'big top', circuses had been held either in permanent buildings or outdoors.

Music Hall

Music-hall songs provide the dull with wit,
just as proverbs provide them with wisdom.
W. Somerset Maugham (1874–1965)

This form of public entertainment developed in the eighteenth century from 'taproom concerts', which were popular in English city taverns. A number of Acts of Parliament were passed to restrict music and entertainment in taverns. These had precisely the opposite effect and resulted in the rapid development of specially constructed halls, where smoking and drinking were permitted, to accommodate the demand.

The first dedicated music hall was built in 1852 by Charles Morton (1819–1904). He called it Morton's Canterbury Hall, and featured acts were Harry Lauder (1870–1950), Dan Leno (1860–1904) and Vesta Tilley (1864–1952), the biggest names of the time. As a form of popular entertainment music hall went into decline in the 1920s with the advent of 'talking pictures'. Several halls were converted into cinemas.

Musicals

Comic Opera

Modern musicals are descended from comic operas such as *The Beggar's Opera* by John Gay (1685–1732), which debuted in 1728. Composers of comic operas borrowed popular songs of the day and rewrote the lyrics to suit the plot. Tunes by Handel and Purcell were commonly used. Robert Walpole (1676–1745), who was the Prime Minister of the day, and the butt of Gay's satire in *The Beggar's Opera*, arranged for Gay's next opera *Polly* to be banned.

Operetta

The first operetta, which bridged the gap between opera (*see* Art) and the musical, was *Orpheus in the Underworld*, composed by Jacques Offenbach (1819–80) and first performed in 1858. As a German composer living in Paris Offenbach experienced huge difficulties because opera was a government monopoly in France and he was seen as the main competition.

Minstrel Shows

The pioneers of minstrel shows as we know them today were Dan Emmett's Virginia Minstrels. In 1843 Emmett (1815–1904) staged an African-American spoof version of the Tyrolese Minstrel Family, who toured the USA from 1840, with a series of musical comedy sketches, which featured fake European music. He offered full shows of white performers with 'blacked up' faces, performing song and dance routines.

African-American impersonation shows declined in popularity towards the end of the nineteenth century, but enjoyed a brief revival on British television in the 1950s and 60s. However, this form of entertainment died out as society grew to regard 'blacking up' as offensive.

Musical and Musical Comedy

The first modern musical is believed to be *The Black Crook*, which opened at Niblo's Gardens in New York on 12 September 1866. The production was based on a book by Charles Barras.

The first musical comedy was *The Mulligan Guard* in 1878. A uniquely American creation, it packed out the Theatre Comique on Broadway for the whole month of its run. It was produced by and starred Ned Harrigan and Tony Hart.

The first British musical was *Dorothy*. It was staged by George Edwardes, the theatre impresario, with music by Alfred Cellier at the Gaiety Theatre,

London, in 1865. *Dorothy* was a three-act musical, which broke box office records by playing for 931 performances, after transferring to the Prince of Wales Theatre later that year.

The first Hollywood musical was *The Jazz Singer* in 1927, starring Al Jolson (1886–1950). *The Jazz Singer* was also the first feature film to use sound successfully. Jolson's second Hollywood musical, *The Singing Fool* of 1928, set box office records that lasted until *Gone with the Wind* in 1939.

Film

The appearance of motion on a screen, as experienced when watching a film, is made possible as a result of an optical phenomenon known as 'persistence of vision' when a series of still photographs are projected rapidly onto a screen. The main technical innovations involved in producing moving pictures were achieved in France in the 1880s and 1890s by brothers Auguste (1862–1954) and Louis (1864–1948) Lumière, and in the USA by Thomas Alva Edison (1847–1931).

However, a ground-breaking contribution was made in 1889 by William Friese-Green (1855–1921) of England, who invented the cine camera. He recorded a film of the Esplanade in Brighton using paper film negative. Later the same year he replaced the paper with celluloid, which remains the standard material to this day.

The first public screening of celluloid film was hosted by the Lumière brothers on 22 March 1895.

The first international film empire was created by Charles Pathé (1863–1957) of France. The Pathé name is still familiar to modern filmgoers.

The first Hollywood film studio was opened by the Nestor Company in 1911 in the converted Blondeau Tavern. Cecil B. DeMille (1881–1959) and Sam Goldwyn (1879–1974) soon followed, and 15 other film companies were established within a year. The Hollywood film industry grew rapidly to dominate the world of motion pictures.

In 1886, H.H. Wilcox bought an area of land on Rancho La Brea to develop as a residential community for the wealthy. His wife Daeida rechristened the area Hollywood after hearing the name on a train journey. Wilcox paved a road, which he called Prospect Avenue. It became one of the world's most famous streets, known now as Hollywood Boulevard.

The first full-length feature film was *The Squaw Man*, produced in 1914 by DeMille and Goldwyn, who went on, in 1917, to establish a hallowed Hollywood tradition with the first sequel *The Squaw Man's Son*.

The first Hollywood superstar was Mary Pickford (1892–1979) who, in 1927, co-founded the Academy of Motion Pictures, which awards the Oscars annually.

Most of the great film studios originated in this era:

- Paramount Pictures in 1912.

- Columbia Pictures in 1920.

- Warner Brothers in 1923.

- MGM in 1924.

United Artists was formed as a partnership in 1919 between Charlie Chaplin (1889–1977), Douglas Fairbanks (1883–1939) and Mary Pickford (1892–1979), together with director D. W. Griffiths (1875–1948). The other studios could not afford their salaries.

Colour Film

The first colour film was Charles Urban's *Kinemacolour*, which was produced in 1906. Its huge cost prevented it being a commercial success.

Technicolor was developed by German engineer Helmut Kalmus in 1922, and became the industry standard.

Film Sound

The first system to attempt to put sound on film was the Gaumont Chronophone system, which was launched in 1900, but it failed to synchronise sound and vision well enough.

The first usable sound system was the Phone-Bio-Tableaux of 1905, which was developed by Walter Gibbons. The first performer to be heard on the new system was Vesta Tilley (1864–1952) in the same year, but it would be 1927 before the first 'talkie', *The Jazz Singer* with Al Jolson (1886–1950), would incorporate sound fully.

Cinemascope

A physicist, Henri Chrétien (1879–1956), invented Cinemascope in 1928. It is a wide-screen film format and was largely ignored until the 1950s when competition from television as the most popular form of entertainment forced film companies to offer a better film experience to their audiences.

The first Cinemascope film was *The Robe*, released in 1953.

Film Censor

In 1912 the British Board of Film Censors was formed to keep films 'genteel'.

The first designations were: 'U' for Universal, which meant children under the age of 16 were allowed to view and 'A' for Adult, which were deemed unsuitable for the under 16s. 'Adult' did not have the meaning of 'pornographic', it merely meant slightly sexy, or violent, and unsuitable for under-16s.

Film Festival

Usually, film festivals are held annually, for the purpose of evaluating recently released, or shortly to be released, motion pictures. Critics, distributors, film-makers and others having an interest in the promotion of films normally attend. Side attractions include the opportunity for the general public to see film stars close at hand and to sample the glamour of such occasions. It is normal practice for the paparazzi to cluster in any likely spot, such as a hotel pool, where a starlet may be photographed wearing as little as possible.

The first film festival was held in 1932 in Venice, and has been an annual event ever since. Festivals are now held in Berlin, Cannes, Moscow, London, New York and San Francisco.

The Oscars

More properly known as the Academy Awards, the Oscars were first awarded in 1929. The prizes were small golden statues and were first referred to as Oscars in 1931 by Margaret Herrick, a director of the Academy, who thought the statuette resembled her uncle Oscar – and the name stuck.

The winners of the first Oscars were:

Leading Actor: Emil Jannings (1884–1950) for *The Last Command* and *The Way of All Flesh*. Unlike today, when the suspense is maintained right to the last moment, in 1929 the winner was known several days before the event. Jannings, who was German, had booked to return to Europe and asked to be presented with the award ahead of the actual ceremony. His wish was granted and he became the first ever recipient of an Academy Award.

Leading Actress: Janet Gaynor (1906–84) for *Seventh Heaven*.

Best Director: Frank Borzage (1893–1962) for *Seventh Heaven*.

Best Picture: *Wings*.

The first family to produce three winners was the Huston family: Walter (1884–1950), John (1906–87) and Angelica (b. 1951).

The first British winner was George Arliss (1868–1946), who played British Prime Minister Benjamin Disraeli in the 1929 film *Disraeli*. Arliss had specialised in portraying Disraeli in his one-man stage show and was regarded as a 'natural' for the part.

The first use of the sealed envelope for announcing winners was in 1941.

The first African-American winner of the Leading Actor Award was Sidney Poitier (b. 1927) in 1963 for *Lilies of the Field*.

The first African-American actress to win the Leading Actress Award was Halle Berry (b. 1966) in 2002 for *Monster's Ball*.

The first African-American Oscar of any discipline was for the Best Supporting Actress Award won by Hattie McDaniel (1895–1952), who portrayed 'Mammy' in *Gone with the Wind* in 1939.

The first radio broadcast of the Oscars was in 1944.

The first TV broadcast of the Oscar ceremony was in 1953, and 1966 was the first year the ceremony was broadcast in colour.

GRAMOPHONE

Thomas Alva Edison (1847–1931), the great American inventor, produced the forerunner of the gramophone, the phonograph, in 1877.

Emile Berliner (1851–1929) coined the word 'gramophone' in 1894 as a trademark for his new and improved design of phonograph. Berliner's machine used flat discs in place of the cylinders that were used in phonographs.

Jukeboxes

The name 'jukebox' may have derived from the Elizabethan word 'jouk', meaning to move quickly or dodge, or the African-American slang term 'jook' meaning to dance.

The first coin-operated machine to play recorded music was installed on 23 November 1889 by Louis Glass (1864–1936) in the Palais Royal Saloon in San Francisco. He linked an electrically operated Edison phonograph to four listening tubes, each of which was separately coin-operated. The term 'nickel in the slot machine' was coined to describe it.

The first jukebox as we would recognise it today was invented in 1905 by John C. Dunton of Grand Rapids, Michigan. The customer had a choice of 24 pre-selected recordings, each of which was on a cylinder.

Jukeboxes went into decline during the 1930s and 1940s until demand was stimulated by better sound quality and the advent of rock and roll music in the 1950s.

Hit Parade

The original British number-one hit in the record sales chart was 'Here in My Heart' by Al Martino (b. 1927) in October 1952. In 2006 Al is still singing for his living.

The first sheet music sales chart was topped by the Ink Spots in Jan-uary 1950 with 'You're Breaking my Heart'.

The original number one in the US Billboard 'Hot 100' chart was 'Wheel of Fortune' sung by Kay Starr (b. 1922) in March 1952.

In 1949, Todd Stortz bought the ailing radio station KOWH in Omaha and revitalised its fortunes by pioneering the radio format of the Top 40 record hits, played on a countdown to number one.

Radio Luxembourg adopted the same format and broadcast the Top 20 throughout the 1950s and 1960s.

Compact Disc (CD)

The CD, a moulded plastic disc for the reproduction of sound, was devel-oped by Philips Industries (Netherlands) and demonstrated in 1980 at the Salzburg Festival by Herbert von Karajan (1908–89), the lead con-ductor of the Berlin Philharmonic Orchestra.

At the launch event, von Karajan said, 'All else is just gaslight', a reference to the fact that CDs were the recorded music format of the future. The prototype CDs were designed for 60 minutes of music. It is rumoured that von Karajan used his influence with Philips to promote the longer 74-minute CD, in order to accommodate Beethoven's Ninth Symphony, which was his favourite piece of music.

Philips and Sony (Japan) worked together on more than one hundred classical and jazz recordings and launched CDs into the recorded music market in 1982.

Digital Versatile Disc (DVD)

In 1995, Philips/Sony demonstrated their new format MMCD (Multi Media CD). In the same year Toshiba/Warner demonstrated their new format SD (Super Disc). The two consortia agreed to combine the best of both formats to produce the single standard format DVD.

DVD (Rom) and DVD (Video) were launched in Tokyo in November

1996, and in the USA in August 1997. The first DVD was sold in Europe in 1998.

Electric Guitar

The electric guitar was crucial to the development of rock and pop music. Lloyd Loar of the USA developed the original prototype in 1924, and his first commercial model, the Vivi-Tone, was launched in 1933. It was a flop.

Moog Synthesiser

Robert Moog (1934–2005), a US engineer, invented the synthesiser in 1964. He developed his ideas from building Theremin* electronic music kits at home. He sold around 1,000 of these before starting to make his own instruments, collaborating with two composers, Herbert Deutsch and Walter (later Wendy) Carlos (b. 1939).

After the success of Carlos's album *Switched on Bach*, which was the first album produced using only electronic instruments, the Beatles and Rolling Stones bought synthesisers and the word 'Moog' passed into pop legend. After his synthesiser company went bankrupt, Robert Moog returned to producing Theremin instruments.

The word 'Moog' is one of the most mispronounced words in music. It should be pronounced to rhyme with 'vogue'.

* Theremin instruments were named after Leon Termen (1896–1993), a Russian cellist, who, in 1917, developed an electronic machine which could make music by combining two different high-frequency sound waves. Soviet leader Vladimir Ilyich Lenin owned a Theremin instrument and had lessons on how to play it from Termen himself.

Pop Music

The 'Big Bang' year in pop/rock music was 1954. Elvis Presley released 'That's Alright Mama' with Sun Studios, and Bill Haley released 'Shake Rattle and Roll'.

Pop stars – their first number-one hits
Bill Haley and the Comets (previously the Saddlemen)
Shake Rattle and Roll – 1954 (USA)

Little Richard
Tutti Frutti – 1955 (USA)

Elvis Presley
Heartbreak Hotel – 1956 (USA)

Buddy Holly (with the Crickets)
That'll be the Day – 1957 (USA)

Cliff Richard
Living Doll – 1959 (UK)

The Beatles
Please Please Me – 1962 (UK)
or depending on which UK chart compiler is believed
From Me to You – 1963 (UK)

The first recording made by John Lennon, George Harrison and Paul McCartney was 'If You'll be True to Me'.

The Beach Boys
I Get Around – 1964 (USA)

Michael Jackson
Ben – 1972 (USA)
Jackson was a member, along with four of his brothers, of the Jackson Five, which had a number-one hit with 'I Want You Back' in 1970.

The Rolling Stones
It's All Over Now – 1964 (UK)

Spice Girls
Wannabe – 1996 (UK)

Note: there is still some debate over the details of some of these entries.

First Album to Reach One Million Sales

The soundtrack to *The Sound of Music* in 1963

Groups – their original names

Famous name	Original name
Blondie	Angel and the Snake
Creedence Clearwater Revival	The Blue Velvets
Bill Haley and the Comets	Bill Haley and his Saddlemen
The Beach Boys	Carl and the Passions
The Supremes	The Primettes
Simon and Garfunkel	Tom and Jerry
Sonny and Cher	Caesar and Cleo
Black Sabbath	Polka Tulk
Mamas and Papas	The New Journeymen
The Temptations	The Elgins
The Beatles	Johnny and the Moondogs (also The Quarrymen)
Buddy Holly	Charles Hardin Holley
Cliff Richard (later Sir Cliff)	Harry Webb

FAMOUS PEOPLE

COVERING: US Presidents, British Prime Ministers, Other World Leaders, the Ancients, Actors and other Show-business People, Writers, Singers, Great Artists, Others.

The famous exist in the public gaze, and the man in the street wonders: how did they get there ... where did they spring from ... what did he do before he became the Pope or a film star?

What did Hitler do to make ends meet before he ran Germany? Was there something odd about Julius Caesar? Did Sean Connery have a 'proper job' before he started acting?

Public images hide as much as they reveal, and what lies hidden is the most intriguing of all. What you see is not always what you get. Some famous people change their birth names for showbiz or political reasons. Alternatively a new name might be adopted just because the real name is so awful. Imagine, for example, what the parents of the Hollywood film star John Wayne were thinking, by naming him Marion. Why would the great Chinese leader Chiang Kai-shek need four names at different times of his life? Diana Fluck – who is she?

You may also be surprised to learn that George Washington was once an officer in the British Army, and one of the best-known Hollywood 'tough guy' stars began his career as a female impersonator. Perhaps not so difficult to imagine is that a recent British Prime Minister failed to qualify as a bus conductor, went on to work in a bank and then achieved the highest office in the land. His origins reveal other little-known facts. Another Prime Minister invented soft ice cream. Before they became famous, one star worked as a zoo attendant, one a concert pianist and three worked for the US Postal Service.

This chapter reveals the surprising or little-known origins, or back-grounds, of famous people. It could be their original names, or the careers they pursued, before the one that made them famous. It could be a snippet of information that just completes that ever-elusive picture.

US Presidents

George Washington
Tobacco farmer
As a Lieutenant Colonel in the British Army he surrendered to the French at Fort Duquesne

Thomas Jefferson
Lawyer
Planter

Abraham Lincoln
Mill manager
Postmaster
Lawyer

Harry Truman
Farmer
Lead mine owner (failed)
Oil prospector (failed)
Haberdashery shopkeeper (failed)
Partner in a bank (failed)
County Court Judge
Entered the US Senate in 1935.

Became President when Franklin Roosevelt died towards the end of the Second World War. Truman had met Roosevelt only twice and took office having almost no knowledge of the current Second World War plans.

'I never give the general public hell. I just tell them the truth and they think it's hell. Harry Truman

John Kennedy
Inherited colossal wealth from his father's liquor smuggling during Prohibition.
Served in the US Navy in the Second World War

Lyndon Johnson
Schoolteacher
National Youth Administrator

Richard Nixon
Performed in amateur theatre
Liutentant Commander in US Navy
Applied and failed to become an FBI agent
Lawyer
The only man to have been elected to two terms as Vice-President and two terms as President

People have got to know whether their President is a crook. Well I'm not a crook. Richard Nixon

Gerald Ford
US footballer
Lieutenant Commander in
US Navy

Jimmy Carter
Peanut farmer
US Navy officer

Ronald Reagan
Film actor
Union boss

You can tell a lot about a fellow's character by his way of eating jellybeans. Ronald Reagan

George H. Bush
Fighter pilot in the Korean War
(bailed out after aircraft was hit)

Bill Clinton
University teacher

I'm not going to say this again. I did not have sexual relations with that woman, Miss Lewinski. These allegations are false. Bill Clinton

George W. Bush
Oilman
F-102 pilot in the Texas Air
National Guard
Part-owner Texas Rangers Baseball
team

British Prime Ministers

(Since the Second World War)

Clement Attlee
Lawyer
Social worker

Winston Churchill
Descendant of Duke of
Marlborough
Half American on mother's side
War reporter in the Boer War
Took part in the last British Army
cavalry charge, under Lord Kitchener

Anthony Eden
Fluent in Persian
Won the Military Cross in 1917 in
the First World War

Harold Macmillan
Grandson of Macmillan the book
publisher
Wounded three times in the First
World War and on one occasion
moved himself off the 'sure to die'
stretcher

'I was determined that no British government should be brought down by the action of two tarts.
HAROLD MACMILLAN
(on the Profumo affair)

Alex Douglas-Home

Last member of the House of Lords to become Prime Minister
Last Prime Minister to be appointed by the monarch

Harold Wilson

Contracted typhoid in 1931
University lecturer
Member of Liberal Party before joining Labour
President of the Board of Trade at the age of 30

'In politics, a week is a very long time. HAROLD WILSON

Edward Heath

Awarded an organ scholarship at Oxford University
Served in the Royal Artillery in the Second World War

James Callaghan

Tax Inspector
Lieutenant in the Royal Navy
Callaghan is the only man to have held all three great offices of state before becoming Prime Minister

Margaret Thatcher

Research chemist at British Xylonite
Food chemist at J. Lyons, developed soft ice cream
Lawyer

John Major

Bus conductor (failed)
Garden gnome manufacturer
Bank clerk

Tony Blair

Father became a Communist, later a Tory
Rock band guitarist
Lawyer
Pat Phoenix, a leading actress in *Coronation Street*, campaigned for Blair in 1983

OTHER WORLD LEADERS

Yasser (Yassir) Arafat
Real name: Muhammad Al-Ra-Uf
Al-Qudwah Al-Husayni
Studied civil engineering at the
University of Texas
Qualified as a civil engineer and
became a businessman

Pope Benedict XVI
Real name: Joseph Alois Ratzinger
Member of the Hitler Youth
German Army deserter
Allied prisoner of war
Professor at several German
universities

Julius Caesar
Full name: Gaius Julius Caesar
Suffered from epilepsy
Studied oratory in Greece
Slept with Pompey's wife

Mahatma Ghandi
Real name: Mohandas Karamchand
Gandhi
Married at 13
Barrister in England
Political activist in South Africa
Survived a lynching attempt

Chiang Kai-shek
Given name at birth: Chung-Cheng
(which means Balanced Justice)
'Milk name': Jui-Yuan (which

means Auspicious Beginning)
aka: Jiang Jieshi (which means
Between the Rocks)

Lenin
Real name: Vladimir Ilyich Ulyanov
Born into a middle-class family

*Liberty is precious. So precious it
must be rationed.* LENIN

Pope John Paul II
Real name: Karol Wojtyla
(pronounced Voyteelah)

Joseph Stalin
Real name: Iosif Vissarionovich
Dzhugashvili
Studied for the priesthood
Bank robber

Leon Trotsky
Real name: Lev Davidovich
Bronshtein
Murdered in Mexico by Stalin's
agent

THE ANCIENTS

Pythagoras
Famous for his theorem 'the square on the hypotenuse is equal to the sum of the squares on the opposite two sides'. He also invented the eight-note music scale, having heard the different 'notes' from unequally sized anvils being struck by blacksmiths.

Aristotle
Private tutor to Alexander the Great

Plato
Real name: Aristocles
Amateur wrestler
Nicknamed 'Plato' because his wide shoulders gave him a 'plate-like' appearance.

ACTORS AND OTHER SHOW-BUSINESS PEOPLE

British

Dave Allen
Real Name: David Tynan O'Mahoney

Michael Caine
Real name: Maurice Micklewhite

Sean Connery
Milkman
Winner of 'Mr Scotland'

Daniel Day-Lewis
Son of the Poet Laureate Cecil Day-Lewis

Diana Dors
Real name: Diana Fluck

Alec Guinness
Real name: Alec Guinness De Cuffe
Advertising copywriter

Nigel Havers
Researcher on the *Jimmy Young Show*
Father was Attorney General of the UK

Benny Hill
Milkman in 1940s (before 'Ernie the Fastest Milkman in the West' – his most famous character)

Glenda Jackson
Checkout till operator at Boots the Chemist

David Jason (now Sir David)
Stage electrician

Sir Ben Kingsley
Real name: Krishna Bhanji

Christopher Lee
Served in the RAF – mentioned in despatches
British Intelligence

James Mason
Architect

Buster Merriwether (Granddad in *Only Fools and Horses*)
Bank manager

Helen Mirren
Real name: Ilynea Lydia Mironoff

Peter Ustinov
White Russian
Father was British spy

American

Woody Allen
Newspaper joke writer

Pamela Anderson
Nude calendar model – *Playboy*

Louis Armstrong
Nickname: Satchmo (short for 'satchel mouth')

Fred Astaire
Real name: Frederick Austerlitz

Lauren Bacall
Real name: Betty Perske

Humphrey Bogart
Real name: Humphrey de Forest Bogart
Son of a famous New York surgeon and a margarine demonstrator
(The distinctive feature of his set upper lip was the result of a shell wound received in the Second World War.)

Yul Brynner
Born in Siberia
Trapeze artist

James Cagney
Half Norwegian on mother's side
Began stage career as a female impersonator

Gary Cooper
Educated in Dunstable, England
Tour guide in Yellowstone National Park
Political cartoonist
Stunt horse rider

Bing Crosby
Real name: Harry Lillis Crosby
Adopted 'Bing' from his favourite
comic strip, the Bingville Bugle
Postal clerk

James Dean
First appearance on film was in a
Pepsi Cola advertisement
Last appearance on film was in a
road safety advertisement (Dean
died in a motor accident within
days)

Cecil B De Mille
Owned a girls school

Walt Disney
Assistant post office letter carrier

Troy Donahue
Real name: Merle Johnson
In *The Godfather* Donahue was cast
as Don Corleone's son-in-law,
Merle Johnson

Robert Downey Jr
Shoe salesman

Richard Dreyfuss
Conscientious objector in the
Vietnam War

Robert Duvall
Son of a US Navy admiral

Clint Eastwood
Firefighter
Lumberjack
Steel-mill furnace stoker
Swimming instructor and lifeguard

Peter Falk
Lost right eye at the age of three
from a malignant tumour
Worked as an efficiency expert for
Connecticut State Budget
Department

Henry Fonda
Journalist

Harrison Ford
Carpenter

Jodie Foster
Real name: Alicia Christian Foster

Judy Garland
Real name: Frances Gumm

Greer Garson (1940s film star)
Achieved BA (Hons) at University
of London

Cary Grant
Real name: Archibald Leach
Born Bristol, England
Acrobat
Song and dance man
Stilt walker
Juggler
Lifeguard

Dustin Hoffman
Janitor
Attendant in mental hospital

Bob Hope
Real name: Leslie Townes Hope
Born in Eltham, England

Rock Hudson
Real name: Roy Scherer
Post office letter carrier
In 1985 Hudson became the first
famous person to die of AIDS

Charles Laughton
Hotel clerk

Stan Laurel (of Laurel and Hardy)
Real name: Arthur Stanley Jefferson
Music hall and American
vaudeville

Jack Lemmon
Pianist in a beer hall

Jayne Mansfield
Concert pianist and violinist

Lee Marvin
Plumber
US Marine
Marvin became the world's first
'palimony' case after splitting with
live-in girlfriend of six years

Robert Mitchum
Heavyweight boxer
Aircraft fitter
Stage hand

Marilyn Monroe
Real name: Norma Jean Baker
(or Norma Jean Mortenson)
Nude calendar model on the cover
of the first issue of *Playboy*

Paul Newman
Second World War naval radioman

Jack Nicholson
Office boy in MGM Cartoon
Department

Al Pacino
Theatre usher
Porter
Superintendent in an office
building

Gregory Peck
Medical student

Sidney Poitier
Physiotherapist

Anthony Quinn
Irish-Mexican son-in-law of Cecil
B. De Mille

Robert Redford
Pavement artist in Paris at the
age of 19

Martin Sheen
Real name: Ramon Estevez
Janitor
Soda 'jerk'
Half Irish, half Spanish

Kevin Spacey
Real name: Kevin Fowler
Stand-up comedian in comedy
clubs

Sylvester Stallone
Expelled from fourteen schools in
eleven years
Zoo attendant
Porn film actor (*The Party at Kitty
and Stud's* and *Italian Stallion* – 1970)
Pizza demonstrator
Theatre usher

Barbara Streisand
Switchboard operator
Theatre usherette

John Wayne
Real name: Marion Morrison

Mae West
During the Second World War an
inflatable yellow lifejacket was
named after her

European

Brigitte Bardot
Real name: Camille Javal

Greta Garbo
Latherer in men's barber shop

Audrey Hepburn
Real name: Edda van Heemstra
Hepburn-Ruston
Dancer with Ballet Rambert
Appeared in her first film as Edda
Hepburn

Gina Lollobrigida
As a fashion model she used the
name Diane Loris

WRITERS

William Shakespeare
Poacher on Charlecote Park,
Sir Thomas Lucy's estate in
Warwickshire. In later years
Shakespeare was invited back to the
estate on a deer shoot, but was so
short-sighted that he was not
allowed to handle a crossbow.

Nevil Shute
Designer of R100 airship, sister
ship of the famous R101 that
crashed

Edgar Allan Poe
Classics scholar

Raymond Chandler
High-flying oil-company executive
Became a naturalised British citizen

in 1907 so that he could take the
Civil Service exam

Daniel Defoe
Reporter

Barbara Cartland
Step-grandmother to Princess
Diana

Mark Twain
Real name: Samuel Langhorne
Clemens
Twain had heard the leadsman on
the paddle steamers calling out the
depths of the river, from knots, or
'marks', on a line hanging over the
side. Mark 'twain' indicated the
second knot, which was two
fathoms or 12 feet deep, the safe
depth of water for a steamboat.
He adopted Mark Twain as his
pen name
Gold miner
Reporter
Editor
Mississippi River boat pilot

SINGERS

Boy George
Real name: George O'Dowd

I prefer a nice cup of tea to sex.
BOY GEORGE

Rod Stewart
Grave digger

Stevie Wonder
Real name: Steveland Judkins

GREAT ARTISTS

Leonardo da Vinci
Born illegitimate (illegitimacy was not a stigma during the Renaissance)
His first commercial painting was to decorate a shield, for which his father received 100 ducats (and kept it all)

Michelangelo
Michelangelo Buonarroti Simoni

Raphael
Raphael Sanzio d'Urbino

Rembrandt
Rembrandt Harmenszoon van Rijn

Caravaggio
Michaelangelo Merisi
Double murderer

OTHERS

Mother Teresa
Real name: Agnes Gonhxa Bojaxhiu (Yugoslavia)

The biggest disease today is not leprosy or tuberculosis, but rather the feeling of being unwanted.

St Matthew
Tax collector

St Mark
Born in Libya
Wrote the first of the Gospels in Greek

Albert Einstein
Patent Office clerk (second class). When he was asked to explain his Theory of Relativity, Einstein said

When you sit with a pretty girl for two hours, you think it's only a minute. When you sit on a hot stove for a minute, you think it's two hours. That's relativity.

Thomas Alva Edison
Telegraph operator

Henry Morton Stanley
Real name: John Rowlands. He took his adoptive father's name.

Doctor Livingstone, I presume?

Louis Vuitton

Opened first shop in Paris 1854
Best customer: Empress Eugenie

Christine Keeler

Nude dancer and hostess at
Murray's Cabaret Club

*Discretion is the polite word for
hypocrisy.*

Casanova

Trainee abbot

Charles Manson

Failed an audition to be a member
of the Monkees pop group (but this
may be an urban myth)

FOOD AND DRINK

COVERING: Agriculture, Cookery, Types of Food, Diets, Beverages, Kitchen Equipment.

AGRICULTURE

It is believed that agriculture – cultivating soil, harvesting crops and raising livestock – began in the Middle East about 9000 to 7000 BC.

The ox-drawn plough was invented in Mesopotamia (modern-day Iraq) around 4500 BC.

COOKERY

The origins of cookery are uncertain, but in all probability began in the Palaeolithic period. Cooked food is thought to have originated from the chance discovery of burned animal carcasses after a forest fire. The meat would have been tastier and easier to chew than it was when raw.

French Cuisine

For most of the twentieth century French cuisine has been recognised as the most sophisticated in the West. Its pre-eminence originated in 1533 when the Florentine Catherine de Medici (1519–89), at the age of 14, married the Duc d'Orléans, (1519–59), who was later to become Henry II of France. Catherine brought her staff of Florentine chefs, who taught the French a thing or two about refining their, up until then, rather crude methods of cooking.

Cookery Books

The first recorded cookery book was written by Archestratus of Gela, a Sicilian Greek who lived around 350 BC. He called his book *Hedypatheia* (The Life of Luxury).

Archestratus travelled throughout the Greek world of Sicily, Italy, Asia Minor and Greece to record recipes. He emphasised the use of fresh seasonal ingredients with sauces to enhance flavours. He also recorded cooking techniques and combinations of flavours from around the empire.

In the second century BC, the Greek Athenaeus wrote *The Learned Banquet*. The book contained many wonderful recipes, but was not strictly speaking a cookery book, as it was written in a style more like a novel.

He also wrote a series of 15 books called *Deipnosophistai* (*The Gastronomers*), which covered most aspects of the ancient Greek and Roman world. In the book, Athenaeus imagines learned men, including some real people from the past, meeting at a banquet and discussing food and other subjects. The work contains around 800 quotations from writers from antiquity.

The earliest and most important Latin cookbook *De Re Coquinaria* (*On Cookery*) was written by Marcus Gavius Apicius (14 BC–AD 37). In his book, Apicius showed the changes in taste and style of the Roman upper class leading up to the fall of the Roman Empire. Some of the dishes Apicius wrote about still feature in regional Italian food. Pliny the Younger (*c.*AD 62–113) claimed that Apicius force-fed geese to enlarge their livers to produce the best pâté: the forerunner of pâté de foie gras.

Recipes in *De Re Coquinaria* included casseroled flamingo and nightingale tongues. Apicius entertained lavishly, but lived beyond his means and found himself in financial difficulties. Sad to say, he decided to poison himself rather than face the consequences.

In the thirteenth century Kublai Khan's (1215–94) personal chef, Huou, wrote *The Important Things to Know About Eating and Drinking*. The majority of the book was dedicated to a collection of soup recipes, with household advice thrown in.

The first American cookbook was the delightfully titled *American Cookery or the Art of Dressing* written by Amelia Simmons and first published in 1796.

TYPES OF FOOD

Bread

Loaves have been found in 5,000-year-old Egyptian tombs, and are displayed in the British Museum, but the first evidence of bread goes back further still.

The origin of bread lies with the Neolithic Stone Age people who made solid cakes from stone-crushed barley and wheat about 12,000 years ago. Archaeologists have discovered a millstone, thought to be more than 7,000 years old, which was used for grinding grain.

The Bible contains several references to bread, including the parable of the 'loaves and fishes', and the ancient Greeks and Romans used both unleavened and leavened (risen) bread as a staple food.

Pizza

The basis of pizza, unleavened bread, has been around for centuries, and historical writings record that the ancient Egyptians, Greeks and Romans all used a form of flat unleavened bread as a base for vegetables.

The invention of the first modern pizza is credited to Neapolitan restaurant owner Raffaele Esposito. His Pizza alla Margherita combining pizza crust, tomato sauce, mozzarella cheese and basil – the red, white and green of which matched the colours of the Italian flag – was produced to commemorate the visit of Queen Marguerita (1851–1926) to Naples in 1889.

The first pizzeria in the USA was opened by Gennaro Lombardi in Spring Street, New York, in 1905.

Chicago Deep Dish Pizza is jointly credited to Ike Sewell, a Texan businessman, and Ric Riccardo, who opened Pizzeria Uno, serving their newly invented pizza in 1943.

Potatoes

The potato was cultivated in South America for approximately 2,000 years before it was introduced into Europe by the Spanish. Potatoes were brought to England from the West Indies by Sir Walter Raleigh (1552–1618).

Tomatoes

Cultivated in South America, tomatoes were introduced into Europe by the Spanish in the early part of the sixteenth century. Home grown tomatoes were first eaten in England in 1596, from the garden of John Gerard, a barber surgeon.

Cheeses

How can you govern a country that has two hundred and forty-six varieties of cheese?
CHARLES DE GAULLE (1890–1970)

The first cheese is thought to have developed around 4000 BC as a result of Sumerian herdsmen storing their daily ration of milk in dried calf stomachs. The milk combined with the natural enzyme of rennin left in the stomach and then curdled, becoming cheese.

Cheese was described by Homer in the Odyssey in about the seventh century BC.

In Greece, whey was separated from curds by using a wicker basket called a *formos*, which became *fromage*, the French word for cheese.

Stilton was first made in the mid-1700s in Melton Mowbray by Mrs Frances Pawlett (1720–1808). It was Britain's first blue cheese and remains a market leader.

Biscuits

The word 'biscuit' derives from the Latin *bis coctum*, meaning 'cooked twice'. In the USA they are known as 'cookies'.

The biscuit is first recorded in the twelfth century. Richard I (1157–99) (also known as Richard the Lionheart) took 'biskits of muslin' to the Crusades.

Beginning in the seventeenth century, the English Navy supplied mass-produced biscuits for their sailors because they lasted longer than bread on extended sea voyages.

The Garibaldi biscuit was baked to commemorate the visit of Giuseppi Garibaldi (1807–82), founder of modern Italy, to London in 1864.

Biscuits (cookies) were first brought to America by British and Dutch immigrants in the seventeenth century.

The first known recipe for brownies was published in the Sears Roebuck catalogue of 1897, and the same catalogue sold the brownie mixture.

Chocolate chip cookies were invented by Ruth Graves Wakefield of Whitman, Massachusetts, in 1937. She chopped pieces of sweet chocolate into some cookie dough, assuming it would melt into the mixture during cooking. To Wakefield's surprise, the chocolate held its shape, a taste sensation was born, and the rest is history.

Fortune cookies are an American invention, introduced by the so-called Chinese forty-niners (Chinese labourers working in the 1849 California gold rush), and were not eaten in China until the 1990s when they were advertised as 'Genuine American Fortune Cookies'.

Sausages

The word sausage is derived from the Latin *salcicius*, meaning salted and preserved meat, not necessarily in a skin, which was to be cooked and eaten hot. Various forms of sausage were known in Babylonia, ancient Greece and Rome.

Homer mentions goat-meat sausages in the Odyssey in about 700 BC, and ancient Greeks were certainly eating cooked sausages by 9 BC. Sausages were introduced into Britain by the Romans.

Sausages were known as 'little bags of surprises' in Victorian England. This expression came from the uncertain contents. In the days when product labelling was nearly a century in the future, it was not unheard of for sawdust to be included.

The origin of the nickname 'banger' for a sausage came about during the Second World War, when sausages contained so much water that they had a tendency to explode during frying.

Ice Cream

In the first century AD, the Roman Emperor Nero (AD 37–68) ordered runners to pass buckets of snow from the mountains in the north, along the Appian Way, down to Rome. The snow was mixed with red wine and honey to be served at banquets.

The Chinese may have invented a form of half-frozen fruit-flavoured ice cream in the first millennium AD. Marco Polo (1254–1324) returned to Venice from his trip to the Far East, with ancient recipes for concoctions made of snow, fruit juice and fruit pulp.

The first documented record of milk being added to the icy slush to produce a form of modern ice cream was in 1672 when it was served to King Charles II (1630–85) of England.

The first company to sell ice cream from tricycles was Wall's in 1924. The new means of distribution was launched with the slogan 'Stop me and buy one'.

The Wall's company sold sausages in winter and ice cream in summer, to 'equalise the seasonality'.

Margarine

Margarine was invented and patented in 1869, by the exotically named food chemist Hippolyte Mege-Mouris (1817–80). The first mixture consisted of beef fat, cow's udder and chopped sheep's stomach. The French government had offered a prize to anyone finding an acceptable substitute for butter, and the deeply unappetising Mege-Mouris creation won.

Modern margarine was created in 1915 by adding hydrogen to the mixture to harden it to the consistency of butter. The raw ingredients were almost irrelevant, as flavourings were added at a later stage of the process.

Canned Food

In 1810, Nicholas Francois Appert (1750–1841), a French chef, published a method for preserving food in tin cans. With his invention, Appert won the 12,000 franc prize which Napoleon Bonaparte had offered for the best method of preserving food for his troops on long marches.

Frozen Food

The practice of freezing food to preserve it can be traced back to 1626, and commercial production of frozen food began in 1875, but early food-freezing methods suffered by freezing the food too slowly. Slow freezing broke down the cell walls of the foodstuff, and failed to preserve texture, appearance and flavour.

In the 1920s Clarence Birdseye (1886–1956) developed two methods for quick freezing fish. While he was working as a fur trader in Canada, Birdseye had observed how the Inuit (Eskimo) people preserved fish by rapid freezing, in readiness for the harsh Artic winters. He bought a simple electric fan and, using buckets of salt water and ice, devised an industrial method of flash-freezing food under pressure and packing it in waxed cardboard boxes. In 1924, Birdseye put his first frozen fish on sale, and founded the frozen food industry as it has evolved today.

Starting with an initial investment of only US$7, Birdseye sold out his patents in 1929 for US$22,000,000. The product range was rebranded Birds Eye.

Chocolate

The Aztecs and Maya discovered the stimulation value of the cacao tree in around AD 600 and made a nourishing drink from the cocoa beans. They called it *xcoatl*, and in 1519, served the bitter drink to Hernan Cortes (1485–1547), the Spanish conquistador. He took it with him on his return to Spain, where it remained secret for over 100 years.

The first chocolate factory in America was set up by John Hannan and Dr James Baker in Dorchester, Massachusetts, in 1765.

The first chocolate bar in Britain was sold by Fry & Sons in 1847. John Cadbury (1801–89) started selling chocolate in 1849 at Bingley Hall in Birmingham.

Chewing Gum

The ancient Greeks chewed mastic gum, a product of the mastic tree. Other ancient cultures in India and South America, also enjoyed the benefits of chewing raw gum.

The first modern chewing gum was invented by Thomas Adams of New York in 1869 after a meeting with Antonio Lopez de Santa Anna (1794–1876), the exiled ex-President of Mexico, who told him of *chicle* gum which the native Mexicans had been chewing for years. Initially Adams tried to market a blend of *chicle* gum and rubber as a substitute material for carriage tyres, but this failed. He then began selling it as a flavourless, but chewy ball to be used as chewing gum, calling his product 'chiclets'.

The first British chewing gum was Beeman's Pepsin gum, which was launched in 1890 and produced in Merton, Surrey. It failed as a product, and it wasn't until 1911 that Wrigley's produced a successful chewing gum for the British market.

Crisps

American restaurant owner George Crum invented crisps – or potato chips, as they are known in the USA – in 1853 after the railway and shipping magnate Cornelius Vanderbilt (1794–1877) had complained about the thickness of the French fries being served in Crum's New York restaurant. Crum was angered by these remarks and decided to serve up deep-fried paper-thin potato chips. To Crum's surprise, Vanderbilt approved the new product. Crum's potato chips became a well-known delicacy, which he called Saratoga Chips.

Mass-marketing of crisps began in the USA in 1926 when Mrs Laura Scudder began to sell them in waxed paper bags. Mrs Scudder invented the airtight bag to keep the crisps fresh, by ironing together pieces of waxed paper. Until that time, crisps were distributed in large tins, which resulted in the last crisps out of the tin usually being stale.

DIETS

The earliest recorded 'fad' **diet** was that which was followed by William the Conqueror (1028–87). William grew so fat that he confined himself to his bedroom, ate no food, and drank only alcoholic drinks. In 1087, at the Battle of Mantes, near Rouen in France, the strap holding the saddle on his horse gave way under the strain, and William died from the injuries he suffered as he fell on the pommel of the saddle.

William Banting (1796–1878) is the first person known to have deliberately **regulated his weight** by controlling his food intake. Banting's diet, which included reducing his carbohydrate consumption, was supervised by Dr William Harvey. The results were first published in Banting's booklet, *Letter on Corpulence Addressed to the Public*, in 1863. The booklet went on to become a worldwide best-seller.

The Atkins Diet, which achieved cult status in 2001/2, began with the publication of *Dr Atkins' Diet Revolution* in 1972 by Dr Robert Atkins (1930–2003). At his death, Atkins weighed 260 lb (more than eighteen stone).

Weight Watchers began in 1961 with the efforts to lose weight of an obese Brooklyn housewife, Jean Nidetch (1923–present). Nidetch held meetings in her home to discuss ways of losing weight, and within a few months people were queuing on the street to attend. In 1963 Nidetch created Weight Watchers, and formalised the ideas that had developed from her meetings.

BEVERAGES

Tea

According to ancient myth, in 2737 BC, a handful of dried leaves from a tea bush blew into a pot of boiling water, into which the Chinese Emperor Shen Nung (Divine Farmer) was staring (*see also* History of Medicine p. 136). There is no record to say why the pot was being boiled, or why the Emperor was staring at it, nor why the leaves had been dried. The story relates that the resulting brew was henceforth known as *tchai* and became China's national drink during the T'ang Dynasty (AD 618–906).

Outside China, the Arabs were the first to mention tea in AD 850.

The first time tea was seen in Europe was in 1560, when it was introduced into Portugal by Father Jasper de Cruz, a Jesuit priest.

The first to be sold publicly in England was in 1657. Milk was not added to the brew until 1680.

The first tea imports to America were in 1650 by Peter Stuyvesant (1612–72), the last Dutch Director General of New Amsterdam (New York).

The most famous 'tea party' was the so-called Boston Tea Party of 1773, in which a cargo of tea was emptied into Boston Harbour in protest against excessive English excise duty. The protest signalled the start of the American War of Independence (*see also* War p. 322).

Iced tea was first served in 1904 at the St Louis World's Fair by a tea plantation owner.

Tea bags were accidentally invented by American tea importer Thomas Sullivan, who gave his customers samples of tea in silk bags. Mistakenly they put the entire bags into the pot and the tea bag was born.

Thomas (later Sir) J. Lipton (1850–1931) patented the tea bag in 1903 and a four-sided tea bag in 1952.

Coffee

Before AD 1000, the Galla Tribe of Ethiopia began to eat ground coffee beans mixed with animal fat for extra energy. It is recorded that a goatherd called Kaldi had noticed his goats jumping around with increased energy after chewing berries from the coffee bushes growing wild in his fields. He tried them and found renewed vigour when he became tired, supposedly becoming the first person to benefit from a caffeine 'shot'. News of the added energy to be gained from Kaldi's 'magic' beans spread rapidly throughout the region, and coffee consumption became a national habit.

Coffee was first imported to Constantinople in 1453 by the Ottoman Turks, and the world's first coffee shop, Kiva Han, opened there in 1475. By the sixteenth century, coffee drinking had spread throughout Asia, and coffee houses began to serve as public gathering places in Persia, in the same way as taverns.

The first English coffee house was opened in 1652 in St Michael's Alley, Cornhill, by a Turkish immigrant, Pasqua Rosee. Such was the spread of coffee houses and their allure as places of learned discussion, that they were dubbed 'penny universities', the cost of a cup of coffee being one penny.

Edward Lloyd opened his coffee house in London in 1668. It was used principally by merchants, seafarers and bankers and eventually grew to become Lloyd's of London, the centre of the world insurance market.

Ninety per cent of the world's coffee production can be traced back to a single bush, stolen by French naval officer Gabriel Mathieu do Clieu in 1723. A seedling was transported to Martinique in the Caribbean, and, within 50 years, almost 20,000,000 bushes had been propagated.

The first coffee drunk in America was in 1607 introduced by Captain John Smith, one of the founders of Virginia. Later, after the Boston Tea Party in 1773, coffee drinking became a patriotic duty, so that British tea would fall out of favour and lose its market.

The Maxwell House brand was founded in 1886. It was named in honour of the Maxwell House Hotel in downtown Nashville. The coffee served there was blended by Joel Cheek, a local wholesale grocer. The hotel burned down in 1961.

The first instant coffee was produced in Chicago in 1901 by chemist Satori Kato.

The first decaffeinated coffee was marketed in Germany and France under the Sanka (contraction of *sans caffeine*) brand in 1906. The product was the result of experiments organised by food scientist Ludvig Roselius on a batch of ruined coffee beans. Roselius, one of the founders of the Kraft Food Company, introduced Sanka into the USA in 1923.

The first freeze-dried coffee (under the Nescafé brand) was introduced in 1923 in Switzerland. Nescafé supposedly called their Blend 37 brand after Didier Cambresson, who completed the whole of the 1937 Le Mans 24-hour race on his own after his co-driver failed to show up. Cambresson was driving Car 37 and came in 37th. It is claimed he kept going by drinking only the new Nescafé brand.

Starbucks opened its first coffee shop in 1971 in Pike Place Market, Seattle. The original coffee shop named after the first mate in *Moby Dick*, was started by an English teacher, Jerry Baldwin, a history teacher, Zev Siegel, and a writer, Gordon Bowker, and is still trading. By 1992 when it floated as a public company, it had 165 coffee shops. In 2005, the total stood at more than 11,000 outlets.

Beer

Tests on ancient pottery jars from present-day Iran reveal that they were in use for holding beer up to 7,000 years ago and archaeologists have unearthed clay tablets dated 4300 BC from Babylonia, revealing the earliest recipe for producing beer.

The early Romans were drinking beer from the fifth century BC.

During the late Middle Ages in England, beer was used as a form of payment, even of taxes.

The first beer brewed in America was on the estate of Sir Walter Raleigh in 1587. The colonists had sent messages to England requesting better beer supplies, but then decided to brew their own.

The first commercial brewery in America was set up in New Amsterdam (now New York) in 1612.

There were over 2,000 breweries in the USA in 1880. By 1935 the number had reduced to 160. By 1992 most of the breweries had been consolidated into just five giant breweries which controlled 90 per cent of US beer consumption.

Lagering techniques were developed in the period 1820–40, resulting in a lighter tasting beer, but still with dark colouring from hard German water. The first modern lager beer, with a characteristically light golden colour, was produced in Pilsen, Bohemia (now in the Czech Republic), in 1842 by 29-year-old brewer Joseph Groll. Groll used the soft local water to produce his lager. The type of beer was named after the town, and became Pilsener or Pilsner.

The first canned beer was Kreuger Cream Ale, sold in 1935 by the Kreuger Brewing Company of Richmond, Virginia.

Guinness, which is a stout, has been brewed at the St James's Brewery in Dublin since 1759. Arthur Guinness signed a 9,000-year lease for £45 a year. Contrary to the myth that the Guinness brewed in Dublin uses water from the river Liffey, it actually comes exclusively from the Lady's Well in the Wicklow Mountains.

Beer Widgets

Brewers had struggled for years to devise a way to produce bottled and canned beer, which, when poured, would successfully imitate the creamy head on draught beer. The invention of the beer widget solved the problem in 1985.

The widget was invented by William Byrne and Alan Forage, and patented by the Irish brewer Guinness. It works by releasing nitrogen into the beer, to produce foam, after the can or bottle has been opened.

Draught Guinness in a can, the first beer with a widget, was launched in March 1989.

The original use of the term 'widget' was in the 1924 play *Buxton on Horseback*, as a product manufactured by one of the characters.

Wine

The Neolithic people of the Near East and Egypt are credited with producing the first wine between 8500 and 4000 BC. Pottery jars used for storing wine were developed around 6000 BC.

Buried jars, dated between 6000 and 7000 BC, have been unearthed in the Chinese village of Jiahu, containing a wine-like liquid.

Winemaking is recorded on the walls of Egyptian tombs dating from 2700 BC and shown to be part of ceremonial life. As grapes were not grown in ancient Egypt, it is most likely they were imported from the Near East.

Champagne

> *'I drink champagne when I win, to celebrate, and drink champagne when I lose, to console myself.*
> NAPOLEON BONAPARTE (1769–1821)

The creation of the sparkling wine champagne was supposedly a collaborative effort between two great cellar-masters of the monastic orders of Pierry and Epernay in the Champagne area of north-east France.

With their abbeys only two miles apart, Frère Jean Oudart and Dom Pierre Perignon (1638–1715) are jointly credited with producing the first successful champagne in the late seventeenth century. Although the principles established by Dom Perignon hold good today, modern dating techniques have the earliest sparkling wine as having been produced around 1535.

Scotch Whisky

The origins of Scotch are uncertain, although it is known that the ancient Celts in Ireland understood distilling before AD 1200. They called their drink *uisge beatha* (the water of life).

The first evidence of a distilling process from the eighth century BC has been uncovered in China.

By the sixth century AD, distilling was taking place in England, but the first mention of distilling in Scotland appears in the Exchequer Rolls of 1494, which list sufficient malt to produce 1,500 bottles of Scotch. This suggests that an industry was already supplying an established demand.

Brandy

Although there is some evidence of brandy being known in the twelfth century, it is generally thought that an unknown Dutch trader invented brandy in the sixteenth century. In an effort to save storage space, he started boiling his wine to cause the water in it to evaporate. The resultant liquor became *brandewijn* meaning 'burnt wine'.

KITCHEN EQUIPMENT

Refrigerator

(*See also* Inventions, Refrigerator p. 168)

The freezing properties of ammonia were discovered in 1868 by French scientist Charles Tellier (1828–1913), leading directly to the development of the refrigerator. Unfortunately for him, he failed to patent his idea and ended up dying in poverty.

Toaster

Making toast in front of an open fire began as a way of using stale bread, and was known to the ancient Romans.

The electric toaster was invented in 1891 in England and produced by Crompton & Co.

Microwave Oven

In early 1946, Dr Percy Spencer (1894–1970) of Raytheon Corporation accidentally discovered the possibility of cooking by microwave during experimental work with magnetrons, which produced microwaves for use in radar. He found chocolate bars in his jacket pocket had mysteriously melted when he ran low-level microwaves.

The patent for the microwave oven was filed in late 1946, and the first oven branded the Radarange, went on to the professional catering market in 1947. The Radarange stood over six feet tall and was sold at more than $5,000.

Tappan Corporation introduced the first domestic microwave ovens in 1955 at $1,295 each.

HEALTH

COVERING: History of Medicine, Diseases and Cures, Ears, Eyes, Heart, Kidneys, Mind, Teeth, Drugs.

Health is one of our biggest preoccupations. This chapter highlights the origins of the main developments in health and the battle against diseases, with thumbnail sketches of the routes some pioneers took.

'When you don't have any money, the problem's food. When you have money, it's sex. When you have both, it's health.
J. P. DONLEAVY (b. 1926)

HISTORY OF MEDICINE

One cannot practise a science well unless one knows its history.
AUGUSTE COMTE (1798–1857)

Prehistory

Neolithic man used stone tools with a cutting edge to lance abscesses and let blood.

Evidence has also been found in the Petit-Morin valley in France that around 20000 BC, using the same stone tools, Neolithic man was also performing delicate and successful operations, such as removing discs of bone from skulls. The holes in the skulls show evidence of healing, which indicates that the patient survived. Whether this very difficult operation was for the purpose of releasing evil spirits or for the relief of pressure inside the skull is unknown, although it is thought that magic formed a major part of medical treatments, and that the doctor and the priest would have been the same person.

At Ur in Mesopotamia, 6,000 years ago, the ancient Sumerians had begun to base their medicine on astrology.

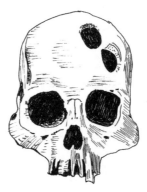

Chinese

Traditionally, the Chinese have tested the effectiveness of herbal remedies on themselves rather than using animals. The earliest known practitioner of herbal medicine was the Emperor Shen Nung, who lived around 2800 BC, and who is reputed to have tasted hundreds of different herbs in his quest for medical cures. Shen Nung is venerated as the father of Chinese medicine, and is thought by some scholars to have invented acupuncture.

The system of yin and yang, the belief that nature is in harmony when the yin and yang (male and female) elements are in balance, is also attributed to Shen Nung.

Chinese legend also records that Shen Nung invented the plough and was the first to drink tea after some dried tea leaves blew into his cup of boiling water one day (*see* Food and Drink, Beverages p. 128).

Babylonian and Egyptian

By 2000 BC, the ancient Babylonians had begun to base their medicine on religion. Surgeons were answerable directly to the state, and the code of the profession had established savage punishments for medical failure, whereas when practising medicine as priests the surgeons were answerable only to God.

In 1500 BC, the ancient Egyptians began the practice of cauterising – sealing by burning – wounds, to stop bleeding.

Indian

Ayurveda, the ancient Indian system of healing, is the oldest holistic (whole body) system in existence. It was first expounded by Dhanvantari in around 1500 BC, but not written down until 200 BC. The Ayurvedic system teaches the elements of surgery as well as knowledge of plants, herbs, aromas, colours and lifestyle. It is thought that Ayurveda may have developed out of earlier texts, dating from 3000 BC, which include instructions in spirituality and behaviour. The *Atreya Samhita*, one of the Ayurvedic books, is the oldest medical book in the world.

Injuries to the nose were common in the first millennium BC. The maiming of prisoners of war by cutting off their noses, and the slitting of noses in combat was common. In 500 BC Sushruta of India was the first to conduct a successful rhinoplasty (reshaping the human nose). Sushruta described how a strip of skin could be left partly connected to the forehead and grown over the place where the nose had been cut off.

Greek

Ancient Greece consisted of a collection of city states, which were independent of each other. Despite this independence, the states shared common ground in their attitudes to healthy lifestyles and the treatment of illness.

Aesculapius According to ancient Greek mythology, the greatest of the ancient Greek surgeons was Aesculapius, who was born a mortal but made into a god in the fifth century BC. Aesculapius was said to be the son of Apollo, who himself was regarded as the god of medicine, until Aesculapius usurped that role.

Alcmaeon of Croton The dawn of scientific medicine came with the Greeks between 600 and 700 BC. In 550 BC, the Greek Alcmaeon of Croton (b. 535 BC) pioneered experimental medicine and produced the first ear trumpet. He also discovered the optic nerve and was the first to consider the brain to be the centre of intellectual activity.

Pythagoras In 530 BC, the Greek philosopher and mathematician Pythagoras (582–496 BC) founded the world's first medical school in the town of Croton, in what is present-day southern Italy. The school was founded around the time when the practice of medicine had begun to acquire professional status.

Hippocrates The Greek mathematician Hippocrates (460–380 BC), who was born and brought up on the island of Kos, wholly rejected the superstition and magic of primitive medicine. Hippocrates was the first to introduce scientific method to the treatment of illnesses and recommended that doctors should accurately record all their treatments for the benefit of other doctors who followed. Hippocrates also introduced the idea of patient confidentiality to medical practice, and is widely regarded as the 'father of medicine'.

Doctors still swear the Hippocratic Oath, which is regarded as the foundation of Western medical ethics, 'I swear by Apollo the healer; by Aesculapius; by health and all the powers of healing, that I will use my power to help the sick to the best of my ability and judgement.'

Herophilus of Chalcedon The first public dissection of a human body was performed by Herophilus of Chalcedon (320–260 BC) in 300 BC. He is credited with being the first to carry out scientific explorations of what lay within the human body, and is regarded as the 'father of human anatomy'. He was the first to consider the brain, not the heart, as the seat of consciousness, and was the first to distinguish between motor and sensory nerves. The study of anatomy advanced enormously under his guidance and was continued by his rival Eristratus. With their deaths, advances in human anatomy ground to a halt until Leonardo da Vinci (AD 1452–1519) accurately drew the inner workings of the body, more than a thousand years later.

Galen of Pergamum The greatest Greek contributions to the furthering of medical knowledge came from Galen of Pergamum (129–200 BC). He wrote over 400 treatises, of which 300 were lost in a fire. He proposed that careful hygiene, good diet and plenty of exercise were important factors in health care, and made an outstanding contribution to the understanding of the cardiovascular system. Galen was summoned to become surgeon to the Roman Emperor Marcus Aurelius (AD 121–180), and after Marcus's death, to his son, the Emperor Commodus (AD 161–192).

Soranus of Ephesus Known as the birthing doctor, between AD 98–138 Soranus of Ephesus was the first to make an in-depth study of obstetrics, the branch of medicine dealing with the care and treatment of women before, during and after childbirth. Sonanus realised that women's reproductive anatomy led to unique medical problems that men could not experience. He fought against superstition and misunderstandings for most of his life, writing widely on the delivery of babies.

Roman

In AD 379 after a severe famine, St Basil the Younger (AD 329–79), who had been a school friend of the Roman Emperor Julian (AD 331–63), sold his family land, bought food to feed the starving and founded the world's first hospital in Caesarea, in what is present-day Israel.

The first European hospital was opened in Rome in AD 400. The building was funded by Fabiola – later St Fabiola – (d. AD 399), a Roman noblewoman, who was a member of the wealthy Fabia family. Divorced from her first husband, who had abused her, and left widowed by the death of her second husband, Fabiola had ambitions to become a hermit and live in Jerusalem. She travelled to Bethlehem in AD 395, but her involvement with the hospital led her to return and she became a nurse instead.

General

The first English hospital was built in York in AD 936 and was originally dedicated to St Peter. The hospital was rededicated to St Leonard in 1137 after a fire, but it closed 400 years later with the dissolution of the monasteries.

The first European medical school was established at Montpellier in southern France in AD 1220. In 1181, the Lord of Montpellier had given his permission for anyone to come and teach medicine within Montpellier, no matter where they came from. The school attracted teachers and students from as far away as Scotland.

The first organised school of medical teaching began in about AD 1260 with Thaddeus of Florence (1223–1303), who taught at the University of Bologna.

The first hospital in the New World was founded in Mexico in 1524 by Hernando Cortes (1485–1547), the Spanish conqueror.

The first animal-to-human bone graft was performed in 1668 by Job van Meekeren of the Netherlands when he grafted part of a dog's skull into the wounded leg of a Russian soldier.

Plaster of Paris was first used as a bandage material in 1852 by Anthonius Mathijsen of the Netherlands.

The speech centre of the human brain was discovered in 1861 by the French doctor Paul Broca (1824–80).

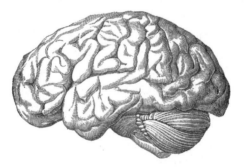

The first to use plaster of Paris to treat spinal injuries was American orthopaedic surgeon Lewis Sayre (1820–1900) in 1877.

The first appendix operation in Britain was carried out by Dr H. Hancock in 1848, although there are reports of a British Army surgeon called Amyan performing an appendectomy as early as 1735.

The first successful appendix operation in the USA was carried out in Davenport Iowa in 1885 by Dr William West Grant. The patient was 22-year-old Mary Gartside.

The first artificial incubator for premature babies was developed in 1888 by German obstetrician Karl Crede (1819–92). Electricity was not widely available, and the air inside had to be warmed by a kerosene lamp.

The first lumbar puncture operations – driving a needle into a patient's spine to sample spinal fluid – were conducted independently of each other in 1891, by Walter Winter in England and Heinrich Quinck in Germany. Anaesthetics were not available.

The first surgeon to use rubber gloves while performing an operation was William Halstead of Johns Hopkins Hospital in the USA, in 1894.

The surgical mask was invented by William Hunter of England in 1900.

The National Insurance Act came into effect in Britain in 1911. The Act made it compulsory for employers to collect revenues from every employee's pay to fund medical treatment.

The National Health Service came into being in 1948.

The World Health Organisation was established in 1948.

X-rays

While he was investigating the properties of light in his laboratory at the University of Würzburg in Germany on 8 November 1895, Wilhelm Conrad Roentgen (1845–1923) discovered X-rays. After seven weeks of further research, to satisfy himself that the results were both genuine and repeatable, Roentgen presented his report to the medical establishment. By January of 1896, the world was gripped by 'X-ray mania', and within a few months X-rays were being widely used as diagnostic tools. Acclaimed as a miracle worker, Roentgen refused to patent his discovery, and in 1901 he was awarded the first Nobel Prize for Physics.

The first ever X-ray picture was of Roentgen's wife's left hand. The image clearly shows her wedding ring.

DNA

More properly known as deoxyribonucleic acid, DNA was made famous the world over in 1953 when James Watson (b. 1928), Francis Crick

(1916–2004), and Maurice Wilkins (1916–2004) announced they had discovered its structure.

Watson, Crick and Wilkins received the Nobel Prize for Physics for their discovery of the famous double helix shape of the DNA molecule. However, they most definitely did not discover DNA itself. It had actually been identified in 1869 by Swiss scientist Johann Friedrich Miescher (1844–95) working in Tübingen in Germany (*see also* Questionable Origins p. 210).

CAT Scanner

The CAT (Computer Assisted Tomography) scanner is a machine that takes X-rays from different angles. It was developed in the UK by EMI, and launched in 1973. The price of individual machines started at £100,000. Godfrey Hounsfield (1919–2004), who led the development team, received the Nobel Prize for Medicine in 1979 and was knighted in 1981.

In Vitro Fertilisation (IVF)

The world's first test tube baby, Louise Joy Browne, was born in Oldham, Lancashire, on 25 July 1978. Louise's birth was made possible by the pioneering IVF process. Elizabeth Carr, who was born in 1981, was the first American test tube baby.

Blood

In 1628, William Harvey (1578–1657) published his most important book, *An Anatomical Study of the Motion of the Heart and of the Blood in Animals*. In the book, Harvey describes how blood is pumped around the body by the heart, returns to the heart and is recirculated. The book was controversial at the time and lost Harvey many patients.

Blood transfusions were attempted in Europe from 1628 by Giovanni Colle, a professor in Padua in Italy, but because of the incompatibility of blood types it was not until 1654 that another Italian, Francesco Folli (1624–85), actually achieved the first successful blood transfusion.

It was not until the early twentieth century that the Viennese physician Karl Landsteiner (1868–1943) identified the four human blood types, enabling routine and non-life-threatening blood transfusions.

Blood pressure was discovered and reported in the preface of a book on plants written in 1727 by the Reverend Stephen Hales. Pressure was measured by inserting a tube directly into the vein of an animal and noting how high the blood rose in the tube.

Human blood pressure was first accurately measured in 1856 by J. Faivre of France, following the work of the German physician Karl von Vierordt (1818–85), who in 1855 developed the inflatable cuff to stop the arterial blood flow so that blood pressure could be measured in a non-invasive way.

Brain

Early man has practised brain surgery since Neolithic times, and Hippoc-rates himself left copious notes on how to treat head injuries and depressions.

In 1926, the pioneering brain surgeon Harvey Cushing (1869–1939) was the first to use electrodes to cauterise blood vessels during brain surgery.

DISEASES AND CURES

Smallpox

An acute viral infectious disease, smallpox is characterised by fever and pockmarks on the skin, and could be fatal. It has now been eradicated.

The first vaccination for smallpox was developed in 1796 by Edward Jenner (1749–1823) and by 1801, 100,000 people had been vaccinated in England.

Earlier in his life, at the age of eight, Jenner had survived an extremely risky treatment, which was supposed to prevent him contracting small-pox for the rest of his life. He was subjected to variolation, the forerunner of inoculation, which had been introduced to Britain by Lady Mary Wortley Montagu (1689–1762), a noted eighteenth-century writer. The treatment involved taking pus from the sores in the body of a dead victim of smallpox and inoculating it directly into the patient. Variolation had been successfully used in China for centuries, but dosage was very difficult to control as the individual patient's reaction was impossible to predict. The whole treatment included three weeks' isolation from non-infected people.

After an intensive worldwide inoculation programme conducted by the World Health Authority, it was announced on 8 May 1980 that small-pox, which had blighted humanity for thousands of years, had finally been eradicated from the world; the first, and so far only, disease ever to be conquered.

Pasteurisation

The process known now as pasteurisation was invented in 1862 by French chemist Louis Pasteur (1822–95) after he had performed experiments proving his germ theory, which maintains that micro-organisms cause fermentation and the formation of mould. After establishing the cause, Pasteur set about finding a means of preventing the formation of moulds in liquids such as milk by pasteurisation.

Pasteur also managed to save the French silkworm industry, which had been blighted for years by a disease called pébrine that killed great numbers of silkworms. By eliminating the microbe that caused the disease, Pasteur brought the pébrine under control.

Tuberculosis

Hippocrates (460–380 BC), writing in about 410 BC, identified a form of tuberculosis called phthisis, and by the nineteenth century almost 25 per cent of all deaths in Europe were being caused by the disease. In adults, the bacillus spreads in the lungs and destroys the respiratory tissues and then attacks the air passages, at which stage the patient becomes infectious. In 1882, the German doctor Robert Koch (1843–1910) discovered the microbe that causes tuberculosis, but it was not until the development of the antibiotic streptomycin, in 1943, that successful treatment was possible.

Streptomycin was discovered in 1943 by Albert Schatz (1920–2005) after performing his research at Rutgers University, New Jersey, USA. His supervisor Selman Waksman (1888–1973) took all the credit for the discovery, as well as the Nobel Prize in 1952. However, Schatz successfully sued Waksman for a share of the streptomycin royalties.

Polio

A viral infection, polio attacks the muscle-controlling nerves of the brain and spinal cord, resulting in paralysis. There is no cure for the disease, but in 1952, Dr Jonas Salk (1914–95) discovered a vaccine that would prevent its onset. The vaccine was made available to the public on 12 April 1955, and in a remarkably humane gesture Salk refused to patent his vaccine, holding that he had no desire to profit personally from his discovery, merely to see the widest possible distribution for the greatest possible good.

Malaria

In 1880, the French physician Charles Louis Alphonse Laveran (1845–1922) discovered that malaria is caused by a protozoan (a single cell organism). For his work in the field he was awarded the Nobel Prize in Medicine in 1907.

In 1898, Sir Ronald Ross (1857–1932) discovered the life cycle of the malaria parasite as it develops in the malaria mosquito, and in the human host. He was awarded the Nobel Prize for Medicine in 1902.

From the end of the Second World War to the 1970s, the pesticide DDT was used to destroy local mosquito populations, helping to eliminate malaria from certain parts of the world. However, a ban has been in force since those times, and the mosquito population has steadily increased.

Acquired Immune Deficiency Syndrome (AIDS)

AIDS is a condition in which the body's immune system becomes weakened due to the contraction of the human immunodeficiency virus (HIV). Those infected are susceptible to infections that eventually result in death. It is now believed that HIV is a new virus to emerge in the human population. Previously, it was an ancestral virus that infected monkeys.

AIDS was officially recognised for the first time on 18 June 1981 in California and New York. It was originally thought to be a sexually transmitted disease restricted to homosexual men, but it was quickly discovered that it could be transmitted to anyone through transfusion of contaminated blood or the use of contaminated intravenous needles. AIDS can also be transmitted from mother to child during pregnancy.

There was 'false evidence' that a 25-year-old British sailor, David Carr, had died from AIDS in 1959. This was dismissed after exhaustive testing of saved tissue samples on both sides of the Atlantic.

The first accidental blood transfusion victim of AIDS was the unfortunate Don Coffee in 1981.

The first British person to die of AIDS was Terrence Higgins in 1982.

EARS

Hearing Aids

The first reference in literature to a hearing aid is a reference by Homer to a speaking trumpet in the *Iliad*.

The first man-made auditory tube or ear trumpet was made in 550 BC by the early Greek medical writer and scientist Alcmaeon of Croton. These first examples were intended not to provide the hard of hearing with a tool to help their hearing, but as an aid to hearing at distance, such as at sea in times of war, and on the hunting field.

In approximately 300 BC the ancient Greeks were importing sea-shells into Phoenicia to be used as ear trumpets. The shells were hardened and then painted, to make them more marketable.

The first modern ear trumpet was described by the Belgian scientist and high-school rector Jean Leurechon (1591–1670) in his book *Récréation Mathématique*, published in 1624.

The first British maker of ear trumpets was Bevan of London in 1715.

Around 1790 **Alessandro Volta**, who developed the electric battery, discovered that the auditory system could be stimulated by electricity, when he put metal rods into his own ears and gave himself a 50-volt electric shock. The result of Volta's experiment was that he heard noises like 'a thick boiling soup'.

Modern hearing aids owe their existence to the first commercial hearing aid to use a carbon microphone. It was produced by the Dictograph Company of the USA in 1898.

By 1954, hearing aids were small enough to be built into spectacle frames, and fully digital hearing aids, worn within the ear, were introduced in 1995.

The first cochlear implant was carried out on Ron Saunders in Melbourne, Australia. Professor Graeme Clark of Melbourne pioneered the technique during the 1970s.

The cochlear implant is often referred to as a bionic ear, as it is effectively an implanted hearing aid for the profoundly deaf and the very hard of hearing. Unlike traditional hearing aids, the cochlear implant does not amplify sound, but stimulates the auditory nerves with minute electrical impulses.

After approval by the US Federal Drug Administration, the first cochlear implant in the USA was performed in 1984.

EYES

Alhazen (Abu Ali al-Hasan ibn al-Haythen) (AD 965–1039) was a brilliant Arab mathematician, who was born and lived in Basra, in Persia (now in present-day Iraq). Alhazen was the first to establish, through experimentation, that people see things because rays of light pass from an object to the eye. Until Alhazen's research, it had been generally thought that the eyes sent out invisible rays to detect objects.

Alhazen also described the magnifying properties of lenses, but his observations were not appreciated until the thirteenth century through the work of the British scientist/monk Roger Bacon (1214–94).

Spectacles

The Roman Emperor Nero (AD 37–68) used to look through a highly polished emerald to watch gladiators fighting. Polishing it into a lens shape gave the emerald magnification properties.

The invention of spectacles is attributed to Salvino d'Armato (d. 1317) who introduced his invention in Florence in 1268. His spectacles had no side arms, and had to be balanced or held on the nose.

The side arms on spectacles were not added until the eighteenth century in Paris when short arms were added to a pair of specs to hold them to the sides of the head. In 1727, the English optician Edward Scarlett extended the arms to fit over the ears.

The first painting to portray a person wearing spectacles was by Thomasso de Modena in 1352, showing an elder of the church, Hugh de Provence, peering at a manuscript.

The first printed book on ophthalmology was published in 1474. The title of the book was *De Oculis Eorumque Egritudinibus et Curis*, which had been written by Benvenuto Grassi in the twelfth century.

The invention by Johann Gutenberg (1398–1468) of the printing press in 1456 triggered the production of reading glasses as all ranks of society began to read the printed word.

Bifocal spectacles are popularly understood to have been invented in 1784 by the great American scientist and statesman Benjamin Franklin (1706–90). However, there is historical evidence that Samuel Pierce, an English optician, may have invented them in 1775.

The first US President to wear spectacles was George Washington (1732–99), who wore them from 1776. Washington was also noted for wearing false teeth made of wood.

Varifocals (also known as progressives) were introduced in the 1960s. They are bifocals without the boundary between the reading and distance parts of the lens being visible.

Optical Surgery

The removal of cataracts from the eye was pioneered in 1748 by Jacques Daviel (1693–1762), the optician to Louis XV of France. He cut out the opaque lens from beneath the cornea, the hard coating of the eyeball. There were no anaesthetics.

Spanish ophthalmologist Ignacio Barraquer Barraquer (1884–1965) devised a method of cataract removal by suction in 1917.

Contact Lenses

Leonardo da Vinci drew sketches showing several forms of contact lens in 1508.

Many attempts were made to produce contact lenses, including by French philosopher René Descartes (1596–1650), but the first commercially available contact lenses were introduced by William Feinbloom, a New York optometrist, in 1936. Bifocal contact lenses became available in 1982.

HEART

In 1707, John Floyer (1649–1734), one of the three great medical pioneers of Staffordshire (the others were Erasmus Darwin and William Withering), invented a stopwatch to measure the human pulse.

Pacemaker

The artificial heart pacemaker is designed to regulate the beating of the heart when the heart's natural pacemaker is not effective. In 1862, English surgeon W. H. Walshe suggested the use of electrical impulses to control the heart's rhythm. It fell to Canadian electrical engineer John Hopps to design and build the first heart pacemaker in 1950. The early models were fitted outside the body and had to be plugged into a wall socket.

The first pacemaker implanted into the body was designed and fitted by Dr Rune Elmqvist (1906–96) at the Karolinska Hospital in Solna,

Sweden, in 1958. The first implanted pacemaker patient, Arne Larsson, survived until 2001, having been fitted with no fewer than 22 throughout his life.

Heart Surgery

During the Second World War, doctors made enormous advances in blood transfusion, anaesthetics and antibiotics, which led to the development of modern surgery. A young US Army surgeon, Dr Dwight Harken, removed fragments of shrapnel from the still-beating hearts of soldiers by inserting his finger into the wound hole, locating the shrapnel, and pulling it out through the same hole in the heart.

The problem faced in open-heart surgery is that once the heart is stopped to perform the surgery, the surgeon has only four minutes to complete the procedure before the patient's brain is irreparably damaged due to lack of oxygenated blood pumped by the heart. In 1952, Dr Bill Bigelow (1913–2005) of the University of Minnesota, who had studied the habits of hibernating animals, had the idea of reducing the patient's temperature from 98 to 81 degrees Fahrenheit. As a result, doctors were able to extend the operating time from four to ten minutes.

The heart-lung machine was developed by John Gibbon (1903–73) of Philadelphia in 1953 to overcome these difficulties. By connecting the patient to the machine, it left the heart in a still condition for the operation, allowing the surgeon ample time to perform the complex procedures.

The first successful open-heart surgery took place on 15 May 1953 on 18-year-old Cecilia Bavolek who was connected to the heart-lung machine for 27 minutes. Dr Gibbon performed the operation.

The first successful hole-in-the-heart operation was performed on 2 September 1952 by Dr F. John Lewis and Dr Walton Lillehei (1918–99). The patient was a five-year-old girl.

The first heart bypass surgery was performed in 1967 by Argentinian cardiologist Dr Rene Favaloro (1923–2000) in Cleveland, Ohio.

The first human heart transplant was performed by Christiaan Barnard (1922–2001), a cardiac surgeon at Groote Schuur hospital in Cape Town,

South Africa, on 55-year-old retired grocer, Louis Washkansky (1913– 67), on 3 December 1967. Washkansky died 18 days later from pneumonia, not from failure of the new heart. The donor was Louise Darvall (1943–67), who had died after a car accident.

On 23 January 1964, three years before the first human heart transplant, Boyd Rush became the first human to receive a transplanted heart. While he was waiting for a human donor heart, Rush's own heart failed and in a last-ditch attempt to preserve Rush's life, the pioneering surgeon James D. Hardy (1903–87) of the United States transplanted a chimpanzee's heart in its place.

The new heart immediately began to take over the role of the diseased heart, but within a few hours Rush's body rejected it.

Robot-assisted Heart Surgery

One of the most exciting areas of medicine currently being developed is the introduction of robot assistance. This operating technique developed out of the need to control the greater hand tremors experienced by surgeons when conducting operations using minimally invasive surgery.

In traditional heart surgery, the chest is opened and the surgeon is able to put his or her hands physically inside the cavity to make incisions close to the organ. In minimally invasive surgery, the incision may be no bigger than a few millimetres. The instruments are therefore much longer, and this added length leads to normal hand tremors being magnified.

With robot assistance, the surgeon is also able to conduct the operation from a remote location, even from another country.

The first robot-assisted heart bypass operations were performed in late 1998 on 17 patients by Dr Ralph Damiano, at Pennsylvania State Hospital, USA.

KIDNEYS

The artificial kidney (dialysis machine) was invented by Willem Kolff (b. 1911) during the Second World War, with the first machine being tested in 1943. In the great humanitarian tradition, Kolff refused to patent his invention. Kolff was born in the Netherlands but moved to the USA in 1950, and subsequently worked on development of an artificial human heart at his new home at the Cleveland Clinic Foundation.

Early experiments with kidney transplants began in France in 1909, with diseased human kidneys being replaced by animal kidneys. There were no survivors.

Before tissue and blood-type matches, and the human immune system were fully understood, all human-to-human kidney transplants failed. Researchers began to realise that the body rejects that which it does not regard as its own, and a way was sought to combat these rejections.

In 1947, Charles Hufnagel (1916–89) was a young surgeon working in Boston. In a desperate last-ditch attempt to save a patient's life, he transplanted a dead patient's kidney into the forearm of a young woman whose own kidney was so diseased that she had been given only hours to live. The woman was too weak to move to an operating theatre, so the surgical team worked in her room with only rudimentary lighting to illuminate the operation. The kidney began to function immediately it was connected to her blood supply. Although the transplanted organ died after a few days, it had provided sufficient breathing space for the woman's own kidneys to revive, and she made a full recovery.

The first successful kidney transplant was performed by Dr Joseph Murray (b. 1919) on 23 December 1954, at the Peter Bent Brigham Hospital in Boston, USA. He took a kidney from Ronald Herrick and transplanted it into his identical twin brother Richard, allowing Richard to live for another eight years. Ronald remains alive today, as does Dr Murray, who was awarded the Nobel Prize for Medicine in 1990.

MIND

The first mental hospital in England was built in London in 1247 near to the present-day site of Liverpool Street Station. The hospital was named the Bethlehem Hospital, but was also known as Bethlem or Bedlam.

Mesmerism Anton Mesmer (1734–1815), who was born in Austria, practised his branch of medicine in Paris. Mesmerism, a form of hypnotism, was used in an attempt to treat mental illness.

The first mental hospital in the USA was the Institute of Pennsylvania Hospital that was built in 1859.

Psycho-analysis was pioneered by Sigmund Freud (1856–1939). His first book, *Studies on Hysteria,* was published in 1895 with his seminal work, *The Interpretation of Dreams,* published in 1899. Freud based his analytical practice on his theory of 'unconscious motives' and the analysis of dreams, which were subjected to his 'talking cure'.

Before psycho-analysis, the principal treatment for mental illness was to restrain the patient physically, and often to subject him or her to a terrifying array of quack remedies such as surprise ice-cold showers, being kept in total darkness for days at a time to induce docility, and spinning round, strapped into a revolving chair, for long periods. Most treatments ensured the patient (or victim) was never cured.

The first lobotomy for the relief of schizophrenia was performed in 1930 by Portuguese neurologist Egas Monitz (1874–1955). The procedure involved the insertion of medical instruments through the eye sockets to sever the frontal lobe nerves of the brain. He won the Nobel Prize for Medicine for his development of the lobotomy operation, and became the only Nobel laureate in the field of psychiatry.

Since the 1960s psychiatric drugs have made the lobotomy obsolete.

Electro-shock treatment was first used in Italy in 1930 for cases of severe depression. With electro-shocks, typically one amp is administered, using up to 500 volts. Two thousand years earlier, Scribonius Largus (*see* below) experimented with neuro-stimulation by holding patients in water and allowing torpedo fish to administer severe electric shocks. Patients with gout experienced temporary pain relief.

Tranquillisers were first used in psychiatry in 1952 to restrain violent patients.

Prozac, the world's first and still most widely prescribed antidepressant drug, was launched by the Eli Lilly drug company of the USA in 1988. The level of serotonin, a neuro-transmitter chemical in the brain that carries messages between nerve cells, is thought to influence appetite, aggression and mood. Prozac works by increasing the levels of this chemical transmitter, and the use of the drug was the first example of biochemistry being used to control mood.

Sex Change (Gender Re-assignment)

In the modern era, the first person to undergo male-to-female surgery was US GI Christine Jorgensen (1926–89). The surgery, which took place in Denmark, began in 1952 with the removal of the male organ, and after a long healing period, the process was completed in 1954.

The first British sex change patient was April Ashley (b. 1935). Dr Bureau of Casablanca conducted the operation on 11 May 1960 in Morocco. April Ashley now lives in California, having married and divorced the Hon. Arthur Cameron Corbett.

Teeth

There was never yet philosopher
That could endure the toothache patiently.
Much Ado About Nothing, WILLIAM SHAKESPEARE (1564–1616)

In 1700 BC, the Babylonians used gold and silver to make artificial teeth, and Egyptian mummies have also been discovered with false teeth. The pre-Roman Etruscans were able to fix bridges between teeth to fill gaps.

The first to advocate the use of fillings rather than extraction for partially decayed teeth was Scribonius Largus (AD 14–54) in AD 47. He made the dubious claim that the process of removing decay with the use of a knife was painless.

The first to use gold for fillings in teeth was Giovanni Arcolani in 1493.

The first ivory false teeth were made around 1700 by German physicians, using the ivory from elephant and walrus tusks. Even human teeth from cadavers were used.

Porcelain false teeth were introduced in France in 1774.

The first dentures set in a plate were produced by London silversmith Claudius Ash in 1845. The artificial teeth were set in an 18-carat gold plate, which incorporated springs and swivels to fit different mouth shapes. Claudius Ash established his business in 1829 and it continues to this day as part of the Plandent Group.

The first to recognise that nitrous oxide gas has anaesthetic properties was the Cornishman Humphry Davy (1788–1825) in 1799. As he was a research scientist, not a doctor, the medical profession ignored his findings until 1844.

The anaesthetic property of cocaine injected into the gums was discovered in 1862 by Czech researcher Dr Damien Schroff (1802–87). Because cocaine has serious addictive properties, research on synthesising a substitute took place from 1880. An artificial substitute, Novocaine (aka procaine), was formulated in 1905 by German chemist Alfred Einhorn. It has been used as a dental anaesthetic ever since.

Drugs

Penicillin

The first person to study the anti-microbial capabilities of penicillin mould was the French physician Ernest Duchesne (1874–1912) in 1897, working at the Military Health School in Lyon. Despite his meticulous experiments, the Institut Pasteur, noting Duchesne was only 23, ignored his findings. In 1904 Duchesne contracted tuberculosis and died in 1912 without his findings progressing any further.

The antibiotic and antiseptic properties of penicillin were first discovered by Alexander (later Sir Alexander) Fleming in 1928. When he presented his results to the Medical Research Club, Fleming was horrified but not initially discouraged when his colleagues in the club ignored his low-key presentation of 'a powerful anti-bacterial substance'.

The establishment continued to ignore Fleming's findings and it was in 1939 when he attended the Third International Congress of Micro-biology in New York that he found American researchers were also working on penicillin. It was only in 1940 that the medical profession, under pressure from the effects of the Second World War, fully accepted penicillin as an antibiotic.

Industrial manufacture of penicillin began in 1942.

Aspirin

As early as 1829 scientists Johann Buchner of Munich and Henry Leroux of France had discovered that an extract from the willow tree called salicin could provide pain relief for headaches. However, the problem with salicin was that it caused stomach inflammation, and could cause vomiting of blood. In 1853 a German chemist, Charles Gerhardt (1816–56), found a way of preventing stomach inflammation by mixing the compound with sodium, but he had no desire to market his discovery.

In 1897 Felix Hoffman (1868–1946), working for the Bayer chemical company in Germany, rediscovered Gerhardt's formula and produced the product in powder form. Bayer created the trademark Aspirin and marketed it as a powder until 1915, when Aspirin in the form of tablets were first put on sale. The trademark Aspirin was lost by Bayer as part the reparations
Germany was forced to pay under the terms of the Treaty of Versailles in 1919 following their defeat in the First World War.

Viagra

The USA drug company Pfizer developed Viagra, initially as a treatment for angina. In clinical trials it failed to display any benefits for angina but reports noted that it had the marked side-effect of inducing strong sexual arousal in the male laboratory assistants. Viagra first became available in the USA in 1998 and in the UK in 1999. Originally it was only available on a doctor's prescription, and within three years of being launched sales of Viagra had topped one billion dollars worldwide.

INVENTIONS

COVERING: Computers, Parachutes, Newcomen Engines, Photography, Sewing Machines, Bunsen Burner, Cash Register, Radar, Sonar and Asdic, Electricity and Electrical Appliances, Photocopying, Smoking, Safety Pins, Useless Inventions.

*Today, every invention is received with a cry
of triumph, which soon turns into a cry of fear.*
BERTHOLT BRECHT (1898–1956)

However useful an invention may seem right now, and however difficult it may appear to be able to improve on it, someone somewhere will either find a way to improve it, or produce a different solution. It is in the nature of men and women to seek ways to improve the way life is lived, and throughout history the products of their combined imaginations and experiments have brought tidal waves of inventions.

Some inventions such as television, vacuum cleaners, motorcars or corkscrews become everyday objects. Some, like the Claxton Earcap, don't.

Some inventions, like computers, telephones, aeroplanes and the artificial heart have significantly improved life for the population of the world. Others, like the tobacco resuscitator, have more in common with implements of torture. They should be used on the inventor first to see if he likes it. Here are just a few inventions and their origins.

COMPUTERS

There is no reason why anyone
would want a computer in their home.
KEN OLSEN (b. 1926), as President of Digital Equipment

There are numerous claims as to what was the first computer. Here are
some:

The Abacus

A device used for mechanical addition, subtraction, multiplication and
division the abacus does not require the use of pencil and paper and is
good for any base number, but normally in groupings of ten.

There are two forms of abacus: one uses counters on a board with special markings, the other uses beads strung on wires fixed into a frame.
The counters or the beads are used to assist with addition, subtraction,
multiplication and division, by using one set of beads to count each of
the tens, hundreds and thousands.

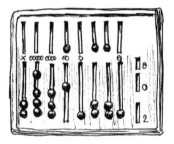

It is thought that the abacus was invented by the Babylonians and may
have been used as early as 2400 BC, but the more commonly accepted
dates are between 1000 and 500 BC. There is also evidence of a similar
Chinese invention as early as 3000 BC and the Aztecs had a form of
abacus from about 1000 BC. The abacus was in common use by the
Japanese up to the 1920s.

Mechanical Computers

The Antikythera mechanism was built in 87 BC by an unknown craftsman to calculate the new moons. It had a specially designed gear ratio of 235:19.

A mechanical calculating machine was designed by Leonardo da Vinci (1452–1519) in 1500.

A logarithmic calculating device was developed in 1620 by Edmund Gunter (1581–1626) of England. This is widely regarded as the first successful analog device. Analog computers perform operations in parallel steps, meaning they can perform more than one operation at a time.

The slide rule was invented in 1621 by the clergyman and mathematician William Oughtred. It is another version of an analog computer and consists of three interlocking strips, normally wood or plastic, which are calibrated so that positioning the strips relative to each other enables arithmetical calculations to be made.

The first mechanical digital calculating device was built by Blaise Pascal (1623–62) of France in 1642.

A 'difference engine' was built by the English mathematician Charles Babbage (1791–1871) in 1822 to improve significantly the accuracy of the calculations in the production of arithmetical tables. Difference engines had first been conceived in 1786 by J.H. Mueller of Germany but did not leave the drawing board.

Babbage's fantastic and complex machine is considered to be the most beautiful computer ever built. It works on the principle that it only ever needs to be able to subtract numbers. The British Museum possesses a working model of Babbage's difference engine.

Electronic Computers

Digital computers work on the principle of binary code, using only 0 and 1 for all calculations, storage, retrieval and instruction.

The modern computer came into being in 1939 when the Bulgarian-American physicist John Vincent Atanasoff (1903–95) built the first electronic digital computer. Atanasoff, whose father had emigrated from

Bulgaria to the USA in 1889, hired Clifford Berry, a young electrical engineer, to help him and they named their first machine the ABC (Atanasoff–Berry Computer).

The first electronic brain was built by Alan Turing (1912–54) during the Second World War at Bletchley Park in order to crack the almost unbreakable code of the German Enigma cipher machines. It became known as the Turing–Welchman Bombe, and it made the rapid calculations needed to solve the immensely complex Enigma codes successfully. Turing's great work led to the shortening of the Second World War in Europe.

The algorithm was invented by Alan Turing before the Second World War began. In late 1936, Turing had published a paper *On computable numbers with an application to the Entscheidungsproblem*. With this paper Turing effectively invented the algorithm, which is a set of instructions for accomplishing a task. This in turn led to the conception of Turing's machine, and has now become the foundation of modern computing and the stored computer programme.

A fully automatic large-scale calculator was built in 1944 by Howard Aiken (1900–73) of the USA. It was known as the Harvard Mark I with more than 750,000 parts and was reputed to sound like a roomful of ladies knitting.

The first programmed electronic computer was built in 1946 by J. Presper Eckert (1919–95) together with John W. Maunchly (1907–80). It was named the ENIAC (Electronic Numerical Integrator and Calculator) and contained 20,000 vacuum tubes.

The first stored programme computer was the EDVAC (Electronic Discrete Variable Automatic Computer). It was developed during the late 1940s and introduced in 1952. This followed the definitive paper on the subject entitled *The First Draft* written by Hungarian-born mathematician Johnny von Neumann (1903–57).

The semi-conductor or integrated circuit was invented by Robert Noyce (1927–90) of Fairchild Semiconductor and Jack Kilby (1923–2005) of Texas Instruments, who were working separately and without knowledge of the other's work. Kilby patented the discovery in 1958 and won the Nobel Prize for Physics in 2000. The invention stands as one of the most important of the twentieth century. Transistors, resistors, capacitors and all the associated connecting wires were incorporated into a single miniaturised electronic circuit. The two companies shared information, and helped to create a trillion-dollar industry.

Noyce went on to found Intel, the company that developed the computer microprocessor.

> *'What we didn't realise then was that the integrated circuit would reduce the cost of electronic functions by a factor of a million to one. Nothing had ever been done like that before.*
> JACK KILBY

The computer microprocessor was invented in 1968 by US engineer Marcian 'Ted' Hoff (b. 1937). It is also called a 'microchip' or 'chip', which places all the thinking parts of a computer, such as the central processing unit (CPU) and the memory onto a single silicon chip.

Hoff joined Intel as employee number 12 and his invention was first marketed in 1971 as the Intel 4004. Eighty per cent of the world's computers now operate on Intel microchips.

In 1949 Edmund Berkeley (1909–88) published plans to build SIMON in his book *Giant Brains, or Machines that Think*. SIMON was a desktop machine, about 0.1 cubic metres (4 cubic feet) in size that used relay technology. Some experts regard it as the forerunner of the personal computer.

The first personal computer was introduced by Apple in 1976, named Apple 1.

PARACHUTES

The principle of how parachutes would work had been recognised by Leonardo da Vinci as early as 1480, but the first practical demonstration was conducted in 1783 by French physicist Louis-Sebastien Lenormand

(1757–1839) when he jumped from a tree holding two parasols, landing successfully. There are accounts of a similar experiment in China in 90 BC.

The first parachute jump proper took place in 1797, when Parisian André-Jacques Garnerin (1769–1823) jumped successfully from a balloon, it is said from approximately 1,000 metres (3,200 feet), using a parachute with a basket slung underneath. Garnerin's wife, Jeanne-Genevieve, became the first woman parachutist in 1799. In 1802, Garnerin made the first parachute jump in Britain from 2,440 metres (8,000 feet).

The first successful parachute decent from an aeroplane was in 1912 by US Army Captain Albert Berry (1852–99).

Parachutes were not issued to pilots in the First World War. Aircraft were in shorter supply than men, and High Command held the theory that pilots might take the easy way out of a 'dogfight' and bale out, rather than try to save the plane. Hundreds died in burning planes, or baled out without parachutes and fell to certain death.

The 'sail' type of steerable parachute was developed during the Vietnam War in the late 1960s so that pilots baling out at high altitude had a chance to steer themselves back behind their own lines.

NEWCOMEN ENGINES

These atmospheric steam engines, which were designed to pump water from deep mines, were invented by Thomas Newcomen (1663–1729). The first engine was installed in 1712 close to Dudley Castle in the Black Country.

Newcomen had to share his success with Thomas Savery (1650–1716), who had previously taken out a general patent covering all the possible means of pumping water by steam power.

PHOTOGRAPHY

Pre-dating photography, and known in China as early as the fifth century BC, the *camera obscura* (Latin – meaning dark chamber or room) was originally used to observe eclipses of the sun without damaging the eyes. The mechanism consists of a darkened room into which light enters through a small hole casting an inverted image on to the opposite wall, or on to a screen.

By the sixteenth century the *camera obscura* was being used as an aid to drawing. Eminent artists such as the Italian Giovanni Antonio Canale (also known as Canaletto) (1697–1768), used the *camera obscura* to observe images very closely and then produce highly accurate paintings of buildings.

Photography was created when French inventor Joseph Nicephore Niepce (1765–1833) introduced light sensitive paper into a *camera obscura*. In 1816 Niepce managed to record a view from his workroom on to paper, which had been sensitised with silver chloride, but was only able to partially fix the image. It took him until 1826 to make a permanently fixed image on to a pewter plate. The exposure took eight hours and the resulting photo is now held in the library of the University of Texas, USA. Niepce called his discovery heliography (from the Greek for sun drawing), as his images resulted from the exposure of the paper to sunlight.

Niepce also invented a means of extracting sugar from beetroot, as well as a machine which he called a pyreolophore, which used the expanded air in a controlled explosion to create propulsion. The pyreolophore was a forerunner of the internal combustion engine.

A primitive form of photography was already being used in 1839 by Sir John Herschel (1792–1871), the same year that Louis Daguerre announced the first commercial photographic system: the daguerreotype.

In 1841 William Henry Fox-Talbot (1800–77), based in London, patented the more commercial negative–positive system, which is the basis of the modern photographic process.

Flexible film was invented in 1884 and introduced in 1889 by George Eastman (1854–1932) of Eastman Kodak fame.

Colour photography was successfully demonstrated at the Royal Institute in London in 1861 by James Clerk Maxwell. Early colour photography was extremely complex and prohibitively expensive. In 1869, Charles Cros and Louis Ducos du Hauron devised a method of creating colour photographs.

The electrically ignited flash bulb was invented in 1893 by E.J. Marcy.

The first commercially available digital camera was the DCS 100. It was released in 1990 by Kodak and was aimed at the professional market. In January 2004, Kodak announced that production of non-digital cameras would cease at the end of the year.

SEWING MACHINES

The first mechanical device for sewing was patented in 1755. British Patent 701 was granted to Charles Frederick Weisenthal of Germany.

The first sewing machines in the USA were produced in 1839 by Lerow and Blodgett Inc. of the USA. After repairing a Lerow and Blodgett machine, Isaac Merit Singer (1811–65) could see ways to improve the design and patented his own machine in 1851. He formed the Singer Sewing Machine Corporation, which became a worldwide company.

Singer also pioneered hire purchase so that a sewing machine could be taken away for a US$5 downpayment. He retired to England in 1863.

The earliest sewing machine for mass-production of clothing was designed by Barthelemy Thimmonier of France in 1841. It was designed for the production of French Army uniforms but was destroyed by rioting tailors.

BUNSEN BURNER

Most school laboratories are equipped with Bunsen burners, which are used to heat liquids in test tubes. The combustible fuel is a mixture of gas and air, and the temperature is regulated by a simple slide to control the flow of air into the combustion tube.

Bunsen burners were first produced in 1855 by German chemist and physicist Robert Bunsen (1811–99). The original designs were by either Michael Faraday or Peter Desdega.

Cash Register

The cash register was invented in 1879 by barman James Ritty (1837–1918). He opened a factory, which he called the National Manufacturing Company. In 1884 Ritty sold the business to James Patterson for US$6,500.

The name was changed to National Cash Register and the company became a major international business, a forerunner of the early computer industry, and a subsidiary of the massive American Telephone and Telegraph Corporation in 1991.

Radio Detection and Ranging (Radar)

(*See also* War p. 302.)

In 1887, German physicist Heinrich Hertz (1857–94) demonstrated the existence of radio waves. He also demonstrated that they behave like light waves and can be reflected.

A device using radio echo for marine navigation was patented in 1904 by German engineer Christian Hulsmeyer.

Practical methods of using radar for aircraft detection were developed in 1935 by Sir Robert Watson-Watt (1892–1973), a descendant of James Watt. By 1939 he had installed a chain of radar stations across the south and east coasts of England.

During the Second World War, German High Command was concerned about high losses to their night fighters and bombers, thanks to the British radar detection systems. British counter-espionage put it about that Allied pilots were eating large quantities of carrots every day to improve their night vision. The secret of RAF on-board radar was protected for several months.

SONAR (Sound Navigation and Ranging) and ASDIC (anti-submarine detection investigation committee)

Sonar and Asdic are identical systems of underwater detection of solid objects by means of sonic echoes. Both active listening devices were developed during the Second World War; Sonar in the USA, and Asdic in Britain.

ELECTRICITY AND ELECTRICAL APPLIANCES

Thomas Alva Edison (1847–1931) was the pioneer who brought the world's first reliable, low-priced, public electricity supply to New York in 1882. This led to the development of electrical appliances, which could be produced for a mass domestic market.

Dishwasher

American Joel Houghton developed the first dishwasher in 1850. He patented a wooden machine with a hand-turned wheel, which splashed water on dishes. It failed to become a household item.

In 1886, Josephine Cochrane, a wealthy widow in Illinois, USA, invented and patented a dishwashing machine because she was dissatisfied with the treatment her servants were giving to her china and disliked doing the washing-up herself.

After her husband had died, she launched a commercial venture with her machine, which was capable of washing a load of dishes in two minutes. Basically, it consisted of wire compartments, into which the dirty china was placed. These were then put onto a wheel inside a copper boiler. The wheel was turned by a motor as hot, soapy water cleaned the china. The machine was used in hotels and restaurants but not in family homes.

Kettle

The electric kettle was launched in England by Crompton and Company in 1891.

Toaster

General Electric of the USA introduced what they claimed was the first electric toaster in 1909. A competing claim by Hotpoint puts their product launch date at 1905.

The pop-up toaster was invented in 1919 (patent granted in 1921) by American Charles Strite and launched in 1926.

Food Mixer

RAF engineer Kenneth Wood (1916–97) had the idea of a multi-purpose food mixer and launched his first product, the A200, in 1947. He launched the famous Kenwood Chef in 1950.

Air Conditioning

A form of air conditioning has been known in India for hundreds of years. Wet leaves are draped across the entrance to a building. As air currents pass into the building, the air is cooled by the water evaporating from the leaves. The principle of exchanging cool air for hot air is the same in the modern air conditioner.

The modern electric air conditioner was invented by New Yorker Willis Haviland Carrier (1876–1950) in 1902. At the time, he was employed at a printing company, which was experiencing problems with four-colour printing due to inconsistencies in the air quality. Carrier came up with a solution and was awarded a patent in 1906.

Air conditioning for human comfort, as opposed to being part of an industrial process, began in 1924 at the J.L. Hutton Department Store in Detroit, Michigan.

Vacuum Cleaner

A forerunner of the vacuum cleaner was invented in 1901 by British engineer H. Cecil Booth. He developed a petrol-powered, horse-drawn cleaning device, which he called 'Puffing Billy'. The device was for commercial not domestic purposes, and would be parked outside office buildings and shops, with a long hose running inside for the cleaning operation. It was not a commercial success.

The domestic vacuum cleaner as we know it was invented in 1907 by James Spangler, a janitor in Ohio. Dust was thrown up by the carpet sweeper he used in his job and continuously troubled his asthma, so he needed to trap the dust. He connected a fan motor to a broom handle, collected the dust in an old pillowcase and was awarded a patent.

William Hoover (1849–1932), the husband of a customer of Spangler, liked the product so much he bought the company and rebranded the product line Hoover. The name Hoover became the generic term for a vacuum cleaner, and hoovering the verb to describe the action of vacuuming. The company went on to become a worldwide industrial combine.

Refrigerator

In ancient India, Egypt, Greece and Rome, wealthy citizens made use of snow cellars, which were pits dug into the ground and filled with straw and wood. Ice transported from mountains could be stored for several months in this way.

The first domestic refrigerator was developed in 1834 by American inventor Jacob Perkins (1766–1849). The machine worked by manually activating a pump and converting the heat produced into a heat loss between two separate chambers. It was not a commercial success because of the exceptionally long time it took to reduce temperature sufficiently to cool liquids and keep food fresh.

The first commercially successful domestic refrigerator was produced in late 1916 by the Kelvinator Company of Detroit, which is now owned by Electrolux.

Light Bulb

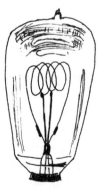

In 1811, the Cornish scientist Sir Humphry Davy (1778–1829) discovered that light is produced when passing an electric arc between two poles. By 1841, Davy's electric arc lights had been installed in Paris.

In 1879, Sir Joseph Swan (1828–1914) of the UK and Thomas Alva Edison (1847–1931) of the USA simultaneously, on opposite sides of the Atlantic, invented the electric incandescent light bulb.

PHOTOCOPYING

Known more accurately as xerography, photocopying was invented in 1937 by Seattle-born Chester Carlson (1906–68). It works by charging paper and powdered ink with opposite static electrical charges. By applying heat to the whole product the ink is fixed to the paper. The massive commercial potential was not realised until the 1950s when photocopying was exploited by the Haloid Corporation, later renamed Xerox.

The first colour copiers were developed in the 1970s.

SMOKING

Experts believe that tobacco was originally used as a hallucinogenic enema in the Americas around the first century BC. The Maya Indians, who occupied the Yucatan Peninsular in South America, developed tobacco as a smoking material between AD 470 and 600.

The first pictorial evidence of smoking is on an eleventh-century pottery vessel found in Guatemala showing a Mayan smoking a roll of tobacco leaves tied with string.

The first Europeans to observe smoking were two Spaniards, Rodrigo de Jerez and Luis de Torres, in November 1492, who were present on Christopher Columbus's (1451–1506) exploration that first sailed to the Americas.

Jerez is thought to be the first non-American smoker. When he returned to Spain he was imprisoned for seven years by the Inquisition having been accused of frightening people with the smoke billowing from his mouth and nose. By the time of his release, smoking was widespread in Spain.

Tobacco was introduced to England in 1564–65 by Sir John Hawkins (1532–95). It was known as 'sotweed' in Elizabethan times.

In 1585 Sir Francis Drake (1540–96), a cousin and protégé of Sir John Hawkins, showed Sir Walter Raleigh (1552–1618) how to smoke tobacco using a clay pipe.

Tabacco, the first English book on the subject of tobacco, was published in 1595.

In 1604 James I of England wrote *A Counterblaste to tobacco*, which strongly denounced the use of tobacco, and in 1629, the first 'No Smoking' signs were being put up in some government buildings in Britain.

The first clinical study into the effects of using tobacco in all its forms was made as early as 1761 by the London physician Sir John Hill (1716–75). Hill linked cancer with tobacco use, and noted the high incidence of cancers of the nose in snuff (powdered tobacco) users.

The cigarette was invented in 1832 by an Egyptian artilleryman at the Battle of Acre in the Turkish–Egyptian war. The gunner had managed to improve the rate of fire of his cannon by rolling the gunpowder in paper tubes. He was rewarded with a supply of tobacco. Having broken his pipe, he rolled the tobacco in the same paper that he had used for the gunpowder and smoked what became the first cigarette.

The first cigarette factory in England was built in 1856.

The first cigar-rolling machine was patented in 1883 by the composer Oscar Hammerstein.

SAFETY PIN

The humble safety pin was the creation of Walter Hunt (1785–1869) of New York. Hunt's wife complained continuously about pricking her finger with the only pins that were available at the time, which were straight, and had to be bent by hand. In 1849, Hunt decided to do something about it. He fashioned a piece of brass wire into the shape we are familiar with today, with a simple catch to shield the sharp end, and was granted a patent.

Unfortunately for Hunt he was badly in debt at the time, and was forced to sell his patent for just $400.

Useless Inventions

Laughable they may be, but useless inventions serve to remind us of things that may have been.

Codpiece

This was worn in fifteenth-century Europe by dandyish males to support their genitalia. Sometimes the codpiece would be decorated with jewellery and generally enhanced to look prominent. By 1580 they had passed out of fashion as they were thought to look lewd.

Chastity Belt

The chastity belt was designed in the Middle Ages to prevent married women engaging in sexual intercourse outside marriage. The belts were normally fitted to the women during the absence of their husbands on the Crusades. They were unpopular and uncomfortable.

Claxton Earcap

Adelaide Claxton patented the Claxton Earcap in 1925, which was supposed to be worn at night by children to correct sticking-out ears.

Phrenology

This is the so-called science of determining a person's character by the shape of his or her skull. Franz Joseph Gall (1758–1828) promoted phrenology in the late eighteenth and early nineteenth centuries.

Tobacco Resuscitator Kit

Invented in England in 1774, the tobacco rescuscitation kit was meant to revive victims of drowning, by injecting tobacco smoke into the rectum.

The idea was to introduce warmth and stimulation to the apparently dead victim, and this was thought to be an entirely rational development, as tobacco was effective in providing both. The devices were placed along the banks of the Thames, by the Royal Humane Society, in the same way that flotation rings are placed today.

Yard-of-Ale Glass

The 'yard-of-ale' glass is a peculiar British drinking vessel, which was first used in the seventeenth century. The glass has a trumpet-shaped opening, a long neck of about a yard in length, and a bulbous container. As the glass is tipped up and the drinker begins to empty the contents, there is a rush of air, which propels the contents towards the opening at far increased speed, creating a wet drinker, to the amusement of onlookers.

The difficulty of drinking from it renders the yard-of-ale glass impractical for normal use, and they are mainly used for betting.

Rocket Mail

The island of Scarp in the Outer Hebrides frequently had to wait several weeks for mail delivery during bad weather and heavy tides. In 1934 an experiment was set up by German rocket engineer Gerhard Zucker to deliver mail across the treacherous half-mile of water by rocket. The rocket exploded on take-off and most of the mail was lost. Two more attempts ended the same way and Zucker returned home.

LANGUAGE

COVERING: Earliest Origins, Indo-European, Greek, Latin, English, Sign Language, Braille, Mathematical Symbols, Slang.

Who does not know another language does not know his own.
HERMANN GOERING (1893–1946)

EARLIEST ORIGINS

Until the eighteenth century and the Enlightenment (a European intellectual movement), most thinking about the origin of language had assumed it began with Adam and Eve in the Garden of Eden. The most recent theory of the origin of language is that simple hand gestures were used as long ago as six or seven million years, shortly after the human line diverged from the apes. Shouting would have been used as alarm calls or emotional outbursts.

About five million years ago, an early hominid, known as *Australopithecus*, started to walk upright, and a more complex form of gesturing was probably used.

Then, two million years ago the brain size increased and hand gestures were used in various combinations to express ideas, and remained as the primary means of communication.

As recently as 100,000 years ago, Homo sapiens may have changed the main means of communication from hand and facial gestures to vocalisations and the use of differing sounds to convey a variety of meanings. Gradually the use of gesturing diminished, although we still use it today to emphasise speech, even during telephone conversations, when the person at the other end cannot see the gestures.

The First Word

'In the beginning was the word.
JOHN 1: 1

After studying 1,000 languages, researchers in Paris have come to the conclusion that 'papa' was the first word ever used. They discovered 'papa' in 700 of the languages studied. From the start of the last Ice Age, roughly 50,000 years ago, it seems that the word 'papa' was part of a common language.

Oldest Spoken Language

The oldest of all spoken languages is almost certainly Mayan, which seems to have been in existence 7,000 years ago when the Maya migrated south into South America.

There are 30 Mayan languages spoken today which are so closely linked that linguists believe they all originated from a single proto-Mayan language.

First Written Language

Cuneiform, the first written language, was developed by the Sumerians more than 5,000 years ago. The strange wedge-shaped letters were a development from earlier pictograms and were formed by pressing shapes into wet clay with a special pen. Cuneiform was the first language able to convey abstract ideas and sounds. There were only two numbers in cuneiform, a vertical wedge for 1 and a sideways wedge for 10.

INDO-EUROPEAN

The original Indo-European language, known as proto-Indo-European, was used around 5,000 years ago. As it did not develop as a written script, historians are not able to pinpoint the precise area in which proto-Indo-European arose as a spoken language, but it is thought most likely to have come either from the inhabitants in an area of present-day Poland or Turkey.

Around 3,000 years ago Indo-European split into two main group-ings, the Germanic and Romance groups. In the second century BC the Germanic group split further into the east, north and west subgroups, of which west Germanic is the ancestor of English.

GREEK

Although the Greek language is widely regarded as the mother tongue of Western civilisation, its beginnings are modest in scale compared with Mesopotamian and Egyptian. The Minoan civilisation developed on the island of Crete in about 2000 BC, and with it developed the beginnings of the Greek language. Minoan civilisation was brought to an end around 1400 BC following the devastating effects of the volcanic eruption on the island of Thera and subsequent conquest by Mycenaean invaders from the Greek mainland.

$$ΑΒΓΔ$$

Linear A

The early form of writing, Linear A, is thought to have been a written script rather than a spoken language. It replaced hieroglyphics in Minoan writing between 1700 and 1600 BC and although it has only 90 symbols Linear A has resisted all attempts to decipher it.

Linear B

Although this is by no means certain, Linear B may have developed out of Linear A. It was in use from 1500 to 1150 BC and was used for writing Minoan Greek. It is thought to be up to 500 years older than the language used by Homer. Linear B was deciphered in 1952 by Michael Ventris (1922–56).

Classical Greek

From around 1200 BC the Dorians migrated down from north-west Greece to occupy central Greece. The remaining vestiges of Mycenaean and Minoan culture were swept away and the country fell into its own Dark Ages, when writing disappeared.

Around 750 BC, Classical Greece emerged as a collection of city states, with heavy involvement in maritime trade, literature, politics and philosophy. It reached its zenith in the fifth century BC.

In 338 BC, Philip II of Macedon (382–336 BC) had established Macedonian supremacy in Greece. His son, Alexander the Great (356–323 BC), spread Greek culture and language to other countries.

Modern Greek

The modern Greek language has the longest continual existence of any of the Indo-European languages, having begun to emerge in the fourteenth century BC and continued through to the present day. The language evolved came from ancient Greek, then Koine, which was the common language from the fourth century BC to the fourth century AD, then on through Byzantine Greek, from the fifth to the fifteenth century AD. Greek as we know it today has been spoken since the fifteenth century. Linguists place the actual starting date at 1453, the Fall of Constantinople to the Ottoman Turks.

The Greek Alphabet

This was the first recognisably modern alphabet, the revolutionary feature being the use of five letters to signify the five vowel sounds. Both the Roman alphabet, now used throughout Western Europe, and the Cyrillic alphabet, which is used in the six Slavic languages (Russian, Bulgarian, Serbian, Ukrainian, Belarusian and Macedonian), are based on the Greek model.

LATIN

The Romans would never have had time to conquer the world if they had been obliged to learn Latin first of all.
HEINRICH HEINE (1797–1856)

An Indo-European language, Latin is the ancestor of the modern Romance languages: Italian, French, and Spanish. It was first spoken from the seventh century BC by small groups of people living along the banks of the river Tiber. The use of Latin rapidly spread as the Roman Empire conquered Europe and the Mediterranean coasts of Africa.

Latin was the most widely used scholarly language in Western civilisation until the late Middle Ages, and was the language of the Roman Catholic liturgy until the late twentieth century. During the Classical period there were three types of Latin in use:

Classical written Latin.

Classical oratorical Latin, used in public speaking and prayer.

Colloquial Latin as used in everyday speech.

The Roman (Latin) Alphabet

This alphabet is now the most widely used writing system in the world, including as it does English and most of the European languages. It was developed around 600 BC from the Etruscan alphabet and can be traced right back to the North Semitic alphabet which was in use in Syria and Palestine in around 1100 BC. The earliest surviving example of the Roman alphabet in use is on a seventh-century BC cloak pin. It says, MANIOS MED FHEFHAKED NUMASIOI, which means 'Manius made me for Numerius'. The pin was probably a little love token.

There were only 23 letters in the Classical Latin alphabet. During medieval times the letter 'I' was used for both 'I' and 'J', and the letter 'V' was used for 'U', 'V' and 'W'. Hence the 26 letters in the modern English alphabet.

Roman and Italic typefaces, or fonts, commonly used in modern printing, developed from legal and commercial script used in fifteenth-century AD Italy.

ENGLISH

English is a member of the Indo-European family of languages, which includes most modern European languages (*see* above).

Old English

Also called Anglo-Saxon, there are four known distinct dialects: Northumbrian (northern England and south-east Scotland), Mercian (central England), Kentish (south-east England) and West Saxon (southern and south-west England). It is thought to have been spoken by King Alfred in the ninth century AD. The language had three genders, male, female and neuter and was spoken from around AD 500 to 1100. Anglo-Saxon dominated the Celtic speakers who were pushed westwards into Wales, Cornwall and Ireland and northwards into Scotland. The Viking invasions, beginning in AD 850, added many new words and roughly 15 per cent of modern English can be directly traced back to Old English.

Middle English

The Norman Conquest, beginning in 1066, introduced Old French (also known as Anglo-Norman). This developed into Middle English, which was in use from around 1100 to 1500 AD. Middle English of the late fourteenth century would be recognisable today as English.

Early Modern English

William Shakespeare (1564–1616) strongly influenced early Modern English (1500–1800). He not only recorded certain words for the first time, but also invented words such as 'dwindle' and 'leapfrog'. In total there are around 2,000 words that can be attributed to Shakespeare.

Late Modern English

The many new territories held in the British Empire, which at its peak covered a quarter of the globe, influenced late Modern English (1800–present). For instance, words such as bungalow, shampoo and jodhpur are Indian. New technologies have brought new words to describe things that hadn't previously existed; words such as vaccine, nuclear, typewriter and microchip.

American English

England and America are two countries divided
by a common language.
GEORGE BERNARD SHAW (1856–1950)

The English spoken in America began to change immediately after colonisation began in around 1600. The American lexicographer Noah Webster (1758–1843) compiled dictionaries and what he called 'spelling books' specifically to help Americans adopt their own standard of language, and to create uniformity. Webster's books were published between 1783 and 1828, and he named the language, which he was institutionalising, 'Federal' English.

There are three periods in the development of American English:

Colonial: 1607 to 1776

National: 1776 to 1898

International: 1898 to present

Sign Language

It is almost certain that simple sign language, in the form of shoulder shrugs, pointing with the arms and fingers, and facial grimaces, is older than speech itself.

The first form of sign language, which is known to have been specifically created for the deaf, was developed by the Italian Giovanni Bonifacio in 1616.

After a chance encounter in the 1750s with two deaf sisters, who managed to communicate with each other by hand signals, Abbe Charles-Michel de l'Epee (1712–89) developed sign language as a form of communication for the deaf in its modern form for spelling French words. French Sign Language (FSL) was also able to express whole concepts with a single sign, and remains in use today. De l'Epee came from a wealthy Versailles family, and funded the world's first free school for deaf children from his own money.

American Sign Language (ASL) was developed in 1816 from FSL when it was taken to the USA. ASL is now the fourth most common language in the USA.

Deaf sign languages are independent of their spoken counterparts. British and American are almost unintelligible to users of the other language, and yet their spoken counterparts are almost identical.

BRAILLE

A form of written communication, Braille uses raised dots on paper or metal to enable blind people to read.

In 1821, French Army captain Charles Barbier invented what he called 'night writing'. The invention made use of a 12-dot code which had been developed for battlefield conditions specifically to eliminate the need for speaking during the hours of darkness, when silence was vital. To demonstrate his new code, Barbier visited a school for blind boys, at which one of the pupils was Louis Braille (1809–52).

Braille was very interested in the system, but considered it too complex, so he set about simplifying it down to six dots. The dots were arranged in different positions to represent the letters of the alphabet, and the Braille system has now been adapted into almost every language in the world.

Braille, who was born near Paris in 1809, had accidentally blinded himself in one eye at the age of four while playing with an awl, a sharp-pointed instrument for marking surfaces or punching small holes. He lost the sight in his other eye as a result of an infection and became totally blind.

MATHEMATICAL SYMBOLS

Plus and minus signs

The earliest known printed use of + and – signs is in the book *Mercantile Arithmetic*, which was published by Johannes Widmann in 1489. He used the signs to indicate surpluses and shortages in cargoes.

Henricus Grammateus began the use of + and – for addition and subtraction in his book *Ayn Neu Kunstlich Buech* in 1518. The new signs were not adopted in England until publication of *The Whetstone of Witte*, which was written in 1577 by the leading English mathematician Robert Recorde (1510–58). The = sign, meaning 'equals', was also introduced by Robert Recorde in 1577.

The English rector and mathematician William Oughtred (1575–1660) was the first to use x as a multiplication symbol. He introduced the x in his great work *Clavis Mathematicae* (*The Key to Mathematics*), which was published in 1631.

The division sign ÷ (known as an obelus) was first used by Johann Rahn (1622–) in his book *Teutsche Algebra*, which was published in 1659.

SLANG

It is thought the use of slang harks back to animism, the first religion. In animism, it was believed that all objects had an external aspect which could be perceived by the senses, and an invisible aspect, which could only be perceived by a specially gifted person. Thus the use of slang was developed to refer obliquely, rather than directly, to an image (*see also* Dictionaries p. 80).

MASSIVE STEPS

CONVERING: the Modern World, the Industrial Revolution, Communism, Consumerism, Great International Co-operations, the Cold War.

> *Don't be afraid to take a big step if one is indicated.*
> *You can't cross a chasm in two small jumps.*
> DAVID LLOYD GEORGE (1863–1945)

THE MODERN WORLD

Michael Faraday (1791–1867) is considered by many to be the greatest of all experimental scientists and the originator of modern society.

Faraday was born near London, the son of a blacksmith, and in his youth he was apprenticed to a bookbinder. One of the bookbinder's customers, William Dance, gave Faraday tickets to a series of lectures by the Cornish scientist Sir Humphry Davy (1778–1829), the inventor of, among many other things, the safety lamp for miners. Listening to Davy's lectures stimulated Faraday's interest in scientific experimentation. He quickly applied for a job, but Davy had no position to offer.

Early in 1813, Davy had to dismiss his chemical assistant for fighting in the main lecture hall. This incongruous act had far-reaching consequences for the future of civilisation. Faraday heard about the incident, applied for the newly vacant post, and was engaged as Davy's temporary assistant. Shortly afterwards, Davy embarked on a European lecture tour, and took his new assistant along. During the tour the leading scientists of the day met Davy to exchange views and scientific data. The tour provided an unconventional but unique scientific education for the young Faraday, and on his return to London he soon began to conduct his own experiments.

The experimental work he completed laid the foundations for:

- Radio

- Electric motors

- Electricity generators

- Electrical dynamos

- Electro-plating of metals

- The theory of molecular structure

- The magnetic fields of galaxies

- An early version of the Bunsen burner

Among many other discoveries, Faraday also:

- Developed a type of glass with a high refractive index.

- Discovered a number of organic compounds including benzene.

- Evolved what was then the radical theory that space was not 'nothing', but a medium capable of supporting electrical and magnetic forces.

- Discovered that light could be bent by magnetism.

- Demonstrated the relationship between electricity and chemical bonding.

It is difficult to imagine how different modern society would be without the work of Michael Faraday, and Albert Einstein kept a picture of him on the wall of his study, regarding him as having provided the foundation of his own studies.

THE INDUSTRIAL REVOLUTION

The term 'Industrial Revolution' refers to, and describes, the process of global change from agricultural and handicraft economies to ones dominated by industry, machine manufacture and automatic processing.

Arnold Toynbee, (1889–1975), the English economic historian, coined the term 'Industrial Revolution' to describe English economic development in the years 1760 to 1840.

The area around Coalbrookdale in Shropshire, the site of the world's first iron bridge completed in 1779, is generally accepted as the cradle of the Industrial Revolution. The area was rich in resources, having ample supplies of coal, iron ore and limestone within easy reach. The navigable river Severn, which ran through the middle of Shropshire, provided both a convenient means of transport to the docks, and abundant water for processing.

The local workforce was only too willing to give up the prevailing seasonal agricultural pay, to take advantage of the higher pay and year-round work offered in the exciting new factories springing up along the banks of the river.

The six main drivers of the Industrial Revolution in Britain were:

- New materials (iron and steel).

- New forms of energy (steam, electricity).

- The invention of new machines (agricultural and industrial).

- The factory system.

- Improved communication and transport.

- The application of science.

To compete with Britain, which had become the dominant force in the world's economy, other European nations underwent the same process of change. Russia and Japan were slow to respond, leaving it until late in the nineteenth century to embrace change. America quickly got into its stride and embraced industrialisation with fervour.

The second Industrial Revolution began around 1850 with the advent of the chemical industry, the electrical industry and the spread of rail-roads. By the time the second revolution came into being, the world and its civilisation had already been changed for ever.

COMMUNISM

The founding doctrine of communism is the liberation of the proletariat: the class within society, which lives solely by selling its labour.

In 1847 Frederick Engels (1820–1925) wrote the draft programme for the Congress of the League of the Just, which became the Communist League.

The Communist Manifesto was written in 1848 by Karl Marx (1818–83) and Frederick Engels. The manifesto grew out of the perception that poverty was not just an unfortunate consequence of capitalism, but a deliberate creation of the capitalist system. According to the manifesto, capitalism was controlled by the bourgeoisie, and the poverty of the proletariat was seen by Marx as an essential tool in creating wealth. According to Marx, the 'labour theory of value' allowed the bourgeoisie to grow massively rich through exploitation of the proletariats' labour.

The revolutionary proposal put forward in the Communist Manifesto was that all the means of production and distribution should be owned communally, not by an elite cadre of wealthy businessmen. This looked rather appealing and just, changing as it did the need for greed and distributing commonly held wealth according to the needs of the whole population rather than the wants of a few. Marx proposed that this would eliminate poverty almost at a stroke. Millions listened.

The Bolshevik leader Vladimir Ilyich Lenin (1870–1924) (original surname, Ulyanov) took the idea of Communism–Marxism forward with dramatic speed in the Bolshevik Revolutions of 1917, during which he seized power in Russia, and created the world's first communist state.

Unlike the capitalist democracies, which had matured over almost 2,000 years, within the next half-century, communist regimes – almost all led by dictators – took control of China, Cuba, and North Korea. Major areas of Eastern Europe also fell under the influence of Communist Russia as the Soviet Empire expanded. At the height of its power, from the 1930s through to the late 1980s, almost half the world's population was governed under some form of communism. Political commentators everywhere expected further growth.

In the mid-1980s, the British and US governments under Margaret

Thatcher (b. 1935) and Ronald Reagan (1911–2004) took rigid stances on freedom and economics in opposition to the Soviet Union, which Reagan referred to as the 'Evil Empire'. This began the process that led Mikhail Gorbachev (1931–present), as the last President, to break up the Soviet Union, and restore forms of capitalism and democracy to Russia and its former vassal states during the late 1980s and 1990s.

European communism's domination ended abruptly between 1989 and 1991, but in 2006, more than 20 per cent of the world's population remains under communist control in China, North Korea, Cuba, Laos and Vietnam.

CONSUMERISM

The consumer is not a moron, she's your wife.
DAVID OGILVY (1911–99) (Advertising executive)

The groundbreaking book, *Unsafe at any Speed – the Designed-in Dangers of the American Automobile*, was written by a young American lawyer, Ralph Nader (b. 1934), and published in 1965 to massive public acclaim.

Nader claimed in his book that in the 1950s and early 1960s hundreds of occupants of motorcars were dying every year in accidents that could have been prevented. Better design (not to be confused with styling) and the installation of safety features were the changes he advocated.

Nader asserted that, rather than coming to agreement between themselves on universal standards of safety, the big car manufacturers were continually wasting their time and efforts by lobbying the US government to prevent safety measures being introduced on a compulsory basis.

Resulting from the impact his book had in the USA and Europe, among other things the fitting and wearing of seat belts was made compulsory. Almost as importantly, the capacity of tyres and suspension to support a fully loaded vehicle had to be proven. Crash testing was introduced (even on Rolls-Royces), and air bags were eventually fitted as standard.

Nader's campaigns affected most industries. Consumers began to realise they had powerful rights, and they demanded improved safety and better information. Governments on both sides of the Atlantic responded with stricter controls. Among other things, the individual contents of prepared foodstuffs were compulsorily listed to show the amounts of additives.

Before the publication of Nader's book, consumers had a tendency to trust big corporations and, at least subliminally, to associate big business with safe products, and government with being trustworthy. Consumers' rights under the law, led to landmark court cases against companies that foisted unsafe products on to the general public. It was no longer enough for a producer to claim *caveat emptor* (let the buyer beware). Once the genie was out of the bottle on corporate responsibility, continuous improvements were instituted in aviation, food, air pollution, water pollution, forestry, and the behaviour of lawyers, among others.

Nader also campaigned against mass advertising, on the premise that it creates false desires in consumers, and he argued strongly against sensationalism in the daily news.

GREAT INTERNATIONAL CO-OPERATIONS

Occasionally, in the face of technological advances and the threat of public pressure, nations co-operate to make life better and improve conditions for everyone, not just their own voters. Nationalism and intolerance are put aside to allow great advances to take place.

International Telegraphic Union (ITU)

The International Telegraphic Union was set up in 1865, originally with 20 member countries, to co-ordinate all international telegraphic traffic. The Union was the initiative of the French government. It was authorised and ratified at the 1865 Paris Convention (Convention Telegraph-ique Internationale de Paris) to:

- Regulate radio frequencies.

- Assist with technical and operational matters.

- Promote telegraphic development in countries not yet 'telegraphed'.

Britain was originally excluded from participation in the ITU, finally being admitted in 1871.

Despite the first telegraphic message being sent in 1844, until the ITU Agreement in 1865 there had been no common international telegraphic traffic standard. As each country used a different system, messages had to be transcribed and handed over at the border. The messages then had to be translated and retransmitted using the neighbouring country's telegraphic system.

It has been renamed the International Telecommunication Union.

Universal Postal Union

The Universal Postal Union was set up in 1874 under its original name of General Postal Union. The name was changed in 1878.

The objective of the union was to organise and co-ordinate postal services throughout the world. The most important agreement was that postage paid at source in one country would cover the cost of delivery in another. It was also agreed that all national stamps would be accepted in all other countries.

World Post Day is held on 9 October each year, the anniversary of the establishment of the UPU.

Red Cross and Red Crescent

Both the Red Cross and Red Crescent were the brainchild of Swiss businessman and humanitarian Jean Henry Dunant (1828–1910). The decisive moment came for Dunant in the aftermath of the 1859 Battle of Solferino, in the Franco-Austrian War. He witnessed helpless, wounded soldiers lying on the battlefield, being systematically bayoneted or shot to death.

Dunant had been involved in the organisation of emergency aid for both French and Austrian wounded, and had been sickened by the suffering on both sides. In a single day, the total killed was over 5,000 and the total wounded was over 23,000. Dunant was strongly affected by the mistreatment of the wounded and determined to make changes.

In 1859, he proposed the formation of societies for the relief of suffering, by all countries, and was awarded the first Nobel Peace Prize in 1901.

The Geneva Convention of 1864 committed all the signatory governments to care for all the wounded, whether enemy or friend. From 1906, at the insistence of the countries of the Hapsburg Empire, the Red Cross became the co-ordinating body in Christian countries, and the Red Crescent in Muslim countries. The cross was regarded as a potent symbol of Christianity and unsuitable for predominantly Muslim countries.

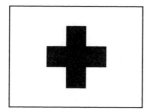 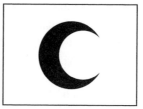

Hague Tribunal

The Hague Tribunal is the popular name for the Permanent Court of Arbitration (PCA) based at The Hague in Holland. The PCA was established in 1899 by a convention of the First Hague Conference as a means to resolve international disputes. The initiative came from Czar Nicholas II of Russia (1868–1918).

There are currently 104 states that are party to the treaty.

League of Nations

Following the initiative of the British Foreign Secretary Edward Grey (1862–1933), the League of Nations was proposed by US President Woodrow Wilson (1856–1924) at the Paris Peace Conference of 1919. Wilson's objective was to create an organisation with enough strength to prevent future conflicts like the First World War. After Wilson returned home from Paris, the US Senate refused to ratify US membership of the League of Nations.

After failing to prevent the Second World War, the League of Nations dissolved itself and transferred all its services and property to the United Nations.

United Nations

The United Nations (UN) was formed with the intention of 'encouraging international co-operation in solving economic, social, cultural and humanitarian problems'. The name 'United Nations' was formally adopted on 24 October 1945 to mean the organisation as it is recognised today, an association of peace-loving nations that accept the obligations of the UN Charter. The original 'Big Four' were the USA, the Soviet Union, the UK and China, with France added, later and offered a permanent seat on the Security Council.

The term 'United Nations' originally referred to the Allies in the Second World War, who had agreed their wartime alliance in 1942. The agreement prevented any individual nation seeking a separate peace treaty with any of the Axis powers (Japan, Germany and Italy). The three war leaders, Roosevelt, Stalin and Churchill, agreed the original Charter, which included objectives on humanitarian aid and human rights in addition to the peacekeeping role of the organisation.

Universal Declaration of Human Rights

The Universal Declaration of Human Rights was completed by the United Nations Commission on Human Rights in June 1948 and adopted by the General Assembly in December of the same year.

Eleanor Roosevelt (1884–1962), the widow of US President Franklin D. Roosevelt (1882–1945), and Chairwoman of the Committee that drafted the Declaration, described it as the 'Universal Magna Carta for all mankind'. The Declaration was universally adopted, with the exception of six abstentions by the Soviet Bloc, plus Saudi Arabia and South Africa.

North Atlantic Treaty Organisation (NATO)

After the signing of the North Atlantic Treaty in 1949, NATO was formed to provide a counterweight to the growing and perceived threat of aggression from the Soviet Union. The USA and Canada formed a military alliance with ten European countries, Belgium, Denmark, France, Iceland, Italy, Luxembourg, Netherlands, Norway, Portugal and the UK.

NATO was instrumental in maintaining peace in Europe for more than 40 years, not only from the Soviet threat, but also between other previously warring European nations.

The Metric System

The new system of measurement was developed in France during the eighteenth century to provide a uniform system of measurement to replace the widely differing systems then in existence. Metric measurement includes weight, volume, length, area, capacity and temperature and is based on multiples being to the power of ten. It is intended that measurements can be understood throughout the world, and universal standards adopted in places such as research laboratories.

Frenchman Charles Maurice de Talleyrand-Perigord, Prince of Benevento, Bishop of Autun (1754–1838), known more popularly as Talleyrand, and Sir John Riggs Miller (d. 1798) of England, jointly championed the metric system in the 1790s.

By 1840 France made metrication mandatory. The metric system was also made legal in the USA in 1866, but not mandatory. At the Metric Conference of 1875 in France, 17 additional countries signed the Treaty of the Metre. Britain signed in 1884, to make the metric system a common international measurement.

The Postmaster General, Tony Benn (b. 1925), headed the British Metrication Board set up in 1969. The metric system was finally adopted in Britain in 1970 and the currency was decimalised in 1971, although to this day there remain many anomalies. The remaining imperial measurements include miles, pints (of beer) and acres.

Organisation of Petroleum Exporting Countries (OPEC)

A fair price for oil is anything
you can get plus ten to twenty percent.
ANON

Established in 1960, OPEC was formally constituted in January 1961 by Iran, Iraq, Kuwait, Saudi Arabia and Venezuela. Its stated aim is to co-ordinate the petroleum policies of its members. Effectively OPEC is a cartel set up to control the volume of oil produced by each of its member states. By controlling the volume, OPEC also controls the price of oil, and therefore controls a major part of the economy of the world. OPEC countries hold around 70 per cent of the world's oil reserves.

THE COLD WAR

The Cold War can be dated from 1947, and was so called because no direct, armed conflict took place. The Cold War was brought about after the end of the Second World War, by the mutual suspicions of the USA and its allies on the one side, and the Soviet Union and its allies on the other.

It was a war that was also, at times, fought by proxy. Armed conflicts in Vietnam and Angola were such proxy wars between the two opposing cultures of the West and East.

The leaders of the USA and Soviet Union officially agreed the end of the Cold War in 1989.

Hotline

In 1963, at the height of the Cold War, the first Hotline was installed between the White House in Washington, and the Kremlin in Moscow (where it was known as the 'Red Telephone'). It was commissioned after the Cuban Missile Crisis of 1961, during which the world had watched with bated breath as the two superpowers faced each other with nuclear weapons. The leaders of the USA and the Soviet Union agreed they should find a means to speak directly and immediately to each other. The line was made available, with no interference other than by their respective interpreters, at any time of day. Up to that point, there had been a real danger of accidental nuclear war being triggered by deputies, while the leaders were unable to contact each other.

The original apparatus used for the Hotline was an old teleprinter (an electro-mechanical device similar in appearance to a typewriter, for transmitting the written word between two points, via simple electrical wires). A real telephone was not installed until 1970.

Although it was a co-operation between only two nations, the Hotline had worldwide safety implications.

The Warsaw Treaty of Friendship, Co-operation and Mutual Assistance (Warsaw Pact)

The Warsaw Treaty was signed in May 1955 to form an alliance between Eastern Bloc countries, led by the Soviet Union. The Treaty was signed as a counter to the perceived military threat from the NATO alliance, and the perception became more acute once West Germany had been admitted to membership of NATO in 1952.

The participating countries of the Warsaw Pact were the Soviet Union, Albania, Bulgaria, Czechoslovakia, East Germany, Hungary, Poland and Romania.

In 1989 the Warsaw Pact became redundant and it was declared non-existent in 1991.

Money

COVERING: Animal Money, Metal Money, Paper Money, Plastic Money, Electronic Money, Currencies, Banks, Gold Standard, Internet Banking, Pawnbroking, Capitalism, Industry, Taxes, Companies.

Society without a form of money depends on barter, and the chance occurrence of having precisely the equal value of barter goods to exchange in any transaction, the so-called 'double coincidence'.

ANIMAL MONEY

Between 9000 and 6000 BC, in the absence of any other means of recognising value, primitive peoples used cattle as money.

METAL MONEY

In one of the most important and far-sighted decisions in the history of money, between 2250 and 2150 BC, the rulers of Cappadocia, in present day mid and eastern Turkey, guaranteed the weight and purity of silver ingots to help widen the acceptance of metal as a means of exchange. The silver was not yet minted into convenient regular sizes, so ingots depended for their value on weight and size.

Coins

The first rudimentary coins were minted in 687 BC in Lydia in Asia Minor (present-day western Turkey). The coins were variable in shape, but produced to a uniform weight. They were supplanted in 640 BC by regularly shaped coins made from electrum, a naturally occurring amalgam of gold and silver, and usually stamped with a symbol of the city in which they were produced.

The first pure gold and silver coins were minted in 550 BC by Croesus, the King of Lydia (ruled 561–546 BC).

The earliest British coins were small cast pieces of bronze and tin, which circulated from the first century BC.

The mints of Roman Gaul were closed in AD *c.* 395 and supplies of coinage dried up. For two hundred years from AD 435, coins were not used in Britain as money. When they were reintroduced, the population was so unfamiliar with their proper use that the newly minted coins were used principally for ornament.

PAPER MONEY

The Chinese were the first to issue paper money in AD 700. This was because of shortages of suitable metal for coinage. By 1455, the paper money was withdrawn in an effort to curb inflation.

Cheques (US: Checks)

During the English Civil Wars (1642–51), goldsmiths, who were continuously on the lookout for opportunities to profit from the prevailing times, offered their safes as secure places for the depositing of valuables such as precious metals. Depositors would issue written instructions to a goldsmith to pay money to a third person, secured against the value of the deposited article. These written instructions are the forerunners of the modern cheque.

Banknotes (US: Bills)

By 1660 private banks in England and the Stockholm Banco (the predecessor of the Bank of Sweden) had begun to issue banknotes. These banknotes were a natural progression from goldsmiths' receipts, which were used for withdrawing deposits, demonstrating an ability to pay or for securing credit. The Bank of England issued its first banknotes in 1694.

Polymer Money

In 1988, Australia issued the first banknote made of polymer, the A$10 note. The polymer note was an exact duplicate of the paper note it replaced, but incorporated additional security features such as a clear transparent area. Because polymer is non-porous and doesn't soak up stains, the note stays cleaner and lasts longer. When its useful life as a banknote is over, the polymer is shredded and recycled to make other products.

PLASTIC MONEY (CREDIT CARDS)

The use of credit cards originated in the USA in the 1920s. As a way of retaining customer loyalty oil companies and hotel chains began to issue credit cards for use by existing customers, but the cards could only be used at the companies' own outlets.

In 1950 Diners Club issued the first universal credit card for use by the public at any outlet that would accept credit cards in settlement of bills. The American Express card followed in 1958.

ELECTRONIC MONEY

Money became transferable from one bank account to another by electronic means in 1871, when Western Union pioneered the electronic transfer of money in the USA.

CURRENCIES

Pound Sterling

The pound originated in AD 928 under King Athelstan (AD 895–939), who decreed in the Statute of Greatley that England should have a single currency. It was important at that time for Athelstan to establish a single currency as he had over 30 mints throughout England producing coins. With the unification of its currency, England became the first country since the Romans to establish a single unit of currency.

The term 'pound' derives from the value of a pound (16 troy ounces) of pure silver, known as sterling silver. The pound thus became the pound sterling and the £ symbol derives from the first letter (L) of the Latin word *libra*.

The slang for a pound is a quid (London slang: nicker).

US Dollar

The US dollar originated immediately after the USA achieved independence from Britain. There was a shortage of coinage at that time, and Spanish pesos, also called dollars, were in circulation. It was decided in 1792 to adopt the dollar as the unit of currency rather than retain the English pound. The first US Mint was established in Philadelphia and began producing coins in 1794.

The term 'dollar' comes from the Czech currency 'thaler' which was first minted in 1519. Thaler (phonetically 'tarler') was mispronounced in England as 'dollar'.

The $ symbol has an uncertain origin. One theory claims it derives from taking the two initials of the US, superimposing the U on top of the S and removing the horizontal lower portion of the U. There are at least six convincing theories, but no definitive origin.

The slang for a dollar is a buck.

Yen (Japan)

The yen originated in 1871 following the New Currency Act of the Meiji government. The New Currency Act simplified and modernised the complex monetary system of the preceding Edo period, to make it easier to trade with foreign governments. The term 'yen' literally means 'round object' in Japanese and is pronounced 'en' in Japan.

The slang for the yen, on the currency trading floors in London, is 'Bill and Ben', from cockney rhyming slang.

Euro (most EU countries)

The euro was adopted as the unit of currency by 12 of the member states of the European Union on 1 January 2002, becoming the largest monetary changeover in history. The term 'euro' was adopted by the European Council in 1995. The symbol € is a derivative of the first letter of 'euro'.

BANKS

Banking developed between 3000 and 2000 BC in Babylon in Mesopotamia and pre-dates the use of coins. Temples and royal palaces were used to store grain, agricultural implements and precious metals which were deposited by farmers as security against cash loans. The receipts, which were issued for the goods, came to be used as a form of money. Depositors used the receipts to pay their taxes and to pay priests and traders.

The term 'bank' is derived from the Italian word for bench, *banco*. The Lombard Jews in Italy kept benches in the markets for exchanging money and bills. If a banker went bust, his bench was broken up (*banca rotta* in Italian), hence the word 'bankrupt'.

The Bank of England was founded in 1694 by a Scotsman, William Patterson (1658–1719). In return for the privilege of being allowed to issue banknotes the Governor and Company of the Bank of England agreed to lend the government of the day £1,200,000.

The first bank in the USA was the Bank of North America, which opened its doors in 1782, having been proposed, chartered and incorporated in 1781. The first central bank in the USA was the Bank of the United States, which was formed in 1791. Its Congressional Charter expired in 1811.

Alexander Hamilton (1757–1804) is regarded as the 'father' of banking in the USA. He was the first Secretary of the Treasury, founded the Bank of America and also the US Coast Guard, which collected excise duties.

GOLD STANDARD

After the Napoleonic Wars England experienced a period of high inflation. In 1816, to stabilise prices, the British government, which was in control of the most powerful currency in the world at the time, adopted the Gold Standard. This was a commitment by countries to fix the price of their domestic currency in terms of a specified amount of gold. Germany followed in 1871, France in 1878, Japan in 1897 and the USA in 1900.

The Gold Standard ended in 1933 when US President Franklin D. Roosevelt (1882–1945) made the private possession of gold bullion and coins illegal. Jewellery was the only exception.

INTERNET BANKING

Internet banking is the logical evolution of the electronic money transfers of Western Union in the nineteenth century. It was used for the first time in 1990, pioneered by the Wells Fargo Bank. The Nationwide Building Society introducing Internet banking in the UK in 1997.

PAWNBROKING

One of the oldest trades known to man, pawnbroking is the business of advancing a loan to someone who has pledged a possession or possessions as security for the loan. The possession(s) may be redeemed for an agreed payment. It was practised in China as early as 1000 BC, and was also common in ancient Rome and Greece. Modern banking law is partly based on pawnbroking regulations, and many of today's banks have their roots in the pawnbroking business.

CAPITALISM

Otherwise known as the 'Free Market' or the 'Free Enterprise Economy', capitalism is an economic system in which the resources of production and distribution are privately owned. Production is guided, and income distributed, through the operation of the free market, which is based solely on demand for goods or services. (By contrast, in command-based economies, the state owns all the resources and distribution, and sets the rules on how and to whom they will be allocated.)

Marketplaces have existed since the dawn of history. The Pharaohs traded with the Levantine Kingdoms as long ago as 1400 BC, and commodity and money exchanges existed in ancient Rome.

Simple capitalism, also known as mercantilism, originated in ancient Rome and the Middle East at around the same time. Goods would be bought in one place and moved to another place to be sold at a higher price. This form of capitalism prospered and expanded with the Roman Empire, and shrank accordingly when the Roman Empire contracted.

Since the break-up of feudalism in the sixteenth century, capitalism has been the dominant means of production and supply, and has been in continuous development since those days. Between the sixteenth and eighteenth centuries, the English cloth industry provided the stimulus for the growth of industrial capitalism. This form of capitalism uses cash to fund the purchase of machinery, the acquisition of raw materials and the cost of labour, and produces goods for profit. It is distinct from the more ancient commercial capitalism, which is the buying and selling of commodities and currencies.

INDUSTRY

'I believe that the able industrial leader, who creates wealth and employment, is more worthy of historical notice than politicians or soldiers.
J. PAUL GETTY (1892–1976)

The oldest known man-made objects are Oldowan tools, which were made in small batches more than two million years ago, in what is present-day Ethiopia. The key innovation in Oldowan tools was the technique of striking one rock against another, to produce a useful cutting edge or blunt instrument.

The earliest known example of mass-production of standard-shaped tools is known as the Mousterian Industry, named after an excavation site, Le Moustier, in the Dordogne region of France, which produced very large numbers of stone tools such as axes, scrapers, diggers, and spear and arrow points. The tools were also produced in other parts of Europe, the Near East and North Africa, from about 200,000 to 30,000 years ago, by Neanderthal man.

The earliest mass-production factory was thought to have been discovered in southern Jordan by archaeologists 50 kilometres south of the Dead Sea in 2002. The dig revealed thousands of hammers, anvils and other metal objects in a factory producing copper and bronze castings in large quantities. The factory collapsed and was buried in a cataclysmic earthquake in 2700 BC.

Taxes

Taxes played only a minor role in the lives of citizens in the ancient world and were generally used to support wars rather than to fund the national economy. Taxes on consumption were levied in both ancient Greece and Rome, but to maximise revenues the state generally found it easier to collect taxes on imported goods rather than to tax its citizens directly. Julius Caesar introduced a sales tax of 1 per cent, and even earlier there was a 5 per cent inheritance tax in Rome.

A tax on bachelors was levied in the American colonies in 1695 in a bid to encourage men to marry.

The word 'exchequer' comes from the chequered table which tax collectors used from AD 1110 to calculate expenditure and receipts on a grid pattern.

Income Tax

The first general Income Tax was introduced in Britain in 1799 by Prime Minister William Pitt the Younger (1759–1806) to fund the Napoleonic Wars. It was supposedly only a temporary measure, and the rate was set at six pence in the pound – just 2 ½ per cent – when there were 240 to the pound, not 100.

Pay As You Earn (PAYE)

In 1944, PAYE was introduced in Britain. On the day it was announced, Sir Kingsley Wood, the pioneer of PAYE, who had been Chancellor of the Exchequer from 1940 until 1941, collapsed and died.

Value Added Tax (VAT)

Devised by a German economist in the eighteenth century as a tax on the final price, VAT is paid by the purchaser of any product. No matter how many intermediate stages existed between the raw material and the finished product the tax would be a fixed percentage of the final price.

France was the first country to impose VAT in 1954, followed by Denmark in 1967 and Germany in 1968. The Heath government brought in VAT in Britain in 1973 at the rate of 8 per cent, to replace Purchase Tax. The standard VAT rate now stands at 17.5 per cent. Twenty-seven per cent of all tax worldwide is now collected as VAT.

Poll Tax

A local tax, the poll tax is a fixed, per head charge on the voting population (poll is an old English word for head).

The originators of poll tax were the ancient Romans around the first century BC.

An early English version of the poll tax was levied in AD 1380, at the rate of one shilling per individual, by John of Gaunt (1340–99) the regent of Richard II of England. This was a swingeing tax at the time, and provoked the Peasants Revolt of 1381.

The government of Margaret Thatcher (b. 1925) introduced poll tax in modern Britain in 1989 and 1990, after abolishing the rating system for local tax collection. This massively unpopular tax was replaced by the Community Charge, which largely resembled the original rating system.

The 'Capitation' clause in the American Constitution makes it illegal to impose a poll tax in the USA; nevertheless some cities have imposed local poll taxes.

COMPANIES

The ancient Greeks and Romans created the concept of an organisation that, as a separate legal entity, could survive the lives of the individual members.

Limited Company

In this corporate organisation each shareholder's liability is limited to the amount of capital he or she has invested. Before the advent of the limited company, people in business could be personally liable for all the debts of their businesses.

In England, the Joint Stock Companies Act of 1844 made it possible to form a limited company merely by registering it. By 1862 limited companies were widespread, and became the most important form of commercial enterprise in modern economies.

The public limited company (plc) was introduced in 1982 to differentiate between private companies, in which a small number of individuals hold all the shares, and public companies with large numbers of shareholders. The shares in public companies are traded on a stock exchange.

London Stock Exchange

The earliest evidence of organised trading in marketable securities (shares, commodities and so on) is from a list of commodity and share prices issued by John Castaing in 1698, called *The Course of the Exchange and other things at this office at Jonathan's Coffee House.*

All the traders had been expelled from the Royal Exchange for 'rowdiness' and begun to trade in the local streets and coffee houses, of which Jonathan's was one. The Royal Exchange in London had been founded in 1565 by Sir Thomas Gresham (1519–79) to provide a place where general commerce could be conducted. It was opened by Elizabeth I (1533–1603) and became 'Royal' in 1571. It closed for commerce in 1939 and is now a shopping centre.

The first regulated stock exchange opened for business in London on 3 March 1801 on a formal subscription basis.

Deregulation of the market, known as 'The Big Bang', took place in

1986. Trading in shares had traditionally been conducted using the open outcry system. The dealers (known as jobbers) would bid verbally, and in most cases rather loudly, on the floor of the stock exchange to buy or sell shares. With the introduction of deregulation, computer bidding replaced the open outcry system, and the floor of the exchange fell silent.

At the beginning of the Second World War the stock exchange closed for six days. It closed for only one other day during the war, when a V2 rocket hit the building.

The Alternative Investment Market (AIM)

The AIM was launched in 2001 for smaller, fast growing companies. Regulation is less onerous in this market, and share prices liable to be more volatile.

New York Stock Exchange (NYSE)

The world's largest stock exchange opened for business on 17 May 1792 with 24 brokers. The founding document of the New York Stock Exchange is known as the Buttonwood Agreement after the signing of the document by the brokers under a buttonwood tree in Wall Street.

There are now 2,800 companies listed on the NYSE, with a total market value of almost twenty trillion dollars, greater than the total amount of money circulating in the USA. (A trillion is 1,000 billion, or, to put it another way, a million million which equals US$1,000,000,000,000.)

QUESTIONABLE ORIGINS

COVERING: President of the USA, Fosbury Flop, Modern Olympics, Internal Combustion Engine, Pneumatic Tyres, Light Bulbs, 'Discovery' of America, Radio, DNA, Speaking Machine, LSD, First Powered Flight, Bond Girls.

Throughout history people have been incorrectly attributed with achievements, new inventions and discoveries, as this chapter explains.

PRESIDENT OF THE USA

The first President of the USA is generally acknowledged as George Washington (1732–99), who served as President from 1789 to 1797. And yet, in 1781, while Washington, as Commander-in-Chief of the Continental Army, was still leading the war against Britain, John Hanson (1715–83) was elected as the first President of the United States in Congress Assembled. It would be eight more years, and six more presidents, before the presidency would go to George Washington.

In 1776, America had declared its independence from Britain, and in the same year Congress proposed the Articles of Confederation. These Articles were intended to bind together the loose confederation of independent states, but, because of territorial disputes between some of the states, the Articles were not signed until 1781.

John Hanson was instrumental in bringing the last state, Maryland, his home state, into the Confederation. The new Articles of Confederation stipulated that the US should appoint a President each year, and that the person appointed should hold the post for the maximum period of one year in any three. In the year of the signing, 1781, Hanson was unanimously voted in as the first President and served for one year – the period laid down in the Articles.

During his term of office Hanson established the Great Seal of the USA, the post of Secretary of War, the Treasury Department and the Foreign Affairs Department, and he ordered all foreign troops off American soil. The six presidents who followed each had a year in power, until Congress replaced the Articles of Confederation with the American Constitution in 1789.

In 1789, George Washington was unanimously elected as the first President under the newly written Constitution and served until 1797.

FOSBURY FLOP

Dick Fosbury (b. 1947) of the USA is wrongly credited with being the first to use the then revolutionary style of high jumping, which bears his name. There is no dispute that Fosbury won the 1968 Men's Olympic high jump gold medal using the Fosbury Flop, which no other jumper of the time used. Nor is it disputed that he had independently developed the technique, but he was not the original.

The first person to use the 'flop' method – launching himself at the high-jump bar with an arched back and facing skywards – was Bruce Quande of the USA in 1963, and there are photographs to prove it.

MODERN OLYMPICS

What are termed the Modern Olympics took place for the first time in Athens in 1896.

Nearly half a century earlier, in 1850, Dr William Penny Brookes (1809–95) staged the first Olympian Games in Much Wenlock, a small Shropshire town. The Games were held annually, and by 1865 the spectator numbers at the event had increased to 10,000 with competitors making their way to the Games from all over Europe. Dr Penny Brookes tried to generate interest from the Greek government to stage the same track and field events as were held at Much Wenlock, in Athens. Unfortunately he met with no success.

But then, in 1856, Evangelis Zappa, a wealthy Greek businessman living in Romania, wrote to King Otto of Greece offering to fund a revival of the Olympic Games. Zappa proposed the new Games should be held for all time in Greece. His sponsorship was accepted, and the first of the Zappa-sponsored Olympic Games were staged in Athens. Dr Penny Brookes donated prize money for one of the events. Zappa financed a second Games in 1865 and a third in 1870. The third Games were for elite competitors only and were the last of the Zappa-funded Games.

Baron Pierre de Coubertin (1863–1937), the acknowledged founder of the Modern Olympics, visited Much Wenlock in 1890 at the invitation of Dr Penny Brookes, and a special Games was put on in his honour. The Baron wrote an article in the French sporting magazine *La Revue Athletique*, in which he said, 'If the Olympic Games are revived, it will not be due to a Greek but to the efforts of Dr W P Brookes.'

The Modern Olympic Movement Inspired by his visit to Much Wenlock six years later Baron de Coubertin went on to found the modern Olympic movement, and to stage the first of the modern era Olympic Games in 1896 in Athens. Sadly, William Penny Brookes died a few months before the Games in Athens, unacknowledged and almost unheard of, except in Much Wenlock. The annual Olympian Games continue in Much Wenlock, dedicated, as is a local museum, to the memory of Dr William Penny Brookes.

It is interesting that over two hundred years earlier, Robert Dover's 'Olimpick Games' were being held annually in the Cotswold town of Chipping Campden.

The original Olimpick Games was held in 1612, and held annually until 1852. There was a gap of a century until they were revived in 1951 for the Festival of Britain.

Despite its eminent title, the Olimpick Games was never more than a large village sporting festival, with shin-kicking as one of the events.

INTERNAL COMBUSTION ENGINE

In 1807 Joseph Nicephore Niepce was granted a patent for a pyredophore, powered by coal and resin. In 1826, Samuel Morey (1762–1843), a prolific inventor who lived in Vermont, USA, was granted a patent on an internal combustion engine. Morey wrote a paper on his invention in the *American Journal of Science and Arts* in the year of the granting of the patent, entitled *An Account of a new Explosive Engine*. Morey's invention pre-dates Lenoir's generally acknowledged first successful internal combustion engine by 34 years and that of Otto by 38 years (*see also* Transport p. 286).

PNEUMATIC (AIR-FILLED) TYRES

John Dunlop (1840–1921) is recorded as the inventor of the pneumatic (air-filled) tyre in 1888. However, the pneumatic tyre was actually invented by a 23-year-old Scot, Robert Thomson (1822–73), who applied for a patent in 1845 for what he called an 'aerial wheel'. Dunlop had merely improved the original design, at the request of his son, by filling the tyre with air to help make riding his bicycle more comfortable (*see also* Transport p. 286).

LIGHT BULBS

The great American inventor Thomas Alva Edison (1847–1931), along with his other thousand patents, has received almost all the credit for inventing the electric light bulb in 1879.

However, the light bulb had actually been around since 1809, and was invented by Sir Humphry Davy (1778–1829) in England. Davy connected two wires to a battery and attached a charcoal strip between the other ends of the wires. The charcoal glowed, making the first arc lamp.

In 1875, Henry Woodward and Matthew Evans patented a new version of the light bulb in Toronto. Unable to raise the capital to produce their lamps on a commercial scale, they sold out to Edison, who went on to improve the design and use a lower power electric current.

In 1879, Edison in America, and Joseph (later Sir Joseph) Swan (1828–1914) in England, simultaneously found a way to make the light bulb a commercial proposition by giving it longer-lasting qualities.

Heinrich Gobel (1818–93), an American of German descent, produced an incandescent lamp in 1854, 25 years earlier than Edison and Swan, using carbonised bamboo as a filament. By 1859 Gobel had improved his lamp so that it would last up to 400 hours. He took out a court case against Thomas Edison in 1893, claiming to be the inventor of the electric light bulb. The court accepted Gobel's claim and recognised him, albeit wrongly, as the inventor of the electric light bulb. A few months after the court's decision, Gobel died of pneumonia.

'DISCOVERY' OF AMERICA

Was America discovered by Christopher Columbus (1451–1506) in 1492, as is almost universally taught? Or was it discovered in 1497 by the Portuguese explorer Vasco da Gama (1469–1525) on an expedition sponsored by the wealthy British aristocrat Richard Amerike? Or was it perhaps discovered in the tenth century AD by Vikings?

And now, to make matters even more confusing, there are Chinese claims that Admiral Zheng He went to America in 1421.

On his voyage west in 1492, Columbus was not looking to discover new lands. He had been brought up as a militant Christian, and was looking for a way to attack Muslims unexpectedly from the rear. The man who actually spotted land, most likely the island of San Salvador in the Caribbean, for the first time was Martin Alonzo Pinzon.

Richard Amerike sponsored Vasco da Gama and asked him to name any 'new found lands' after himself. There is a strong possibility that da Gama sailed to the east coast of America and named it America after Amerike.

Admiral He is supposed to have circumnavigated the earth, beginning his journey in 1405, and finally returning to China, not only having discovered America, but also Australia and Africa. This massive journey of 50,000 kilometres (31,000 miles) is depicted on an ancient chart which is now displayed in Beijing.

The Viking explorer Lief Ericsson (c. AD 980–1025) has a strong claim to have been the first European to set foot on the east coast of America after a sea journey westwards from Scandinavia around the year AD 1000. His discovery is recorded in *The Saga of Eric the Red*, a book written in 1387 by Jon Thordharson. (Eric was Lief's father.)

The original occupiers of the land of North America came from Asia, migrating across the land bridge which used to link Alaska with Russia 20,000 years earlier. DNA tests and language comparisons have been conclusive in establishing the link between the Native American population and the East Asians (*see also* Countries and Empires p. 50).

RADIO

Guglielmo Marconi (1874–1937) is widely thought to have invented radio in 1896, and is known as the father of radio. He did indeed pioneer the first long-distance radio broadcasts, and managed to have a patent granted, but Marconi did not invent radio itself.

In 1943, the US Supreme Court overturned Marconi's patent in favour of the Serbian inventor Nikola Tesla (1856–1943), who has now been properly credited as radio's inventor. Tesla died a few months before the final vindication of his work.

DNA

On 28 February 1953 James Watson (b. 1928) and Francis Crick (1916–2004) announced that they had discovered the famous double helical shape of the DNA molecule. Together with Maurice Wilkins (1916–2004) they were awarded the 1962 Nobel Prize for Physiology or Medicine. DNA had actually been identified in 1869 by Swiss scientist Johann Friedrich Miescher (1844–95) working in Tübingen in Germany, but the actual structure had always remained elusive (*see also* Health p. 141).

At a competing laboratory, at King's College, London, Wilkins had been working with a brilliant young scientist, Rosalind Franklin (1920–58), whose pioneering use of X-ray crystallography to look into the structure of molecules was beginning to yield results. Relations between Wilkins and Franklin were not particularly good and in an act of savage betrayal Wilkins revealed Franklin's research results, and the famous

Photo 51, to Watson and Crick. They quickly seized on this windfall and published their own paper, without acknowledging Franklin's work. It is widely thought that the wrong people were awarded the Nobel Prize.

Rosalind Franklin's work has been properly recognised only in recent years. It is one of the tragedies of medical history that she did not survive long enough to reap the reward for her work, dying at only 38 of ovarian cancer. The cancer was almost certainly brought on by her heavy exposure to X-rays (see Health p. 141).

SPEAKING MACHINE

In 1788, Johann Wolfgang von Kempelen de Pazmand (1734–1804) invented the first 'speaking machine'. The device used a set of bellows to pump air across a reed, which in turn excited a hand-varied resonator to produce the sound of a voice. The human voice was reproduced on the Kempelen machine, but not recorded. De Pazmand's device trumped Edison's phonograph by a century.

LYSERGIC ACID DIETHYLAMIDE (LSD)

Generally thought of as a 1960s hallucinogenic drug, LSD was actually synthesised in 1938 by the Swiss chemist Dr Albert Hofmann (b. 1906). When he repeated the experiment in 1943 and accidentally licked his fingertips, he discovered the hallucinogenic properties of LSD.

Hofmann insisted on continuing his experimental work by trying the drug out on himself. Not knowing how much LSD to take, he accidentally took three times what would come to be regarded as the normal dose, and ended up on a massive hallucinating 'trip'.

It was marketed by Sandoz Laboratories in 1947 as a cure for schizophrenia, and became freely available. The first mass-produced LSD specifically for recreational use came from the laboratory of the renegade chemist Augustus Owsley Stanley III in 1965. In 1967 he was sentenced to three years for possession of a huge quantity of the drug – the equivalent of 100,000 doses.

There are plans to hold an international symposium on Hofmann's hundredth birthday in 2006.

THE FIRST POWERED FLIGHT

The Wright brothers, Orville and Wilbur (*see also* Transport), flew their powered aeroplane *Flyer One* for the first time at Kitty Hawk in North Carolina on 17 December 1903, and entered the history books as the pioneers of powered flight.

Yet, in New Zealand on 31 March 1903, farmer Richard Pearse, known as 'Bamboo Dick', flew 150 metres (500 feet) in a powered aeroplane, landed in a gorse hedge and wrecked his machine. He had beaten the Wright brothers by eight months, but Pearse was a man of high standards and refused to claim his rightful place in the history books. He felt that the Wright brothers had landed under control, whereas he had not. However, it does not alter the fact that Richard Pearse was the first human being to achieve flight in a heavier-than-air aircraft under power.

BOND GIRLS

The immortal image of Swiss sex symbol Ursula Andress (b. 1936) emerging from the Caribbean in a white bikini in the first of the James Bond films *Dr No* has become an icon of cinema. Most filmgoers would opt for Miss Andress, who was playing Honey Ryder, as the original Bond Girl.

However, Ursula Andress was beaten to this honour by British actress Eunice Gayson (b. 1931), who appeared in the opening sequence of *Dr No*, playing Sylvia Trench. According to Miss Gayson, she was instructed to take Sean Connery out for a drink to help him relax as he kept fluffing his famous line 'The name's Bond. James Bond.' He accidentally kept giving his own name.

> *If the role demands it, then*
> *naturally I will remove my clothes.*
> URSULA ANDRESS

Religions

COVERING: Animism, Sun Worship, Moon Worship, Judaism, Hinduism, Zoroastrianism, Confucianism, Druids, Christianity, Buddhism, Islam, Shinto, Voodoo, Mormonism, Scientology, Moonies, Atheism.

> *'If God did not exist, it would be necessary to invent him.*
> VOLTAIRE (1694–1778)

ANIMISM

The oldest belief system of all, Animism pre-dates all known organised religions. The word comes from the Latin *anima* meaning breath or soul. It originated in the Upper Palaeolithic Period between 40000 and 10000 BC.

The core belief of Animism is that spiritual beings exist separately from the physical being. In Animism, the breath is the soul. When breathing stops, the soul passes to another life. It holds that the soul passes into plants, animals and even inanimate objects after the death of the person. This is thought by some experts to have been a way for primitive peoples to explain sleep, dreams and death.

SUN WORSHIP

Agrarian societies whose crops and livelihood were dependent on the weather mainly practised Sun Worship. It reached its zenith in ancient Egypt around 2500 BC with one of the most important gods being Ra, the Sun god. The Pharaoh was regarded as the son of Ra and his representative on earth.

Other societies had different names for their Sun god. In Mesopotamia the Sun god was called Shamash, and the ancient Greeks had two

Sun gods, Apollo and Helios. The Incas, Aztecs, Druids and Zoroastrians all worshipped the Sun.

MOON WORSHIP

The Sumerians of around 2500 BC and other ancient worshippers of the Moon held ceremonies on the last day of the year, when the Sun, who was king for a year, was sacrificed to the Moon. Ceremonially, the Sun's genitals are removed, the blood is drunk and the testicles are eaten. Then, during the ceremony, the Moon resurrects the Sun so that life may continue on Earth.

Moon worship is not to be confused with the cult of the Moonies, which is a twentieth-century phenomenon.

JUDAISM

One of the most ancient belief systems, Judaism is the religion of the Jews. It was founded in around 1900 BC by Abraham in Canaan, which was roughly equivalent to modern Israel and Lebanon.

Judaism is the oldest of the monotheistic faiths, which hold that there is only one God, rather than a plethora of many different deities. The name of the Jewish God is Yahweh (Jehovah), and the holy book is the Torah.

Circumcision The Hebrew Bible, the Torah, which according to some was handed down to Moses in 1280 BC, refers to Jehovah's command to Abraham to circumcise himself, his sons, his slaves and servants.

The origin of the practice of circumcision is uncertain, but its roots can be traced back to around 6000 BC and the puberty rites of tribes in north-eastern Africa and the Arabian Peninsula. From 3100 BC the ancient Egyptians circumcised boys between six and 12 years old as a mark of ritual cleansing.

In AD 570 the prophet Mohammed was born supposedly already circumcised. This inspired Muslims to circumcise boys shortly after birth.

HINDUISM

Religious scholars believe it is conceivable that the roots of Hinduism in the Indus Valley in India may stretch as far back as 4000 BC, which would make it the world's oldest organised religion. However, alternative modern theories consider it is more likely that Hinduism was founded around 1500 BC.

Hindus are polytheistic. They believe in many gods and unlike in Christianity, Islam and Judaism, there is no single named god to worship. Hinduism accepts the view that there is only one reality, but all formulations of the truth are respected. Many Hindu representations of the 'Divine Being' are female, such as Durga, the protective mother, and Lakshmi, the goddess of prosperity, purity, chastity and generosity. Hinduism holds that without honouring female qualities, religion is incomplete.

The holy book of Hinduism is the *Veda*, and the key to Hindu belief is the transmigration of the soul, which produces a continuous cycle of birth, life, death and rebirth. The individual soul enters a new existence once the body has died, and the total of all previous moral conduct will determine the quality of the soul's rebirth.

ZOROASTRIANISM

The ancient religion of Persia (modern Iran), Zoroastrianism, was founded by the prophet Zarathustra (also known as Zoroastra). There is a great deal of debate among academics about when the religion was founded, ranging from between the eighteenth and eleventh centuries BC to approximately 600 BC.

Zoroastrianism is known as 'the three-fold path'. Its motto, as written in the holy book, the *Avesta*, is 'Good thoughts; Good words; Good deeds.' Zarathustra preached that there is only one God, Ahura Mazda,

(Lord Wise). The basic scripture is a set of five poetic songs called the *Gathas*, composed by Zarathustra, each with seven Attributes:

1. Good thought   (animals)

2. Justice and truth   (fire and energy)

3. Dominion   (metals)

4. Devotion and serenity   (earth)

5. Wholeness   (water)

6. Immortality   (plants)

7. Creative energy   (humans)

Zoroastrianism survived invasions of its Persian homeland by Greeks, Muslims and Mongols, and is still practised in India by the Parsees.

In the eighth century AD, the leader of the Parsees made representations to Jadav Rana, the King of Sanjan – modern Gujarat in India – to be allowed to bring his people into India to escape persecution in Persia. The king was reluctant to agree to this request as India was already becoming overcrowded. He filled a cup to the brim with milk to demonstrate that there was no more room. The leader of the Parsees took a spoonful of sugar, dropped it into the cup of milk and stirred it, saying, 'We will be like the sugar in this milk. You will not be able to see us, but we will help to sweeten your lives.' The king accepted the Parsees, with the condition that they adopted local dress and did not prosletyse their religion.

CONFUCIANISM

Man has three ways of behaving wisely.
First on meditation; that is the noblest.
Secondly on imitation; that is the easiest.
Thirdly on experience; that is the bitterest.

FROM *THE ANALECTS* – CONFUCIUS 479 BC

K'ung Fu Tzu (551–479 BC), known in the West as Confucius, founded Confucianism in China in the fifth century BC and it was adopted as the state religion of imperial China.

The two holy books of Confucianism are *Si Shu* and *Wu Jing*, which teach the practical values of benevolence, reciprocity, respect and personal effort, making Confucianism more an ethical and philosophical system than a formal system of religion with a named god.

DRUIDS

The first records of Druidism appear around 200 BC, and Julius Caesar (100–44 BC), gives an account of this religion in his *History of the Wars in Gaul*, written between 59 and 51 BC. Both the ancient Greeks and Romans believed that Celtic magicians, as Druid leaders were thought to be, held special knowledge and the ability to channel their power for good or evil, through gods, spirits and the ancestors. The Roman author and philosopher Pliny the Elder (AD 23–79), who died in the eruption of Vesuvius that buried Pompeii, wrote of Druids being learned men and women having 'oak knowledge', from the ancient words *dru* (oak) and *wid* (know).

There are Druids today and one of the most famous gatherings is the annual Welsh Eisteddfod. They also believe in the transmigration of souls and that they have all descended from a common ancestor.

CHRISTIANITY

Christianity is one of the major monotheistic religions of the world, with a belief in a single named God.

Jesus Christ was born in Bethlehem around 4 BC and it is believed by followers of Christianity that He was the Son of God. Jesus used parables and sermons to make His messages memorable and easily understood, and preached love and forgiveness and tolerance. He began teaching publicly at the age of 30, after He had been baptised in the river Jordan by John the Baptist, and continued for the last three years of His life.

After Jesus' death around AD 30, His authority passed directly to the Apostle Peter (later St Peter), who died in either AD 64 or 69. Peter is regarded by the Roman Catholic Church as the first Pope. The Gospels –

the books recounting the life and teachings of Jesus – were not written until around AD 100, 70 years after His death.

The first Christian church is considered to be St Mark's house in Jerusalem as the one Jesus chose for the Apostles to eat Passover before His crucifixion. The Holy Spirit is said to have descended into St Mark's house on the Day of Pentecost.

St Mark was martyred in AD 68. He was tied to a horse's tail and dragged through the streets of Bokalia in Alexandria for two days. In keeping with the traditions of the day parts of his body were preserved. His head is now in a church in Alexandria, other parts of him are in Cairo and the remainder is in St Mark's cathedral in Venice.

The Roman Emperor Constantine (AD 272–337) converted to Christianity in AD 313. His conversion led to the rise of Rome as the centre of the Christian faith, and the church's influence over the world, which lasts to this day.

Christmas Day was first recognised and celebrated as 25 December in the fourth century AD.

The first Christian church in England was built at Glastonbury in the first century AD and was dedicated to the Virgin Mary.

The first King in England to convert to Christianity was King Ethelbert of Kent. In AD 597 Augustine (later St Augustine) landed in Kent on a mission from Pope Gregory to convert the pagan Ethelbert and spread the faith throughout the country. Ethelbert, whose queen Bertha was already a Christian, converted most probably in AD 597 and allowed Augustine and his followers to stay in an old church in Canterbury. Augustine became the first Archbishop of Canterbury and worked with Ethelbert to draw up the first Anglo-Saxon laws.

The Great Schism of AD 1054 divided Christianity into the Catholic (Western) and Orthodox (Eastern) Churches. The Pope as head of the Western Church, and the Patriarch of Constantinople, as head of the Eastern Church, excommunicated each other in a dispute over whose authority was the greater.

The Coptic Orthodox Church developed as the main Christian Church in Muslim Egypt in the seventh century AD. Copt is from the Arabic *gibt*, which itself is a corruption of *Aigyptios* (Egyptian).

The first Christmas cards originated in 1840. The letter X in the word Xmas is not used just to save writing out the whole of the word Christmas. X is chi, the first letter of the Greek word *christos* – meaning anointed.

Roman Catholicism

The head of the Roman Catholic Church is the Pope (a title which derives from the Latin word for father). Since the ninth century the Pope has also been Bishop of Rome. The full title of the Pope is: Bishop of Rome, Vicar of Jesus Christ, Successor to the Prince of Apostles, Supreme Pontiff of the Universal Church, Patriarch of the West, Primate of Italy, Archbishop and Metropolitan of the Roman Province, Sovereign of the State of the Vatican City, Servant of the Servants of God.

The first Pope was St Peter, the leader of the Apostles and therefore of Christianity until his death in AD 64 or 69.

The first (and so far only) English Pope was Nicholas Breakspear (AD 1100–1159), who reigned as Pope Adrian IV from 4 December 1154 to 1 November 1159. As a novice monk he had been refused entry to an English monastery, so he journeyed to France where he was accepted at the abbey of St Rufus near Arles. He rose to become the abbot and later a cardinal. In this role he was central to the establishment of the Roman Catholic Church in Norway, and was so successful that he was rewarded with the papacy. On 1 November 1159, Breakspear choked and died when a fly that had been in the glass of water he was drinking became lodged in his throat.

New popes are appointed by a process called the Conclave. This is a form of election that began in 1274 and starts 15 days after the death of the previous pope. The 15 days' rule was introduced to allow cardinals time to travel to Rome from all corners of the Roman Catholic world.

Society of Jesus (Jesuits)

The Jesuits were formed in Paris in August 1533 by Ignatius Loyola (later St Ignatius) (1491–1556), a Spanish soldier and nobleman. Ignatius and six other young men, who had met at the University of Paris, formed the first group. They drew up laws which demanded chastity, poverty, and pilgrimage to Jerusalem.

On 27 August 1540, Pope Paul III gave his approval to the new order, and by the time of Ignatius's death in 1556, 1,000 Jesuits had been recruited.

Protestantism

The Reformation of the sixteenth century – the movement to protest against the absolute rule of the Catholic Church of Rome – saw the establishment of Protestantism.

The most dramatic single act of the Reformation was the nailing of

95 theses to the door of Wittenberg church in 1517 by the German theologian Martin Luther (1483–1546). The theses condemned greed and worldliness in the Catholic Church.

Luther was an Augustine monk whose teachings inspired the Lutheran and Protestant movements. He married in 1525, setting the example for clerical marriage.

The Reformation led ultimately to the split of Protestantism from the Roman Catholic Church.

Church of England

Christianity in England can be traced to the second century AD, existing independently of the Roman Church. Church records show that English bishops attended the Council of Arles in southern France, which was held in AD 314, more than 200 years before St Augustine (d. 604) was sent by the Pope Gregory to convert England to Christianity in AD 597.

The Church of England as we know it, which is the mother church of the worldwide Anglican Union, has its roots in the reign of King Henry VIII in the sixteenth century. Henry broke away from the Roman Catholic Church when Pope Clement VII refused to approve the annulment of his marriage to Catherine of Aragon. An Act of Parliament of 1534 made Henry (and all future British monarchs) the head of the Church of England and he subsequently refused to recognise the authority of the Pope in England. Another Act of Parliament of 1534 recognised the annulment of his marriage to Catherine of Aragon and his marriage to Anne Boleyn.

Greek Orthodox

The Greek Orthodox Church is a recent addition to the world's Christian religions, and presently has 10,000,000 adherents. After the Greek War of Independence between 1821 and 1832, negotiations were begun with the Patriarch of the Eastern Orthodox Communion for an independent Greek Church. The Church was finally recognised in 1850 and is organised along the lines established by the Russian emperor Peter the Great for the Russian Orthodox Church.

BUDDHISM

A religion of philosophy, Buddhism follows the teachings of Siddhartha Guatama (the Buddha) who, it was previously thought, lived from 566 BC to 486 BC. This has recently been revised to 490–410 BC.

Ashoka the Great ruled the Mauryan Empire, which covered a major part of Asia, from 273 to 232 BC. He converted to Buddhism and gave it his royal patronage, which led to the rapid expansion of the Buddhist faith throughout Asia. The lack of a written gospel from the Buddha helped lead to the formation of more than 400 diverse movements within Buddhism.

The Buddhist holy book is known as the *Tripitaka*, which was not written until more than 400 years after the death of the Buddha. Until then, the method used to preserve his teachings was for student monks to learn them by heart. At group councils of the monastic orders, a senior monk would ask a question and the assembled monks would recite the appropriate teaching. It was the Theravadian monks who wrote down the *Tripitaka* in the first century AD. The teaching of Buddhism is based on the four Noble Truths, which lead to the eight-fold path:

1. Life is disappointing.

2. Suffering comes from the desire for pleasure, power and continual existence.

3. To stop suffering – stop desiring.

4. Stop desiring by following the eight-fold path, being the rightness of:
   Views
   Intention
   Speech
   Action
   Livelihood
   Effort
   Awareness
   Concentration

ISLAM

The adherents of Islam, known as Muslims (those who submit to the will of Allah), believe that Islam has always existed, but was revealed by degrees to ancient prophets. In Islam, God is Allah, and the theology of Islam allows no other belief.

In AD 610 the final revelation was made to the Prophet Mohammed (*c.*AD 570–632) as he meditated alone in a cave. According to tradition, the Angel Jibreel (Gabriel) visited Mohammed and instructed him to recite the word of Allah. During the rest of his life he continued to receive revelations, which were written down as the Qu'ran (Koran).

The other holy book of Islam is the Hadith, which is an account of the spoken traditions attributed to the Prophet Muhammad, which are revered and received in Islam as a major source of religious law and moral guidance.

The American Nation of Islam was founded in 1913 in Newark, by the prophet Noble Drew Ali, born Timothy Drew (1886–1929).

SHINTO

With Buddhism, Shinto is one of the two national religions of Japan. The name Shinto is derived from the Chinese Shin Tao (the way of the gods). It began around 500 AD and, unlike other religions, it has no known founder, no holy book or scriptures, and no religious law. The priesthood of Shintoism is loosely organised and preaches nature worship, love of family, physical cleanliness, hero worship and shamanism.

The Emperor of Japan was always regarded as a god, descended from Amaterasu the Shinto Sun Goddess and mythical founder of Japan, until after the Second World War when Hirohito (1901–89) was forced by the Americans to renounce his divine status explicitly.

VOODOO

As the national religious folk cult of Haiti, Voodoo is followed by at least 80 per cent of the population. The word comes from the Haitian *vodun* meaning a god or spirit. It is a mixture of Roman Catholic rituals and

African magical elements, which were brought to Haiti by African slaves during the time it was a French colony. Voodoo maintains that there is a state between life and death, in which people become 'the undead', which are known as 'zombies'.

MORMONISM

Mormonism is more properly known as the Church of Jesus Christ of Latter-day Saints.

At the age of 22, in 1827, Joseph Smith (1805–1844) began to write the *Book of Mormon*, and founded the Mormon faith. The *Book of Mormon* was completed in 1830, and contained more than 250,000 words (a typical novel contains about 70,000 words).

Smith preached widely and sold the *Book of Mormon* in large numbers so that the Mormon Church acquired many thousands of followers across America. Mormons regarded Joseph Smith as a latter-day prophet at least as important as Moses.

Brigham Young (1801–1877), who had joined Joseph Smith in 1833, took up the leadership of the Church, and in 1847 led the people to Salt Lake City, Utah. (At that time, Utah was in Mexico.) Young visited England in 1840–41 to bring the Mormon message to Europe for the first time.

The Church, which is based on Christianity, believes that God's revelations come through modern prophets such as Joseph Smith and Brigham Young, and that the Holy Trinity exists as three separate entities. Mormons refrain from tea, coffee, smoking, drinking alcoholic beverages and using illegal drugs. Salt Lake City became to Mormonism what Rome is to Roman Catholicism, the de facto capital of the religion.

SCIENTOLOGY

The Church of Scientology began with a bestselling book called *Dianetics: The Modern Science of Mental Health*, written by American science-fiction writer L. Ron Hubbard (1911–86), and published in May 1950. Hubbard, the founding father of Scientology, began preaching his first messages in Phoenix, Arizona, in the autumn of 1951, and by the spring of 1952 the new religion had over 15,000 adherents.

Hubbard introduced Scientology as 'a study of knowledge', and its founding principles are a form of religious philosophy dedicated, through counselling, to the rehabilitation of the human spirit. Hubbard continued to introduce fresh doctrines for the last 34 years of his life. The first church of Scientology was built in Los Angeles in 1954.

From its early days, Scientology and its leaders have faced prosecutions for tax evasion, charges of fraud, and accusations of conspiracy to steal government papers. The Church has also often been criticised for the financial demands it puts on its members, and what are seen as bogus scientific and religious claims.

MOONIES

More properly known as the Unification Church, the Moonies were founded in Seoul, South Korea, in 1954, by the Reverend Sun Moon (real name Yung Myung Moon) (b. 1920).

In 1945, Moon wrote *The Divine Principles*, which became the scripture of the Moonies, but there is evidence to suggest that he stole many of his ideas and teachings from two other cults, which he had earlier been involved with. Moon's overriding claim is that when he was 16 years old Jesus came to him on a mountain in North Korea and asked him to fulfil

His mission on Earth. The Unification Church holds many of the traditional Christian beliefs, but also believes that the death of Jesus was not pre-ordained, and that in the Final Days, Satan will become a good angel. The Reverend Moon claims that he is the Messiah of the Second Coming.

Moon achieved success in his quest to build a new religion after the 1961 coup in South Korea, in which the military led by General Park Chung-hee (1917–79) overthrew the civilian government. In 1971, after a couple of periods in jail, Moon moved his base to the USA where the media named his followers 'Moonies'.

The organisation owns the *Washington Times* and hundreds of other businesses, including a firearms producer.

ATHEISM

The majority of atheists base their non-belief in God or gods on rationalism or philosophy, citing lack of evidence of the existence of a god as the main reason for their lack of belief.

The Greek philosopher Socrates (470–399 BC) was one of the earliest atheists found guilty of insulting Athena (the goddess of wisdom, war, the arts, industry, justice and skills). He was executed by hemlock poisoning.

Sex

COVERING: Ancient Gods of Sex, the *Kama Sutra*, Contraception, Prostitution, Sex in Art, Sex on Screen, Homosexual Sex.

'I know nothing about sex, because I was always married.'
ZSA ZSA GABOR (b. 1919)

ANCIENT GODS OF SEX

Ancient civilisations worshipped gods and goddesses for almost every aspect of everyday life. Sex and love were among the most important.

In Greek mythology Priapus was the god of fertility and male genitalia. Statues of Priapus, showing him with greatly enlarged male genitals, were placed in gardens to encourage crops. (Priapism, named after Priapus, is a painful medical condition in which the erect penis will not return to its flaccid state.)

The ancient Greeks also worshipped Eros, who was their god of lust, love, sex and fertility, and from whom the word 'erotic' is derived.

Aphrodite was the Greek goddess of love, allegedly born in Cyprus. Engaging in intercourse with one of her priestesses was regarded as the same as worshipping Aphrodite.

Roman mythology held that Venus was not only the goddess of love but also the protector against vice and the goddess of sexual healing. As her natural state was to be naked, Venus became a popular subject for artists.

The Roman equivalent of the Greek Eros was the god of erotic love, Cupid, who is mostly portrayed by artists with a bow and a quiver full of arrows, supposedly the arrows of love.

THE KAMA SUTRA

Kama is the ancient Indian god of all things pleasurable, including erotic sex, approximately equivalent to the Roman god Cupid. The word Sutra means a short book.

The well-known book, the *Kama Sutra*, which glories in the enjoyment of sex, was written in India, at some time between the first and sixth centuries AD by Mallanaga Vatsyayana. The book is mainly about sexual behaviour, and contains chapters on sexual positions, foreplay, orgasms, seduction, marriage and many more aspects of sex.

Rather than being merely a 'how-to-do' manual of all things sexual, the *Kama Sutra* includes chapters on kissing, courtly behaviour, and ways of treating partners, both within marriage and outside. It emphasises the importance of the care and mentoring of partners, encourages mutual experimentation to achieve bliss, and dispenses with the Western ideas of guilt, insecurity or shame in sex.

CONTRACEPTION

One of the earliest contraceptives was used by the ancient Sumerians around 2300 BC. This consisted of balls of opium inserted into the vagina and had the added advantage of giving the man and woman a 'high' at the same time.

Ancient Egyptian documents record various methods of contraception, including coitus interruptus, although the link between male semen and pregnancy was not fully understood. Around 1850 BC the Egyptians had taken to using crocodile dung, although it is not certain how it was applied.

In Rome in the first and second centuries AD the Greek gynaecologist Soranus of Ephesus (in present-day Turkey) made a study of the subject of contraception and provided a lucid and detailed account of various methods. Hundreds of years ahead of his time Soranus wrote *Gynaecology*, which was the first book to elevate birth control, obstetrics and gynaecology to a legitimate medical speciality.

The Aztecs, who dominated most of the land that is now Mexico from the twelfth century AD until the Spanish Conquest in the early sixteenth-century, used an unappetising mixture of eagle excrement and extracts of pulp out of the fruit of the calabash tree as a contraceptive.

Condoms have been used for contraception since the seventeenth century. The early versions were made from animal gut or fish membrane.

Giacomo Casanova (1725–98), whose name, along with that of the Marquis de Sade (1740–1814), has become synonymous with sexual excess and depravity, used a squeezed half-lemon, placed 'strategically', to prevent pregnancies in his many conquests.

Mary Wollstonecraft (1759–97) occupies a very important place in feminist literary studies. Her work in male-dominated eighteenth-century England led to social reforms and the better education of young women, particularly in matters of child rearing and birth control. Wollstonecraft held that 'reason' was God's gift to all humans, and in her 1792 book *Vindication of the Rights of Women* she made the comparison between the rights of men and the suffering of women, maintaining that women should be equal partners of men in marriage. She also campaigned for women's sexual freedom.

Her 1789 book *The Female Reader*, a collection of short stories, was published under the pseudonym Mr Cresswick – Teacher of Elocution.

Mary Wollstonecraft's daughter was Mary Shelley, the author of *Frankenstein*, which was first published when she was only 21. She was the second wife of the poet Percy Bysshe Shelley.

The first systematic attempt to educate the population of a whole country in methods of birth control took place in Holland in 1882. The programme was led by Dr Aletta Jacobs (1854–1929), the first Dutch woman to attend university and the only female doctor in Holland at that time. Incurring the wrath of the whole of the Dutch medical establishment, Jacobs began by providing effective contraception to a number of women whose need she deemed to be the greatest. Her work was criticised as threatening to create 'a world without children' and she even experienced criticism from church pulpits by clergymen whose wives were actively consulting her for contraceptive treatment.

Oral contraceptives The three major figures in the development of the oral contraceptive are Margaret Sanger (1879–1966), who, in her eighties, raised the initial US$150,000 to fund the oral contraceptive research project, Frank Colton (1923–2003), who invented Enovid, the first oral contraceptive, and Carl Djerassi (b. 1923), who developed the modern 'pill'.

Margaret Sanger, an Irish-American from a poor working-class family in New York, is widely regarded as the founder of the birth control movement in the USA. She opened a birth-control clinic in 1916 in New York and published *What Every Girl Should Know*, which provided basic information about topics such as menstruation and sexual feelings. Police were alerted, and raided the clinic. Sanger, who had been mailing out birth-control advice, was arrested for distributing obscene material by post, contrary to US Post Office regulations. To escape prosecution Sanger left the USA to live in Europe. She returned in 1917, published *What Every Mother Should Know* and was promptly rearrested and sent to the workhouse for 'creating a public nuisance'.

> *'I was resolved to seek out the root of the evil, to do*
> *something to change the destiny of mothers whose miseries*
> *were as vast as the sky.*
> MARGARET SANGER, 1931

The pill, as the oral contraceptive is widely known, was introduced to the public in 1961. Women were finally able to take necessary precautions themselves, and no longer had to rely on men. The enhanced sensations of condom-free sex and the combined feelings of emancipation from the strait-laced late 1940s and 1950s, ushered in the freedoms of what is known as the 'sexual revolution'.

The modern IUD (intra-uterine device) was pioneered by Richard Richter in Germany in 1909. Otherwise known as 'the coil', it was a small metal or plastic device fixed into the uterus. Since 1960, there have been two main types, inert and active. Inert types include the Lippes Loop and the Margulies Spiral, both of which are made of polyethylene with a barium sulphate addition so that they can be indentified by X-ray. Active IUDs are made of copper with a hormone-releasing agent.

IUDs are usually set into the uterus by means of an inserter tube, which is passed through the cervical canal. The device is secured according to the manufacturer's instructions, and may be left in place for up to four years. Removal of the IUD normally allows fertility to return.

It is still not certain how IUDs prevent fertility, but it was known in antiquity that a foreign body inserted into the vagina had a contraceptive effect. Highly polished semi-precious stones were the devices of choice of the ancient Egyptians.

PROSTITUTION

The big difference between sex for money and sex for free is that sex for money usually costs a lot less.
BRENDAN FRANCIS

In Old Testament times Moses (*c.*1300 BC) laid down various ordinances for the control of venereal diseases as Hebrew law did not forbid prostitution, it merely confined it to foreign women.

Prostitution is said to be the world's oldest profession and was institutionalised in ancient Greek and Roman society. Prostitutes were compelled to wear distinctive dress and pay taxes, unlike in modern Germany where prostitution is officially sanctioned as tax-free.

European prostitutes were imported to America during the early 1700s, helping to service the garrisons of soldiers stationed in New York and Boston. It rapidly expanded into other cities from 1810 onwards.

Prostitution was legal and virtually uncontrolled in the USA until as late as 1910 when the Woman's Christian Temperance Union began campaigning heavily against it. The Mann Act was passed in 1910, forbidding the transportation of women across state borders for immoral purposes.

The first medical supervision of prostitutes was begun in Buenos Aires in 1875.

SEX IN ART

Ever since writing and painting developed, artists have represented sexual subject matters on walls, paper and canvas. The ancient Greeks and Romans had few inhibitions when it came to matters of sex, and the depiction of sex in their paintings reflects their relaxed attitudes.

In the 4,000-year-old Egyptian tomb at Saqqara, two men, Niankhkhnum and Khnumhotep, are shown sharing a passionate kiss and embrace. In general, ancient Egyptian art was not overtly sexual in content; sex was more in the suggestion than in actuality, especially in high art. The Turin Erotic Papyrus, now housed in the Egyptian Museum in Turin, Italy is an exception. The Papyrus, which is of high artistic merit, was painted in the Ramesside period (1292–1075 BC) and contains a series of 12 vignettes. The vignettes vividly depict a rough-looking man having sexual relations with an attractive, almost naked young woman, in a variety of positions, including standing in a chariot. It is thought the papyrus was a satire on the prevailing human manners.

The walls inside some of the surviving buildings in Pompeii, which was almost completely destroyed by the eruption of Vesuvius in AD 79, are covered with graphically lewd murals. It is thought these may have been the walls of brothels.

Pornography

One of the first known writers of pornography was Ovid (43 BC–AD 17), who wrote *Ars Amatoria* (the Art of Love). In his book, Ovid describes not only the techniques of sex but also advises his readers how often to have sex and how to get the most out of it.

The Italian Pietro Aretino (1492–1556) is regarded as the father of modern pornography. In 1524 he wrote a series of 16 sonnets, known as *Aretino's Postures*, to accompany 16 erotic drawings of sexual positions, drawn by Giuliano Romano, a pupil of Raphael. In the sonnets, he uses highly expressive language to describe the sensations of each position. Aretino was lucky to escape being imprisoned.

SEX ON SCREEN

In 1896, within a year of the world's first public showing of a moving picture, Louise Willy was the first actress to appear naked on screen – in the French film *Le Bain* (*The Bath*). Later the same year, Willy appeared in *Le Coucher de la Marie*, in which she performed a striptease.

Also in the same year, the Catholic Church denounced as pornographic a scene in the filmed version of the stage play *The Widow Jones*, showing a couple kissing. The scene lasted for 20 seconds.

The first screen sex goddess was Theda Bara (1885–1955), who appeared for the first time in *A Fool There Was* in 1915.

The first film to show a woman/couple having an orgasm during sex was *Ecstasy*, in 1933, starring Hedy Lamarr (1914–2000). The film was produced in Czechoslovakia, and in 1935 it became the first film to be blocked by US Customs from entering the USA (*see also* Mobile Phone p. 41 and Torpedo p. 311).

The Hays Code (also known as the Production Code) was introduced in the USA in 1930 in part to control the depiction of sex on screen. The code laid down rules which restricted nudity, suggestive dancing, ridicule of religion, drug use and many other aspects of life that could be seen to lower the moral standards of the day. It even included a rule that actors and actresses must both have one foot on the floor at all times during bedroom scenes. The code was strictly enforced after 1934, even prohibiting sexual innuendo, and in doing so severely limited the blossoming career of Mae West (1893–1980). The Hays Code was abolished in 1967.

The first film to be prosecuted under the Obscene Publications Act of Britain was *Last Tango in Paris* released in 1974, starring Marlon Brando (1924–2004) and Maria Schneider (b. 1952).

Sex and the City is a television programme first broadcast on HBO in 1998. It is unique in depicting the careers and sex lives of four single women. The women were living, working and playing in New York, and the show became aspirational viewing across the age groups round the world.

Homosexual Sex

The term homosexual is generally taken to refer to sex between two males, but strictly speaking it is the overall term referring to sex between any same-sex partners. Sex between females is also referred to as lesbianism. The prefix 'homo' is from the Greek meaning 'same', not the Latin meaning 'man'. The first use of the term homosexual was in a pamphlet of 1869 written by human rights campaigner Karl-Maria Kertbeny (1824–82).

In ancient Greek mythology, the gods Zephyrus and Hyakinthus were homosexual lovers. They are commemorated in the writings of Homer from the sixth or seventh century BC and on Greek pottery of the same era.

Plato (427–347 BC) and the playwright and politician Sophocles (495–406 BC) wrote extensively in the fourth and fifth centuries BC on homosexual love. Before that, the first great female poet Sappho, who lived on the Greek island of Lesbos in the seventh century BC, had groups of female admirers, and wrote most of her love poems, which were sometimes of a graphic nature, exclusively to women (*see also* Art p. 15).

SPACE

COVERING: Early Astronomy, Twentieth-Century Astronomy, Rocket Science, the Moon, Conspiracies and Myths, Satellites and Shuttles, Space Flight, Deaths in Space, Miscellaneous.

All space is slightly curved.
ALBERT EINSTEIN (1879–1955)

EARLY ASTRONOMY

Solar Observatory

The first solar observatory was built by Stone Age man at Newgrange, County Meath, Ireland in 3200 BC. Newgrange, which is reliably dated at 600 years older than the pyramids, is a vast stone-and-turf mound within a high wall of white quartz. Within the building is a cross-shaped central chamber into which an 18-metre-long (60-feet) passageway leads.

At dawn on the winter solstice, the shortest day of the year (21 December), the first rays of the Sun shine along the passage, enter the tomb and light up the burial chamber for about a quarter of an hour.

Planets Orbiting the Sun, not the Earth

Accepted church dogma in the fifteenth century maintained that the Earth was the centre of the universe, and the Sun, the planets and stars orbited around it. Any theory to the contrary was likely to be interpreted as heresy by the Roman Catholic Church, and the perpetrator of any such theory faced being put to death by burning at the stake.

Polish-born Nicolaus Copernicus (AD 1473–1543), who worked in Prussia as a mathematician, economist and church governor, began his observations of the heavens in 1497. He came to the conclusion that, contrary to Church teaching, in fact, the Earth and the planets orbited around the Sun. He formed the theory of heliocentricity (as opposed to geocentricity) but did not dare publish his work until 1543, the year of his death.

Philolaus (*c.*480–*c.*405 BC) Although Copernicus was actually the first to publish the theory that the Sun is at the centre of our solar system, someone else was thinking along the same lines almost 1,800 years earlier. In the fourth century BC, the Greek philosopher and mathematician Philolaus, a contemporary of Socrates, proposed that the Earth revolved in a circular orbit around the Sun, although he thought the Sun was a giant glass disc that reflected the light of the universe. Philolaus was also the first to advance the idea that the Earth spins on its axis.

Mapping the Stars

The ancient Babylonians are credited with the earliest knowledge of stars and their movements. As early as 3000 BC they recognised and charted the most prominent constellations visible to the naked eye.

The first person to map the stars was Danish astronomer Tycho Brahe (1546–1601), who created a massive observatory on the island of Hven in 1577, nine years before the invention of the telescope.

By observing the motion of a comet in 1577, Tycho (as he is known) determined that another plank of the Church's teaching about the heavens was incorrect. It had been the Church's position that the Moon and all the planets circled the Earth, each carried along inside its own 'celestial crystal sphere'. Because the comet he was observing travelled without hindrance through the area supposedly bound by the so-called 'spheres', Tycho proved that the spheres did not exist.

The first person to work out the equations for orbiting planets and to show that their orbits were ellipses – flattened circles, rather than perfect circles – was the German Johannes Kepler (1571–1630). Kepler published his findings in *Astronomia Nova* in 1609.

The first person to establish the basic laws of motion, force and gravity that govern the movement of the planets and to prove conclusively that

Kepler's equations worked was Isaac Newton (1643–1727). He published his findings in 1687.

Transit of Venus

In 1639, the amateur astronomer Jeremiah Horrocks (1617–41) of Toxteth, Liverpool, was the first to observe the transit of Venus, when the planet Venus passes in a direct line between the Sun and the Earth.

Johannes Kepler had calculated that Venus would slightly miss in its trajectory when crossing the face of the Sun. Questioning the calculations, Horrocks made a more accurate forecast of the path Venus would take, and he left a church service to make his observation. He focused his telescope onto a card for 30 minutes, so that the Sun could be safely observed. To his relief, his calculation was vindicated when Venus appeared as a tiny black dot moving across the card in front of the Sun.

It has been claimed that Horrocks's observation was the most important 30 minutes in the history of man, leading as it did, to the accurate measurement of the distance of the Sun from the Earth, the size of Venus, and other astronomical measurements. Horrocks's measurement of the Sun formed the basis for Newton's later work.

Telescopes

Gallileo Gallilei is credited with inventing the telescope in 1609, but the English mathematician and astronomer, Thomas Digges is known to have used a device with a convex lens at the front and a reflector at the rear to observe enemy shipping in 1578. He is thought to be the first man to turn a telescope to the skies to observe the stars.

In 1661, James Gregory (1638–1675) designed a telescope using mirrors instead of lenses, but did not build it. Five years later, Isaac Newton independently developed a fully usable, but small, reflecting telescope.

William Herschel (1738–1822) was born in Hanover in Germany and emigrated to Britain in 1757 after serving as a bandboy in the Hanoverian Guards. In 1774 he pioneered the use of mirrors in place of lenses in the construction of large 'reflecting' telescopes. Reflecting telescopes do not suffer the same optical distortions as refractor telescopes, which use lenses. The lack of distortion enables reflecting telescopes to be constructed on a far bigger scale, thus allowing astronomers to view distant objects much more closely.

Using the new type of telescope Herschel discovered distant galaxies. He was also the first to observe the clouds of particles now known as nebulae, and the first to put forward notions regarding the clustering of nebulae.

Herschel was also one of the first astronomers to develop broad ideas about the nature of the universe. He was the first to propose the theory of stellar evolution – the creation, life and death of stars – and concluded that the whole of our solar system moves through space.

In 1781 Herschel discovered Uranus, the first new planet to be discovered since ancient times. As Astronomer Royal, Herschel tried to name the new planet King George's Star after King George III, but it was not accepted. He discovered two satellites of Saturn and two satellites of Uranus. He also discovered infrared radiation and coined the word 'asteroid'.

However, even Herschel was fallible. Among his theories was the belief that all of the planets, and even the Sun, were populated.

First Asteroid

On 1 January 1801, the first asteroid was discovered by the Italian astronomer and professor of theology Giuseppe Piazzi (1746–1826). Piazzi had stumbled on what we now know as the asteroid belt between Mars and Jupiter.

Twentieth-Century Astronomy

Expansion of the Universe

In 1920, Edwin Hubble (1889–1953) of the USA was the first to provide evidence of the expansion of the universe. Hubble's Constant, which was written in 1929, is a law stating that the speed at which the galaxies are drifting apart is constant and has stayed the same for between ten and twenty billion years.

Radio and Radar Astronomy

The birth of radio astronomy occurred in 1932 when 27-year-old US radio engineer Karl Jansky (1905–1950) detected a source of cosmic static. At the time, Jansky was investigating disturbances on the transatlantic telephone cable on behalf of his employer, Bell Telephone Laboratories. He attributed the interference to the interaction between ions and electrons in interstellar space and located the source of the interference as the centre of our own galaxy, the Milky Way.

By the mid-1940s astronomers were using large antennae to study faint radio sources from space and to obtain greater detail of the galaxies than was possible by optical observation.

In 1946, astronomers in Hungary and the USA were able to bounce radar waves off the Moon and detect the reflected wave. In 1958, radar waves were bounced off Venus for the first time.

Quasars (quasi-stellar radio sources), which are on the very edge of the observable universe and the brightest objects known, were discovered in 1960 by Allan Sandage (b. 1926) and Thomas Matthews using radio astronomy.

Pulsars (pulsating radio stars), which are in fact rapidly spinning collapsed stars, were discovered in 1967 by Jocelyn Bell (b. 1943) while checking massive amounts of printout results from a radio telescope. As Bell was only a student at the time of her discovery, the 1974 Nobel Prize for Physics was awarded to her Cambridge tutor Antony Hewish (b. 1924).

Black holes are collapsed stars, which exert such strong gravitational pull that even light cannot escape. Based only on human imagination, the unnamed theory of such entities had already existed for two centuries, before the term 'black hole' was coined in a 1968 lecture given by American physicist John Wheeler (b. 1906).

The first evidence of a black hole, located in the binary star system Cygnus X-1, was found by NASA's Uhuru X-ray satellite in 1972.

The first pictures direct from Mars were beamed back to Earth on 20 July 1976 by the US Mars landing vehicle, *Viking 1*.

The first usable photographs of a comet's nucleus were taken by the European Space Agency's Giotto spacecraft as it flew close to Halley's Comet in 1986.

Venus was mapped for the first time in September 1994 by the US space probe Magellan, using radar imaging techniques. After the completion of its five-year mission Magellan was allowed to sink into the dense Venusian atmosphere where it vaporised.

ROCKET SCIENCE

Rockets began as no more than fireworks, but developed into missiles for use in war and ultimately as vehicles to transport men and machinery into space.

The earliest rockets were developed by the ancient Chinese, although the precise date cannot be determined. Gunpowder was packed into an open-ended tube, and as it burned rapidly the controlled explosion created thrust, causing the forward momentum of the rocket.

The basic equations of rocketry were first calculated by the Russian Konstantin Tsiolkovsky (1857–1935), who completed his work in 1903. He calculated that the required escape velocity from the Earth's gravitational pull for a space vehicle to enter orbit, was eight kilometres per second. He also stated that to achieve the escape velocity it would need a multistage rocket fuelled by liquid oxygen and liquid hydrogen. In his honour, the equation for rocket propulsion is known as the 'Tsiolkovsky rocket equation'. Although regarded as the 'father of rocketry', and the author of 500 works on space travel, Tsiolkovsky spent most of his working life as a high school mathematics teacher.

The first liquid-powered rocket was produced by Robert Goddard (1882–1945) in Massachusetts, USA, in 1926. Goddard's first rocket flew just 12.5 metres (41 feet) high and 56 metres (184 feet) forward, but he had proved his concept would work. For the fuel, Goddard used gasoline and oxygen mixed from separate tanks in the combustion chamber. The immense noise created by his rocket experiments meant that Goddard was forced to move to the town of Roswell, in a remote area in New Mexico, to continue his work.

The US Army failed to grasp the importance of rockets for war purposes.

Leading the German rocket development programme was Wernher von Braun (1912–77). Von Braun was captured after the end of the Second World War and offered his services to the USA. He pioneered rocketry for the US space programme in the 1950s and 1960s, and saw his Atlas rocket launch a man on to the Moon.

The first proton rocket was developed by the Soviet Union in 1965. Proton engines use hydrazine and nitrogen tetrachloride, which are hypergolic fuels. Hypergolic fuels burn on contact with each other, saving the need for an ignition system, and reducing the total weight of the rocket.

THE MOON

The first map of the surface of the Moon was produced in 1647 by Johannes Hevelius. He was born Jan Heweliusz in Poland in 1611 and became a wealthy brewer and city councillor in Dantzig, Germany. He died in Danzig in 1687.

Going to the Moon

Once mankind had mastered the science of rocketry, going to the Moon became a real possibility. Stimulated by their competing interests during the Cold War, and each with the desire to prove superiority, the USA and the Soviet Union poured massive financial and scientific resources into the pursuit of space travel.

The Soviets were the first to fly a rocket close to the Moon, conducting the first unmanned fly-by with *Luna 1* on 2 January 1959. Then the Soviet *Luna 2* was deliberately crashed into the Moon's surface on 14 September 1959 in the first impact landing. A month later, in October 1959, *Luna 3* took the first picture of the far side – the dark side – of the Moon.

It was almost three more years, on 26 July 1962, before the USA conducted their first impact landing.

The first scheduled unmanned soft landing on the Moon's surface was made by the Soviet *Luna 9* on 3 February 1966. The Soviets had planned to make a soft landing on the Moon with *Luna 6* on 8 June 1965, but the spacecraft missed its lunar orbit and flew off into space.

The first USA unmanned soft landing on the Moon was made by *Surveyor 1* on 2 June 1966. Widespread panic had gripped the US space agency NASA, who thought they might yet be beaten to landing a man on the Moon.

The first humans to fly past the dark side of the Moon were Frank Borman, James Lovell and William Anders on-board *Apollo 8*, on Christmas Eve 1968. As *Apollo 8* disappeared behind the Moon there were some very tense people on the ground in Houston. This was the first time anyone had flown out of radio contact with ground control behind the Moon. To put the space capsule into circumlunar orbit, the crew had to fire the engine in a controlled burn while out of radio contact. As the countdown proceeded, tension mounted but *Apollo 8* emerged into full view at the exact second it had been forecast. Although it did not land on the Moon, *Apollo 8* paved the way for all future Moon landings.

The first man to step on the Moon was Neil Armstrong (b. 1930) on 15 July 1969. Armstrong had a very close brush with death in December 1968. He ejected with only seconds to spare from a crashing Lunar Landing Vehicle, which he was testing.

The first word ever spoken from the Moon to Earth was 'Houston', as in 'Houston, Tranquility Bay here. The Eagle has landed.' Most people remember Armstrong's words as he stepped from the ladder to the Moon's surface: 'That's one small step for [a] man, one giant leap for mankind.'

The first word spoken on the Moon (not for transmission to Earth) was 'Contact' as in 'Contact light' spoken by Edwin 'Buzz' Aldrin (b. 1930). Incidentally, the last word spoken from the Moon was 'here' as in 'OK, let's get this mother out of here.' Gene Cernan, December 1972.

CONSPIRACIES AND MYTHS

Moonmen In 1835, the *New York Sun* published a lead story claiming that a new, powerful telescope had managed to focus on small objects on the surface of the Moon. The story claimed that astronomers had seen strange 'man-bat' creatures (half-bat, half-man) flitting across the landscape. In the face of almost universal ridicule, the *New York Sun* was forced to issue a retraction.

No one has ever been to the Moon A 1995 poll by *Time* magazine revealed that 6 per cent of Americans do not believe men ever went to the Moon.

A Fox TV programme, broadcast on 23 February 2001, proposed the theory that the whole of the Moon landing programme had been filmed in a studio. This conspiracy theory was based on such matters as the contrasting directions of shadows, and the fact that the American flag appeared to be waving in a breeze. Each claim has largely been discredited, although there has been a surprising lack of response from the North American Space Agency, NASA.

Urban myth After Neil Armstrong stepped on to the Moon's surface, he is supposed to have said, 'Good luck, Mr Gorski.' This refers to a supposed incident during Armstrong's childhood, when he overheard his next-door neighbour Mrs Gorski shouting at her husband, 'You want oral sex? You'll get oral sex when the kid next door walks on the Moon.'

Michael Collins (b. 1930) was the pilot of the command module *Columbia* that remained in lunar orbit while Armstrong and Aldrin descended to the Moon's surface. On the journey from Earth, the crew had debated what Armstrong should say as he stepped from the lunar landing vehicle. Collins is supposed to have said, 'If you'd got any balls, Neil, you'd say, "Oh my God, what is that thing?" Then scream and rip your mike off.'

Satellites and Shuttles

The first man-made satellite to be launched into space was the Soviet-made *Sputnik 1*, which went into orbit on 4 October 1957. The USA tried to respond by launching *Vanguard* but it exploded on launch. It was rather unkindly dubbed *Kaputnik*.

The first communication satellite was not, as is commonly supposed, *Telstar*, but SCORE (Signal Communications Orbital Relay Equipment), which was developed by the US Army. SCORE was launched, on board an Atlas rocket, on 18 December 1958 by NASA. The satellite's batteries failed after only 12 days. *Telstar* was launched in 1962 to relay transmissions between the USA, the UK and France.

Arthur C. Clarke (b. 1917), author of *2001: A Space Odyssey*, had predicted the future development of communication satellites in a 1945 magazine article. His idea was that satellites could distribute television programmes around the globe. At the time it was considered to be no more than the dream of a science-fiction writer, but, true to Clarke's prediction, *Telstar* was launched in 1962.

The **first commercial satellite** was *Intelsat 1* (also known as Early Bird), which was launched in 1965 by an international consortium led by the USA.

In 1962, NASA planned and designed the first manned, reusable space vehicle, named *X20 Dyna Soar*, which was to be launched from a *Titan 3* rocket. Neil Armstrong was one of the pilots, but the project was abandoned.

The first effective reusable space vehicle, commonly known as a Space Shuttle, was *Columbia*, which was first launched 12 April 1981. On its twenty-eighth mission in 2003, *Columbia* disintegrated on re-entry to the Earth's atmosphere, and was lost with all hands.

SPACE FLIGHT

The first man in space was the Russian cosmonaut Yuri Gagarin (1934–68). On 12 April 1961 he became the first human being to voyage into space on board *Vostok 1*. He completed a single orbit of the Earth lasting one hour and forty-eight minutes.

Gagarin died at the age of 34 while testing an aircraft. There were strong suspicions that his death was no accident, as he had publicly disagreed with a number of Soviet policies.

The first American in space was Alan Shepard (1923–98) on 5 May 1961, in a *Mercury 3* space capsule, which was launched by a Redstone rocket to an altitude of 186 kilometres (116 miles). Shepard's landing point was a mere 483 kilometres (302 miles) away after completion of this 15-minute suborbital flight.

Shepard became the oldest astronaut to walk on the Moon, at the age of 47, in February 1971.

The first American to orbit the Earth was John Glenn (b. 1921). On 20 February 1962 he orbited the Earth several times in *Friendship 7* in a flight of 4 hours 55 minutes and 23 seconds.

Thirty-six years after his historic first flight, Glenn also became the oldest man into space at the age of 77. The only ill effect he suffered was that he looked a bit wobbly after landing.

The first woman in space was Valentina Tereshkova (b. 1937). On 16 June 1963 she completed 48 orbits of the Earth in 71 hours aboard *Vostok 5*. Tereshkova was a textile-factory worker before she enlisted on the Soviet space programme in 1962.

The first American woman in space was Dr Sally Ride (b. 1951). On 18 June 1983 she travelled on board the Space Shuttle *Challenger*.

The first African-American in space was Guion Bluford (b. 1942) on 30 August 1983 on board *Challenger*.

The first Briton in space was Helen Sharman (b. 1963). On 19 May 1991 she became the first British astronaut on board the Soviet *Soyuz TM-12*.

The first space walk was made by Major Alexei Arkhipovich Leonov (b. 1934) on 20 March 1965. Leonov had been launched on *Voskhod 2*.

The first American space walk was made by Edward White (1930–67) on 6 June 1965. He was later to perish in the *Apollo 1* disaster.

The first British space walk was made by Dr Michael Foale (b. 1957) who holds dual US-UK citizenship. In February 1995 he performed the first space walk by a British citizen after a rendezvous with the Russian space station *Mir*.

The first space walk without an umbilical was made by on 7 February 1984 by Bruce McCandless (b. 1937). Using a manned manoeuvring unit (MMU), which was nothing more than a jet pack strapped to his back, he left the safety of *Challenger* on Mission SS-41-B and became the first person to 'walk' in space without being tethered.

The first dog in space was Laika, a mongrel stray who had been caught on the streets of Moscow. On 3 November 1957 she was launched into space on board *Sputnik 2*. There was no way to return Laika safely to Earth and she died in space.

The first monkey in space was Gordo, a squirrel monkey. On 13 December 1958, NASA launched Gordo into space aboard a Jupiter rocket. He survived re-entry but there was widespread condemnation in the media when he drowned in the ocean after his flotation device failed on landing.

The first animals to return safely from space were Belka and Strelka, two Soviet dogs, who returned safely to Earth on 20 August 1960 after a day in space in the company of 40 rats.

The first song in space was 'Happy Birthday' on *Apollo 9*, in 1968.

The first married couple in space was Mark Lee and Jan Davis in 1992.

The first private spacecraft At 11.08am on 23 June 2004, *Space Ship One*, designed by Burt Rutan (b. 1943) with pilot Mike Melvill (b. 1941) at the controls, crossed the frontier of space at 100.12 kilometres (62.21 miles) above sea level. Melvill was a mere 124 metres (410 feet) above the boundary of the Earth's atmosphere, but it was enough to enter the record books.

The first man or woman on Mars Not yet, not yet! But… he or she is said to be walking on the Earth right now. According to NASA's website, new space vehicles combining the best of the Apollo and Shuttle technology will be going to the Moon carrying four astronauts at a time. The Moon will be used as a staging post to launch a mission to Mars carrying six crew members. The mission timetable includes returning to the Moon in 2018.

DEATHS IN SPACE AND SPACE PROGRAMMES

The space programmes of the USA and Soviet Union have cost hundreds of lives. It is a feature of these deaths that they have been caused in almost all cases by a set of unique circumstances. Faults have rarely been repeated.

The first rocket death on any space programme Officially 92 people, but possibly as many as 150, died on 24 October 1960 in the Nedelin Disaster in Russia. This was the first, and remains the largest single space disaster.

The official in charge of the launch, Mitrofan Nedelin cut corners and ignored safety procedures, in a panic to have the launch coincide with the anniversary of the Bolshevik Revolution, and in an attempt to gain favour with Nikita Kruschev (1894–1971), the General Secretary of the USSR. There was a major malfunction with the ignition sequence, and the engines fired up as Nedelin and the team of engineers were still on the scaffolding surrounding the rocket. As spectators tried to run they found the tarmac had melted around them. Many became stuck to the ground and unable to move as flames engulfed them.

The first death on a training programme On 23 March 1961 Soviet cosmonaut Valentin Bondarenko (1937–61) was killed by a flash fire while training in a ground-based simulator. Bondarenko Crater, on the far side of the Moon, has been named in his honour.

The first death on the launch pad On 27 January 1967 in *Apollo 1*, Americans Ed White (1930–67), Virgil 'Gus' Grissom (1926–67) and Roger Chaffee (1935–67) died in their launch capsule when a fault in the 30 miles (48 kilometres) of wiring caused sparks, which ignited in the pure pressurised oxygen inside the cabin. The fire spread rapidly in the oxygen-rich atmosphere, igniting the ethylene glycol fuel mixture, and the astronauts were unable to open the escape hatch.

The first parachute malfunction On 24 April 1967, after the successful re-entry of *Soyuz 1*, the capsule's parachute failed to open properly at 7,010 metres (23,000 feet). The vehicle hit the ground at more than 200 miles (322 kilometres) per hour, and the pilot, Vladimir Komarov (1927–67), was killed instantly, becoming the first person to die on a space mission.

The first death on re-entry On 29 June 1971, *Soyuz 11* had completed the first successful visit to the world's first space station, *Salyut 1*. The spacecraft was on its final approach to Earth, when a valve, just one millimetre in diameter, opened during the re-entry phase, allowing air to escape from the spacecraft.

The three crew members were unable to stop the leak, all the air escaped, and the cabin pressure collapsed to zero within two minutes of the valve opening. The craft landed intact but Georgi Dobrovsky, Victor Patseyev and Vladislav Volkov had been asphyxiated. They were the first to die at the point of re-entry.

The first rocket explosion In 1980 at the Plesetsk Space Centre in the Soviet Union, a rocket exploded on the launch pad killing 50 people.

The first death during lift-off was on 28 January 1986 when the US Space Shuttle *Challenger STS-51L* exploded 74 seconds after lift-off. All seven crew members died.

The first women to die On 28 January 1986, Judith Resnick (1949–86) and Christa McAuliffe (1948–86), crew members on board *Challenger*, died when the spacecraft exploded after launch.

The first private citizen to die on any space programme was Christa McAuliffe on board *Challenger* (see above). Christa was a schoolteacher who had applied for the opportunity to be the first private citizen in space and had been selected from 11,000 applicants.

The first American deaths on re-entry On 1 February 2003, the US Space Shuttle *Columbia* broke up on re-entry. The Columbia Accident Investigation Board found that a piece of insulating foam had broken away on launch and fatally damaged a wing. On re-entry, heat entered the wing through the resultant hole and melted the wing from the inside out. The Shuttle disintegrated, and all seven crew members died.

The first moonwalker to die was Alan Shepard, the oldest man to walk on the moon at 47 and the first American in space. He died of leukaemia at age 74 on 21 July 1998.

MISCELLANEOUS

Asteroids and Comets

The first asteroid rendezvous On 20 February 2001 the US spacecraft *NEAR* (Near Earth Asteroid Rendezvous) soft-landed on the asteroid Eros after orbiting it for 12 months.

The first impact with a comet was by NASA's *Deep Impact* vehicle, 83,000,000 miles away in space. It was deliberately crashed into the Tempel 1 comet on 4 July 2005. The impact velocity was 23,000 miles per hour.

The objective of the mission was to view and analyse the inside of a comet for the first time, and try to discover the role comets may have played in the formation of the solar system. The experiment has so far revealed the existence of water ice on the surface of the comet, and abundant organic material in the interior. It also pinpointed the comet's likely origin, which was the region of space occupied by Uranus and Neptune.

Space Station

The first space station was *Salyut 1*, launched by the Soviet Union on 19 April 1971. It lasted six months, but lost its orbit and disintegrated on re-entry into the Earth's atmosphere. The few small parts remaining after the disintegration fell into the Pacific Ocean.

Space Law

International Geophysical Year (IGY), a worldwide co-operation between over 200 leading international scientists, lasted from July 1957 to December 1958. It coincided with the Soviet Union successfully launching *Sputnik* and the USA launching *Telstar*.

Among the objectives of the IGY was to co-ordinate research into, and observations of, geophysical phenomena such as volcanoes, cosmic rays, Earth's magnetism, rocketry and solar activity. A technical panel was set up to launch the first artificial satellite.

After the two competing launches by America and Russia, the scientists involved in IGY became concerned that the major powers could use space in strategic power games.

The first space law treaty was drawn up in 1967 and signed by 63 countries, including the UK, the USA and the Soviet Union. Called the Outer Space Treaty, it states that:

- No country is allowed to claim sovereignty over celestial bodies.

- No country is to conduct nuclear testing in space.

- No country is allowed to launch military action in or from space.

Space Elevator

In 1895, after visiting the Eiffel Tower in Paris, Konstantin Tsiolkovsky (*see* Rocket Science p. 240) proposed the construction of 'celestial castles' in orbit, attached to the Earth by vast cables.

The theory of the Space Elevator, a massively tall tower extending into space, was first proposed in 1970 by Jerome Pearson. While working at the US Air Force Research Laboratory in Ohio, Pearson published his thoughts on a 'stairway to heaven' and a 'cosmic railway', in the technical journal *Acta Astronomica*. Arthur C. Clarke (b. 1917), author of *2001: A Space Odyssey*, was asked after a talk he had given about the Space Elevator when he thought construction would be feasible. He answered, 'About fifty years after everyone's stopped laughing.'

Sport

Covering: Athletics, Golf, Tennis, Cricket, Boxing, Horse Racing, Association Football, Rugby, Swimming, Cycling, Motor Racing, Basketball, Baseball, Darts, Archery, Snooker, Bog Snorkelling.

Organised sport formed an important part of the ancient ways of life and originated with the Egyptians and Sumerians around 3000 BC. Egyptian games, which are recorded on temple walls, included archery, wrestling, boxing, acrobatics, stick fighting, horse events and ball games.

The Egyptians used sport for training and strengthening the body as well as for recreation and pleasure. During his reign, the pharaoh Zoser the Great (2667–2648 BC) had himself depicted in a mural taking part in a running competition during the Heb Sed festival in 2650 BC. It was considered important for a pharaoh to establish his supremacy in long-distance races, which could be rough events by today's standards. Permitted tactics included barging and hair pulling.

A mural in a tomb in Saqqara, which has been dated 2300 BC, shows children taking part in sports.

Athletics (US: Track and Field)

The earliest organised athletic events were held in Egypt and Sumer in southern Mesopotamia in 3000 BC, as described above. The main participants were the ruling elite, and taking part was considered essential, particularly in the education of the pharaoh.

Greek games began around 1500 BC and by the end of the sixth century BC were being held in four main cities: Olympia – Olympic Games; Delphi – Pythian Games; Nemea – Nemean Games; Corinth – Isthmian Games.

The first Olympic Games took place in 776 BC. They were considered to be the most important of the four games and were staged every four years for over 1,000 years and as they held such an important part of Greek life, the word *olympiad* was coined to indicate a four-year period. During the period, participation was always restricted to speakers of Greek. All of the contestants were men and they all contested the events naked. Women were not allowed in as spectators, even though the original Olympic stadium could hold 50,000 people.

We know the name of the first Olympic champion, Coroebus of Elis, who was a cook. Coroebus won the *stadion*, a sprint race of around 190 metres (207 yards) (a stade). Hence the track became known as the stadium.

The first modern Olympic Games took place in Athens in 1896 (*see also* Questionable Origins p. 206).

First Modern Olympic Athletics Champions

Men champions

Track

Event	Winner	Time			Year
		hrs	mins	secs	
100m	T. Burke (US)			12.2	1896
200m	J. Tewkesbury (US)			22.2	1900
400m	T. Burke (US)			54.2	1896
800m	E. Flack (Aust.)		2	11.0	1896
1500m	E. Flack (Aust.)		4	33.2	1896
5000m	H. Kolehmainen (Fin.)		14	36.6	1912
10000m	H. Kolehmainen (Fin.)		31	20.8	1912
Marathon	Spiridon Louis (Gr.)	2	58	50.0	1896
110m hurdles	T. Curtis (US)			17.6	1896
400m hurdles	J. Tewkesbury (US)			57.6	1900
3000m steeplechase	T. Hodge (GB)		10	00.4	1920
4 x 100m relay	GB			42.4	1912
4 x 400m relay	US		3	16.6	1912

Field

Event	Winner	Height/Distance	Year
		Metres	
High jump	E. Clark (US)	1.81	1896
Pole vault	W. Hoyt (US)	3.30	1896
Long jump	E. Clark (US)	6.35	1896
Triple jump	J. Connolly (US)	13.70	1896
Shot put	R. Garrett (US)	11.22	1896
Discus	R. Garrett (US)	29.15	1896
Hammer	J. Flanagan (US)	49.73	1900
Javelin	E. Lemming (Swe.)	54.83	1908
Decathlon	J. Thorpe (US)		1912

The first year women were allowed to participate in the official Olympic athletics (track and field) events was 1928.

Women champions

Track

Event	Winner	Time		Year
		mins	secs	
100m	E. Robinson (US)		12.20	1928
200m	Fanny Blankers-Koen (Neth.)		24.40	1948
400m	Betty Cuthbert (Aus.)		52.00	1960*
800m	L. Radke-Batschauer (Ger.)	2	16.80	1928*
1500m	L. Bragina (USSR)		41.40	1972*
4 x 100m relay	Can.		48.40	1928
4 x 400m relay	E. Ger.	3	23.00	1972*
80m hurdles	M. Didrikson (US)		11.70	1932

Field

Event	Winner	Height/Distance	Year
		Metres	
High jump	E. Catherwood (Can.)	1.59	1928
Long jump	V. Gyarmati (Hun.)	5.69	1948
Shot put	M. Ostermeyer (Fra.)	13.75	1948
Discus	H. Konopacka (Pol.)	39.62	1928
Javelin	M. Didrikson (US)	43.68	1932
Pentathlon	I. Press (USSR)		1964

*Members of the International Olympic Committee were so distressed at the sight of women collapsing on the track in the 800-metre race in 1928 that no further women's events were run at 400, 800 or 1500 metres until the 1960 Olympics in Rome. The 400 metre and 800 metre events were reintroduced that year, but there was no 1500-metre race until 1972.

The first ever women's modern Olympic champion was Betty Robinson of the USA, who died in 1999.

The International Association of Athletics Federations (IAAF) is the world governing body of athletics and was formed during the Stockholm Olympics in 1912. It was originally called the International Amateur Athletics Federation.

The Amateur Athletic Association (AAA) is the governing body of athletics in Britain and was formed in 1880. The first AAA Championships due to take place that year were rained off.

GOLF

It is claimed that golf was invented in Scotland, but this is by no means certain – the origins of the sport are shrouded in obscurity. Certainly the oldest golf courses and the oldest golf clubs in the world are in Scotland, and the game is controlled worldwide, with the exception of the USA and Mexico, from St Andrews in Scotland. The Royal and Ancient Golf Club of St Andrews, which remains a private members' club, controls the rules of the game, approves changes to the equipment and runs the Open Championship and Amateur Championship.

There are many other contesting claims as to the origin of golf:

Paganica was a game played by the ancient Romans, which involved hitting a wooden or leather ball into a hole with a curved stick. This does sound suspiciously like golf, and *paganica* has perhaps the strongest claim to being the precursor of the modern game. It is said that the Romans brought *paganica* to the countries they conquered throughout Europe in the first century AD, much as cricket spread throughout the British Empire hundreds of years later.

Kolven or *kolf* is known to have been played in Holland in 1297, before golf was recorded as a sport. In *kolven*, a curved stick was used to strike a ball into a hole in a frozen lake. There are paintings of people playing the game, and it is mentioned in some documents of the time, but there are no records of the rules.

Chole is another claimant to be the original form of golf. It was played in northern France and Belgium in the thirteenth century AD, and seems to have existed in different versions. The essence of *chole* was for opposing teams to strike the same ball, but in different directions. Each team could take three strikes at the ball in an effort to score, after which the opposing team could take a single shot to strike the ball in any direction they chose. *Chole* may therefore seem to be more closely related to modern hockey.

Professor Ling Hongling, a Chinese academic based at Lanzhou University, claims that golf was invented in China and was being played in 945 AD. The professor bases his claim on a literary reference he has unearthed in a work called the Dongxuan Records. The reference is to a pastime called chuiwan-chui (hit-ball hit), in which the players hit a ball with a 'purposely crafted' stick.

The earliest records of Scottish golf are from 1457, with the proclamation by King James II of Scotland (1430–60) that golf must be banned. The sport, he said, should be 'utterley cryed down' as it was interfering with his troops' archery practice.

There are records that it was being played in St Andrews in 1552 on the site of what is now the most famous golf course in the world, known as the Old Course.

The first golf club was the Royal and Ancient Golf Club of St Andrews (known as the R & A), formed in 1754 by 'Twenty-two Noblemen and Gentlemen'. It was originally known as the Society of St Andrews Golfers and became 'Royal' in 1834, being the second club so honoured (Perth was the first). Of the ten oldest clubs, the R & A is the only one that still plays golf over its original links, the Old Course. The Old Course does not belong to the R & A, but the club has certain playing rights granted to it by the owners, the St Andrews Links Trust.

Only seaside courses are referred to as a 'links' courses, as they are built on the land that links the sea with the land. By convention, the word 'links' is never used for an inland course.

The Honourable Company of Edinburgh Golfers (also known as Muirfield) claims it was formed in 1744. However, the club ceased to function between 1831 and 1836 as a result of financial difficulties and therefore does not have a continuous existence.

The Royal Burgess Golfing Society of Edinburgh was formed in 1735 (the 'Royal' was granted in 1929 by George V) giving it the strongest real claim to be the oldest golf club still in existence. The club plays over the Bruntsfield Links in Edinburgh.

The first golf club in England was the Royal Blackheath Golf Club, which has a tenuous claim to be the world's oldest golf club. The club maintains that it was formed in 1745, and records actually show golf being played regularly on the heath as early as 1608, although this is not claimed as a club event. Royal Blackheath was certainly formed by 1766, making it the oldest club in England.

James I (James VI of Scotland) (1566–1625) brought his clubs to London in 1603 when he was crowned King of England, and he is known to have played golf on the heath.

The first major golf championship was the British Open Championship. First played in 1860 at Prestwick it is the oldest of the major golf championships and is known simply as 'the Open'.

The first winner of the British Open was Willie Park Snr (1834–1903) of Musselburgh in East Lothian, Scotland. The championship was played over three rounds of 12 holes each and Park's total score was 174.

TENNIS

The word 'tennis' is derived from the French *tenez* (hold) which was used to warn an opponent that a serve was due. The forerunner of tennis called *jeu de paume* (the game of the palm) was played in twelfth-century France and is still played in parts of Paris. The game involved batting a ball across a net with bare hands, and later, wearing gloves. Racquets were introduced into the game in the sixteenth century. The ball, which was made of leather stuffed with feathers, did not bounce.

Lawn tennis as we know it began in the 1870s: Major Walter C Wingfield (1833–1912), a British Army officer, created what he called sphairistike, as an almost direct crib of the ancient Greek game of the same name. Sphairistike was played on an hourglass-shaped court with a net at head height. In 1865 Wingfield tried to obtain a patent for sphairistike, but failed because the Patent Office recognised that the French had already been playing the very similar game of tennis for 700 years. Far from discouraged, Wingfield spent a good deal of the rest of his life promoting tennis.

The All-England Croquet Club had been founded in 1868 and in 1875 was persuaded to set aside a small area of land in Worple Road, Wimbledon, for the playing of tennis. The club was later renamed the All England Lawn Tennis and Croquet Club.

The Lawn Tennis Association was formed in 1888.

The first Wimbledon champion was W. Spencer Gore (1850–1906) in 1877. The final was postponed from Monday 16 July to the following Thursday because of rain. Two hundred paying spectators watched the final from a stand made of three planks of wood. Spencer Gore also played cricket for England.

The first woman champion and first French winner was the legendary Suzanne Lenglen (1899–1938), who dominated the championship from 1919 to 1926.

Lenglen fainted and withdrew from the 1926 Wimbledon singles tournament after being informed she had inadvertently kept Queen Mary, who was sitting in the Royal Box, waiting. Lenglen had been misinformed of her starting time.

The first American winner was Bill Tilden (1893–1953) in 1920.

The first African-American winner was Althea Gibson (1927–2003), who won the women's championship in 1957 and 1958.

The first Davis Cup match was played between the USA and Great Britain in 1900.

In 1899 four members of the Harvard University Tennis Team came up with the idea of a challenge tennis match between the USA and Great Britain. The trophy was provided by a Harvard team member Dwight Davis, after whom the trophy was named in 1945 (it was originally known as the International Lawn Tennis Challenge). The first match was held in Boston, Massachusetts, in 1900, with the USA winning 3–0. In 1905 the competition was expanded with France, Australasia (combining Australia and New Zealand), Belgium and Austria invited to send teams.

CRICKET

The origins of cricket are lost in the mists of history, although in his accounts of 1300, Edward II, King of England (1284–1327), makes reference to playing a similar game against his friend Piers Gaveston (1284–1312).

It is thought that cricket began as a casual game between shepherds in the sheep-rearing area of the south-east counties of England. Sheep would keep the grass short and a woollen ball would be bowled at a wicket gate, which was defended with a shepherd's crook.

During the seventeenth century cricket's popularity increased but without a fixed set of rules. The Hambledon Club, which was formed in 1760, claims its place in cricketing history as being first to lay down the techniques of batting and bowling. Control of cricket was later transferred to the Marylebone Cricket Club (MCC), which had been established in 1787. The MCC drew up the first formal set of rules (known as laws) in 1835. The same laws remain in use today.

The first county match was between Surrey and Kent in 1709.

The first match between gentlemen (amateurs) and players (professionals) took place in 1806.

The first cricket match played at the Lord's Cricket Ground in London, took place in June 1814.

Wisden Cricketers' Almanack was first published in 1864. It has been published annually ever since, including during the two world wars. John Wisden (1826–1884) was a London retailer of cricket equipment and cigars, and had been a star cricketer of the mid-nineteenth century. On one occasion he took all ten wickets (all bowled out) in a North v. South match at Lord's. This is the only time all ten wickets have been clean-bowled in any first-class match.

BOXING

Ancient Boxing

There is recent evidence of boxing matches being held in North Africa and Ethiopia as early as 4000 BC, but the most reliable records show that boxing took place in 1500 BC on the island of Crete. There is no written record of Cretan boxing and most of the evidence is in the form of art. The famous relief on the rhyton at Hagia Triada is dated as sixteenth century BC and depicts a number of sporting poses including boxing. There is also a fresco at Thera, dated 1550 BC, which shows two young men boxing, with each wearing a glove on the right hand.

The Greeks adopted boxing as an Olympic sport in 688 BC, calling it *pygme* or *pygmahia*.

Modern Boxing

The first rules for boxing were known as the London Prize Ring Rules of 1743 written by Jack Broughton (1703–89). They were used for more than 100 years.

In 1865 new rules were developed for boxing by John Graham Chambers of England. To add legitimacy to the new rules Chambers asked John Sholto Douglas, 9th Marquess of Queensberry (1844–1900) to allow his name to be attached to them as sponsor. Queensberry agreed and the new rules were published in 1867. The rules of boxing are referred to worldwide as the Marquess of Queensberry Rules, and Chambers is never heard of.

Until 1892, all boxing contests were conducted using bare knuckles.

The first heavyweight champion, so recognised even though there were no weight divisions at the time, was James Figg (1695–1734) of England. In his whole boxing career Figg only ever lost one bout and claimed to have been ill at the time.

The first heavyweight champion of the world wearing boxing gloves was James J. Corbett (also known as Gentleman Jim) (1866–1933). He beat John L. Sullivan (1858–1918), the last bare-knuckle champion, in 1892 over 21 rounds in New Orleans.

The first British-born heavyweight champion of the world was Cornishman Bob Fitzsimmons (1863–1917), who beat James Corbett on 17 March 1897. Fitzsimmons was never more than a middleweight, but was successful in the heavyweight division as a result of his ferocious punching strength.

The first African-American heavyweight champion of the world was Jack Johnson after he knocked out Tommy Burns in December 1908 in Sydney.

The origin of the expression 'up to scratch' comes from early boxing contests, which were conducted outdoors on the ground with no ring. At the conclusion of each round, a scratch would be drawn in the dirt by the referee, roughly in the centre of where the contest was taking place. To start the next round the boxers were obliged to advance to the scratch (come up to scratch) and face each other. If a boxer was unable to make it to the line, he was deemed to be 'not up to scratch' and lost the fight.

Subsequently the term 'scratch' was adopted in golf to refer to a skilled golfer who was able to play consistently to level par. His handicap was deemed to be 'scratch'.

HORSE RACING

Racing with horses has taken place since man first managed to ride them and harness them to chariots. Horse racing was included in the ancient Olympic Games in 638 BC.

The origins of horseracing, as we recognise it today, can be traced back to the English knights returning from the Crusades in the twelfth century. None of them came back from the Holy Land empty-handed. Several brought back swift-running Arab stallions and mares, which were cross-bred with English horses to add stamina to their speed.

The first recorded horse race in England took place in 1174 at a horse fair in Smithfield, London, although it has been speculated that Roman soldiers raced horses in Yorkshire during the Roman occupation of Britain.

For four centuries, match racing, in which two horses were matched against each other for a wager, was a popular pastime of the wealthy nobility. The sport developed into full professional horseracing during the reign of Queen Anne (1665–1714) between 1702 and 1714. Anne was also instrumental in the foundation of Royal Ascot.

The Jockey Club was formed in 1750 as the controlling body of all horseracing, and remains in control today. In 1793, the Jockey Club authorised the Weatherby family to keep the General Stud Book tracing the pedigree of every thoroughbred horse in Britain. The family has continued the tradition to this day, and the origin of every thoroughbred horse running in Britain can be traced back to just three stallions called the Foundation Sires: the Byerley Turk of 1679, the Darley Arabian of 1700 the Godolphin Arabian of 1724.

The Derby was first run in 1780. It was named after Edward Smith-Stanley, 12th Earl of Derby (1752–1834). At a celebration after the Epsom Oaks in 1779, the Earl of Derby and Sir Charles Bunbury tossed a coin to see who would have the race named after them. Derby won the toss, but Bunbury won the first race in 1780, collecting a prize of £1,000. Derby won his own race in 1787.

The Grand National is regarded as the premier National Hunt event and, despite earlier disputes between historians over the first time it was run, it has now been agreed that the first winning horse was the Duke in 1836.

The Tote was established by Act of Parliament in 1928 so that the government could have some control over, and take a cut of, the revenues generated by gambling on the results of horseracing. It began operating in 1929 and, today, is the fourth largest bookmaker in the UK and distributes its profits 'for purposes conducive to the improvement of breeds of horses or the sport of horseracing'.

The first organised sporting event in the USA was horse racing on Long Island in 1664.

ASSOCIATION FOOTBALL

It has now been officially recognised by the governing bodies that association football, or soccer, began in China more than 2,500 years ago. The ancient Chinese played a form of football known as Cuju, which was popular between 770 and 476 BC. It originated in the Linzi district of the city of Zibo, on the Shandong Peninsula. The rules involved kicking an inflated pig's bladder round an enclosed courtyard and the ball had to be kept in the air, as a score could not be made if the ball had gone to ground. There were several versions of the game, and one even had a goal net similar to the modern one.

The first set of rules which would be recognised today was drawn up in 1848 at Trinity College, Cambridge. Shin kicking, known as hacking, was allowed as a legitimate means of tackling an opponent.

The Football Association (FA) was formed in 1862 from the various associations, such as the Sheffield Association or the Nottingham Association, who came together to hold competitions and set out rules for the game. The word 'soccer' is an abbreviation of 'Association'.

The first professional football club, Notts County, was formed in 1862.

The first football organisation in the USA was the Oneida Football Club. It was formed in Boston in 1862 by 17-year-old Gerritt Smith-Miller, and the first game was played on 7 November 1863. In the seasons 1863–65, Oneida did not lose a game and did not concede a single goal.

The first Scottish club, Queen's Park, was formed in 1867.

The first and oldest football competition in the world is the FA Cup, which was proposed in 1871 by C.W. Alcock. It was first played the following year, 1872, when Wanderers Football Club beat the Royal Engineers FC 1–0 at the Oval. Wanderers went on to defend the trophy successfully in 1873.

Referees were introduced to football in 1871 to avoid what had become regular disputes in professional matches.

The two-handed throw-in was introduced in 1882.

The Football League was formed in 1888 by 12 clubs who met in a Fleet Street hotel.

Fédération Internationale de Football Association (FIFA), the international ruling body, was formed in 1904.

The first FA Cup Final at Wembley Stadium was played in 1923. Estimates vary, but as many as 200,000 spectators may have been crammed in.

The first World Cup between nations was won by Uruguay, who beat Argentina 4–2 in the final in 1930. Neither side could agree on the size of ball to be used in the final. A compromise was reached by using one size in the first half and another in the second.

On 22 April 1909, in Turin, Italy, the Sir Thomas Lipton Trophy was won by the amateur football side of West Auckland FC, representing England. West Auckland beat FC Winterthur, representing Switzerland, in the final, and thus became the first **World Club Champions of football**.

Lipton had donated the trophy, which was planned as an international competition for the best teams in the world. The British Football Association had refused to send a team, so Lipton himself invited West Auckland which was mainly made up of coal miners.

In 1911, West Auckland successfully defended their trophy, beating Juventus of Italy 6–1 in the final. The trophy was awarded outright to West Auckland, and was never contested again.

La Stampa Sportiva, an Italian sports magazine had organised a similar event in 1908, with the Swiss team Servette beating Turin (Torino) 3–1 in the final. This contest set the pattern for the Sir Thomas Lipton Trophy, but, because of the small international presence, the 1908 event was not considered to be a World Cup.

Rugby

The myth endures that rugby was born as a result of a single incident in 1823. During a game of the very individual version of football being played at Rugby School, William Webb Ellis (1806–1872), a pupil, supposedly picked up the ball and ran to the goal line. No hard historical evidence exists to support this romantic story. Nonetheless the Rugby Union World Cup is named the 'Webb Ellis Trophy' in commemoration of the event and the man.

The rules of rugby were first codified in 1845 by three pupils of Rugby School. Until that time, opposing teams would meet to agree their own set of rules before taking to the field. Inevitably, lack of a fixed set of rules had led to disputes and occasional brawling.

In the beginning, a try was called a 'run-in', and no points were scored. By touching the ball down over the try line, it allowed the team to 'try' to convert the touchdown into a goal.

In 1884, the scoring system was changed so that an unconverted try was valued at one point, which could be converted into three points if the goal was scored.

The Rugby Football Union (RFU) was formed in 1871.

The International Rugby Board (IRB), the ruling body of rugby, was formed in 1886.

The Northern Football Union left the RFU in 1895 and from 1920 was called the Rugby Football League. The traditional form of rugby is Rugby Union, which is played with 15 players on each team. Rugby League is played with 13 players and formed the breakaway movement from Rugby Union in 1895 after disputes over making payment to players.

Rugby Union remained amateur, and Rugby League, which was predominantly a northern game, had always been professional, until 26 August 1995, when the IRB declared the Union code open to both amateur and professional players.

American Football, Canadian Football and Australian Rules Football are all descended from rugby.

SWIMMING

The earliest evidence of man's ability to swim is shown on cave drawings, which have been found in the so-called 'cave of swimmers' at Wadi Sora in Egypt, dated at up to 14,000 years old. An ancient Egyptian clay seal, dated between 9000 and 4000 BC, shows four swimmers who are swimming the stroke now known as the front crawl or freestyle.

The earliest written references to swimming date from 2000 BC, occurring in *Gilgamesh*, the *Iliad*, the Bible (Ezekiel 47: 5) and the *Beowulf* sagas.

The first book on swimming was *Colymbetes*, written in 1538 by Nicholas Wynman, a German language professor, mainly as a means of reducing the dangers of drowning.

The first swimming competitions were held in England before 1837. At that time there were six man-made swimming pools in London.

The front crawl was originally known as the 'Trudgen' on account of being developed by Englishman John Trudgen in 1873. Trudgen had copied the style from Native Americans after seeing its use on a trip to South America, although it had been seen in 1844 in London, also being used by Native Americans. This style was thought of as un-English, as the leg kicking created far more splashing than the then current breaststroke.

Milestones

The first indoor swimming pool was built in England in 1862.

The Amateur Swimming Association was formed in 1880.

The first person to swim the English Channel was the Englishman Captain Matthew Webb (1848–83) in 1875, taking 21 hours and 15 minutes to swim from Dover to Calais. Captain Webb died after being sucked into a whirlpool, in the rapids at the foot of Niagara Falls. He was trying to win a prize of £12,000 in what was considered a suicidal feat.

The English Channel was not swum again until 1911 by Englishman T.W. Burgess.

The first woman to swim the English Channel was Olympic gold medallist Gertrude Ederle (1906–2003) of the USA in 1926.

Olympic Swimming

Although the Greeks did not include swimming in the ancient Olympics, it was included at Athens in 1896 in the first of the modern Olympics. Only four events were contested in 1896: the 100 metres, 500 metres and 1200 metres (all freestyle), and the 100 metres for serving sailors!

The first Olympic swimming gold medal was won by Alfred Hajos (born Arnold Guttmann) (1878–1955) of Hungary in the 100 metres freestyle in 1896. Hajos also played soccer for Hungary, and won the Hungarian 400 metres hurdles and discus championships.

CYCLING

The controlling body of world cycling is the Union Cycliste Internationale, based in Switzerland, which was founded in 1900.

Velocipede racing began in France in 1867. The velocipede was the forerunner of the bicycle.

The first race in England took place at Islington in 1869.

The Tour de France was first staged in 1903 allegedly by Henri Desgrange (1865–1940) as a publicity stunt to boost the circulation of *L'Auto*, a national newspaper. The idea came from a journalist on *L'Auto*, Geo Lefevre. The race was won that year by Maurice Garin (1871–1957) of France with a winning margin of 2 hours and 49 minutes, which remains the greatest winning margin in the history of the Tour de France.

In 1994, in an unparalleled act of *entente cordiale*, to mark the opening of the Channel Tunnel, part of the Tour de France took place in England.

MOTOR RACING

In 1887 in Paris, the newspaper *Le Velocipede* announced plans for the first motor car 'reliability trial'. Only one competitor showed up and the race was cancelled. A trial finally took place in 1894 with cars racing between Paris and Rouen. This time 21 competitors took part, and the trial was won by Le Comte Albert de Dion on a steam-driven tractor. The tractor travelled at an average speed of 11½ miles per hour, including a break for a spot of lunch.

The first motor race in the USA was won by Frank Duryea (1870–1967) over an 86-kilometre (54-mile) course in Chicago in 1895.

The first Grand Prix race was the French Grand Prix. The race took place in 1906 over 1,100 kilometres (686 miles) on a 100-kilometre (60-mile) road circuit, close to the town of Le Mans. The first winner was the Hungarian driver Ferenc Szisz (1873–1944), driving a Renault AK 90CV.

The world's first purpose-built, off-road race track was Brooklands at Weybridge in Surrey, which was completed in 1907.

The Monte Carlo Rally first took place in 1911. It was won by H. Rougier in a Turgat-Mery (*see also* Transport p. 273).

BASKETBALL

Uniquely among major sports, basketball has not evolved and developed out of a group activity with long historical roots, but was thought of by a single person, acting alone.

In the winter of 1891, Dr James Naismith (1861–1939), having been appointed athletic director at the YMCA Training School in Springfield, Massachusetts, was faced with the problem of finding a sport to play indoors during the cold winter months of this northern town. He wanted the sport to require skills, mobility and ingenuity, rather than merely to be a test of strength.

Naismith set out to create a game that could be played on a small sports area, and within 14 days had managed to devise a set of rules governing what would become basketball.

The first basketball games took place in late 1891 and were played with a soccer ball. The baskets, which were provided by the school janitor, were peach baskets with closed ends. This meant that play had to stop for the ball to be recovered from the basket by hand, after every goal.

Basketball's popularity spread rapidly through the YMCA movement in many nations, and was introduced into the Olympic programme of 1936.

The National Basketball Association (NBA) was formed in 1946, originally as the Basketball Association of America (BAA). The name was changed in 1949 after teams from the National Basketball League (NBL) joined it.

BASEBALL

In 1744, the English author and book publisher John Newbery (1713–67) produced *A Pretty Little Pocket Book*, in which he referred to a game he called 'base-ball'. As in modern baseball, a pitcher had to throw a ball to a batter, who tried to hit it. To score a 'run' the batter had to run to a base and return. The book was reprinted in the USA in 1762.

The traditional story of the origin of baseball is that in 1839 Civil War General Abner Doubleday (1819–93) formulated the first set of rules for what he called 'town ball' in Cooperstown, New York. Although this story is generally accepted within baseball, it is unlikely to be true. Baseball is thought more likely to have developed out of the English game of rounders, which itself developed out of earlier English games such as 'stool ball'.

Doubleday's nickname in the US Army was 'forty-eight hours' (a 'double day'). He is noted for firing the first cannon shot in defence of Fort Sumter in the Civil War. After the Civil War had ended, Doubleday bought the company that still operates the cable cars in San Francisco.

The American Civil War of 1861–65 witnessed the rapid growth in popularity of baseball among the serving troops, and within ten years of the end of hostilities, professional players began to emerge. The National Association of Professional Base Ball Players was formed in 1871.

The original five members of the Hall of Fame of Baseball elected in 1935 were Walter Johnson, Christy Matthewson, Babe Ruth, Honus Wagner, and Ty Cobb.

DARTS

Played mainly in the public bars of English public houses, darts is another sport with an uncertain origin.

One theory is that soldiers passed time by throwing shortened arrows at the bottom of upturned wine casks. This speculation has some merit, as it is known that English archers used a form of darts as a training aid during the Middle Ages, and that later Henry VIII (1491–1547) played darts. The numbering of the board in its current layout was devised in 1896 by Brian Gamlin.

The National Darts Association was founded in 1953.

ARCHERY

Recreational archery was practised by the ancient Egyptians, although there is no record of any competitions. The ancient Greeks also used archery as a form of recreation.

The earliest book on archery was *Taxophilus:The Schole of Shooting*, which was written by Roger Ascham and published in 1545.

The first recorded archery competition took place in 1583 in England, and archery has been an Olympic event since 1900. The modern sport of archery developed out of the military practice of shooting at targets to sharpen the archers' skills.

SNOOKER

It is thought that snooker may have been invented in 1875, in the English officers' mess at Jubbulpore in India, by Colonel Sir Neville Chamberlain. Chamberlain developed snooker out of the earlier game of billiards, using variously coloured balls, rather than the red and white of billiards.

The first professional World Champion was Joe Davis (1901–78), who won £6 10s in the first event in 1927. Davis went on to win a record 15 times. Snooker was seen as a dying sport until its fortunes were revived by television.

BOG SNORKELLING

The first World Bog Snorkelling Championship was held in 1985, in Llanwrtyd Wells, Wales. Competitors have to swim two lengths of a 60-metre (200-feet) course cut through a peat bog, but are not allowed to use conventional swimming strokes. Flippers and snorkels are compulsory, but wet suits are optional.

Transport

Covering: Water, Air, Rail, Road (Ancient), Road (Modern), Automobiles, Miscellaneous.

Water

Boats and Ships

The first to master the use of boats were the ancient Egyptians. Egyptian rock drawings dated 6000 BC show canoes, dugouts and rafts. These were propelled by manpower and steered by a spare oar mounted on the side of the boat.

The first sails Historians have speculated that the first sails were fashioned out of animal skins, and fixed to rafts to harness the power of the wind for propulsion. The earliest evidence of cloth sails being used comes from Egyptian paintings from 3300 BC.

The stern-mounted rudder There is a depiction of a stern-mounted rudder on a first century AD pottery model of a Chinese junk, which is now in the Kuangchow National Museum.

It was developed independently, with better technology, in the West and is depicted on church carvings of AD 1180. In 1252 the Port Book of Damme in Flanders records ships with stern-mounted, as opposed to side-mounted, rudders.

The first steamboat was successfully trialled in 1787 by American clock-maker John Fitch (1743–98).

The first Mississippi paddle-wheel steamboats were used in 1811.

The first cruise ship was the *El Horria*, weighing 3,762 tonnes, 146 metres (478 feet) long and 13 metres (43 feet) wide, which was launched in 1865.

It is now berthed in Alexandria, Egypt, renamed the SS *Mahroussa*, and used as a state school ship.

The first oil tanker was the *Zoroastra*, owned by Robert Nobel (1829–1926) (the oldest of the Swedish Nobel brothers). The *Zoroastra* was launched on the Caspian Sea in the late 1870s, at the end of an eight-mile long pipeline from the oil port of Baku. However, the 90-metre-long (300-feet) German ship *Gluckauf*, launched in 1886, is often quoted as the first specially designed oil tanker. The *Gluckhauf* ran aground close to New York in 1893, and can still be seen.

Canals

The first major canal was the Great Canal of China, which was begun in the fifth century BC but not completed until AD 1290. It remains in use today.

In 600 BC the Egyptian Pharaoh, Necho II, authorised a canal to be built to connect the Red Sea with the Nile – this was the forerunner of the Suez Canal. Construction was completed by King Darius of Persia between 549 and 486 BC.

The first great Roman canal and aqueduct was the Aqua Appia, built in 312 BC. The canal, which mainly ran underground, was named in honour of the Roman censor Appius Claudius Caecus (340–273 BC). The Appian Way, the great Roman road stretching from Rome to Naples in the west and Brindisi in the east, was also named after Appius Caecus.

The most significant improvement in canal technology was the lock, which was developed in the Netherlands around 1373.

The first canal built in the UK was the ten-mile-long (16 kilometres) Bridgewater Canal, started in 1759 and opened for navigation between Manchester and Worsley in 1761. It was funded by Francis Egerton, 3rd Earl of Bridgewater (1736–1803) to transport coal from his mines at Worsley, and built by James Brindley (1716–72). As a result, the price of coal in Manchester was halved.

Sankey Brook Navigation, which ran from the river Mersey to St Helens was completed in 1757, earlier than the Bridgewater, but part of its length was along an existing waterway.

The first canal in the USA was 22-mile-long Santee Canal built in 1800 in South Carolina, to connect the Santee and Cooper Rivers. After severe droughts in 1817 and 1819, the canal dried up and the bed was planted with corn to take advantage of the fertile soil there. The Santee Canal fell into disuse shortly after the arrival of the railway in 1846.

The Grand Canal in Venice is not strictly speaking a canal, as it was not dug out or cut. It is in fact a seawater channel running between several islands. The shape of the waterway has been determined by the construction of the buildings on the water's edge.

AIR

Balloons

Hot air lifted the first balloons into the sky and modern-day balloons are no different except that the gas-burning equipment they use to heat the air is more sophisticated. Up until the 1930s, when they went out of fashion, airships, or dirigibles, used either hydrogen, which proved to be too dangerous or helium, which was too expensive and impractical.

The first successful attempt by humans to fly was in balloons, notwithstanding the Greek legend of Icarus and tales of other ancient figures who attempted to fly using artificial wings and hang gliders.

Bartolomeu Lourenco de Gusmao (1685–1779), a Brazilian priest, conducted numerous experiments with hot-air ballooning as early as 1709. De Gusmao's third attempt to construct a working balloon succeeded, but no one was on board.

The first balloon to take a man aloft was designed and built by the French Montgolfier brothers, Joseph (1740–1810) and Etienne (1745–99). The lifting medium was hot air, which was generated by burning straw and dry wool.

The first controlled flight was on 20 November 1783 in a Montgolfier hot-air balloon. The physicist Jean-Francois Pilatre de Rozier (1754–85) and the Marquis d'Arlandes spent a leisurely 23 minutes flying over the rooftops of Paris. The event was witnessed by Marie Antoinette (1755–93).

Previously the Montgolfiers had experimented by sending up a selection of animals, including ducks, sheep and hens, before finally allowing men to fly.

Aircraft

According to the ancient Greek myth, Icarus, who lived around 1400 BC, attempted to fly using a pair of wings made for him by his father. The wings were built out of feathers and wax, and in the story, Icarus is supposed to have flown too close to the sun, so the wax in the wings melted, and Icarus fell into the sea and drowned. The Icarian Sea is named in his memory. The accident occurred as Icarus was trying to escape, with his father Daedalus, from imprisonment by the mythical King Minos of Crete. In the legend, Daedalus survived the flight.

The legend of Icarus inspired Brother Elmer, a monk living at Malmesbury Abbey in Wiltshire, to try his luck at the same thing. Around AD 1010, according to recent discoveries by historians, Elmer built a form of paraglider, from a willow or ash frame, with linen or parchment stretched over it. According to the historian William of Malmesbury, writing in the following century, Elmer launched himself from a height of about 18 metres (60 feet), the height of a church, and glided 200 metres (660 feet) until he panicked, crashed and broke both legs.

Brother Elmer survived and wanted to modify his 'aircraft' to try again, but the abbot forbade further flying experiments. Nevertheless Elmer has an authentic claim to be the first person to have flown.

The basic scientific principles of flight were laid down in the early years of the nineteenth century by the barrister and mathematician Sir George Cayley (1821–95).

The first man to fly in a machine that was heavier than air was the German inventor Otto Lilienthal (1848–96). Lilienthal built workable gliders and flew more than 2,000 hours, sometimes with passengers, before crashing and dying near Berlin in 1896. He also experimented with flying models, which had flapping wings, in an attempt to be the first to achieve powered flight.

In 1896, Samuel Langley (1834–1906) built a pilot-less, steam-driven, heavier than air flying machine, codenamed Aerodrome 5. The machine flew over 914 metres (3,000 feet) across the Potomac River in a flight lasting 90 seconds and landed safely at the village of Quantico, Virginia, USA. Langley continued his quest for manned flight for the next five years, but with money and patience running out, decided to quit on 8 December 1903, just nine days before manned flight became a reality.

The first controlled powered flight in a heavier than air machine was achieved by the Wright brothers, Orville (1871–1948) and Wilbur (1867–1912) at Kitty Hawk in North Carolina on 17 December 1903. The brothers tossed a coin to see who would go first. Orville guessed wrong, and Wilbur made history. The flight lasted just 12 seconds, but it led to the Wright brothers building the world's first usable aeroplane in 1905.

It is generally thought that the Wrights' first aircraft was named *Kitty Hawk*, but at the time of its inaugural flight it was called *Flyer I* and was later renamed *Kitty Hawk*. The Wright brothers built their first aircraft (unpowered) of any sort, a biplane kite, in 1899. The kite was followed by gliders in 1901, 1902 and 1903.

Jet Aircraft

The first jet aircraft to fly was the Heinkel He178, which first flew on 27 August 1939 in Germany with Flight Captain Erich Warsitz (d. 1983) at the controls. It was powered by an He S3B jet engine, which had been designed by Hans von Ohain (1911–98) and patented in 1934. The aircraft reached a speed of 400 miles an hour.

On 20 June 1939 Warsitz had piloted the first rocket-powered aircraft, the He176.

The first British jet aircraft was the Gloster E29/39, which flew for the first time on 15 May 1941, piloted by Flight Lieutenant P.E.G. Sayer. The aircraft was powered by a Whittle engine produced by Power Jets Limited. The designer, Frank (later Sir Frank) Whittle (1907–96) had patented his original concept in 1930, but struggled to achieve official recognition of its value.

Whittle and von Ohain are recognised as co-inventors of the jet engine, and met for the first time in 1978.

The first US jet aircraft was the Bell XP-59A *Airacomet*, which first flew on 1 October 1942. The performance was a great disappointment as it was only able to reach a speed of 380 miles an hour. The engine was produced by General Electric of the USA and the aircraft designer was Lawrence Bell (1894–1956), after whom it was named.

The first jet-powered aircraft launched from a ship was the British De Havilland Vampire T11 in 1949, which also became the first jet to cross the Atlantic.

Helicopters

It is generally thought that Leonardo da Vinci (1452–1519) was the first man to design and think of creating a flying machine that could take off vertically. Leonardo had the vision that vertical take-off could be achieved by means of a type of propeller, or air-screw, mounted on the top of the machine. Leonardo's drawing, which is dated 1483, depicts a helicopter-like machine and now resides in the Bibliothèque de l'Institut de France in Paris.

However, around 400 BC the ancient Chinese had already made feathered toys which behaved like helicopters. The Chinese helicopters predated Leonardo by nearly 2,000 years.

French bicycle maker Paul Cornu (1881–1944) built a twin-rotor helicopter in 1907, a mere four years after the Wright brothers' first powered flight. Cornu's helicopter made its inaugural, manned, but all too brief flight of 20 seconds, reaching a height of 30 centimetres (12 inches) on 13

November 1907. After a few more flights without making significant progress, Cornu abandoned the project.

In 1923, the Spanish aeronautical engineer, Juan de la Cierva (1895–1936) invented the autogyro, which was the predecessor of the modern helicopter. Autogyros have a forward propeller instead of a tail rotor, and a rotor on top, which supplements a pair of short wings. Cierva's autogyros were built in England by the Parnall Company.

The first effective demonstration of a helicopter under full control was in 1924 by Etienne Oehmichen (1884–1955) of France. He flew a heli-copter for 1 kilometre (½ mile) within a closed circuit. The flight lasted 7 minutes and 40 seconds.

The first practical helicopter was the German Focke-Wulf FW61 which made its inaugural flight in 1936.

The first recognisably modern helicopter was the VS300 developed by Igor Sikorsky (1889–1972). The prototype first flew in the USA in 1939. Sikorsky was born near Kiev in Ukraine but emigrated to the USA in 1919.

Hovercraft

Neither land vehicles as we know them, nor ships, nor even aircraft, hovercraft, which are also known as ground-effect or air cushion machines, are hybrid machines. They position themselves somewhere on the fringes of each, by taking off vertically and hovering in the air, but always within touching distance of land or water.

The first hovercraft was produced and patented in the UK by Sir John Thorneycroft in 1877, although it was unsuccessful in trials. Christopher (later Sir Christopher) Cockerell (1910–99) invented the modern hovercraft in 1956 and produced his first machine in 1959, naming it the SRN I. The air cushion was created by pulling air from above, using a powered fan. The air was prevented from escaping by a rubber skirt fitted around the outside edge of the machine. In his earliest experiments, Cockerell used an empty Kit-e-Kat tin inside a larger coffee tin and blew air into it with a hairdryer.

Ornithopter

Ornithopters use the same means of propulsion as birds – they flap their wings. Out of a sheep field in Munich, on 26 June 1942, Adalbert Schmid (1880-?) made the first successful motorised ornithopter flight.

Earlier attempts include a 1929 human-powered ornithopter, which had to be towed into the air. The aircraft had Dr Alexander Lippisch (1894–1976) of Germany at the controls. In 1870 there was a French ornithopter, which was powered by elastic bands, and a human-powered ornithopter in 1781, which is rumoured to have flown with Karl Friedrich Meirwein of Germany at the controls.

RAIL

Locomotives and Railroads

Steam

The first steam locomotive to undertake practical work was built in 1803 by the Cornish engineer Richard Trevithick (1771–1833). He attached a steam engine to a chassis and used it for haulage at the Pen-y-Darren Iron Works in Wales. Trevithick also began the tradition of naming the locomotive, which he called the *New Castle*. Unfortunately the engine was too heavy for the poor-quality rails, which regularly buckled and were constantly in need of repair.

The first fully practical steam locomotive for freight haulage was built in 1812 by Leeds mining engineer John Blenkinsop (1783–1831). Traction was provided through a toothed gearwheel that meshed with a rack rail alongside the running rails.

The first passenger steam locomotive was run by George Stephenson (1781–1848) in 1825. Called the *Locomotion* it travelled between Stockton

and Darlington, a distance of around 40 kilometres (25 miles.) In 1828 the boiler exploded, killing the driver.

Track Gauge

George Stephenson arbitrarily chose 4 feet 8 ½ inches for the Stockton & Darlington Railway. This became known as Standard Gauge and remains the uniform gauge for 64 per cent of the world's railways.

Electric

There had been experiments with trains powered by electric batteries as early as 1835, but they had proved impractical.

The first train to draw its motive power from a cable carrying electricity was demonstrated at an industrial show in Berlin in 1879. The engine had a three-horsepower electric motor and carried passengers along a 300-metre (330-yard) track. The locomotive was built by Werner von Siemens (1816–92), the leading German electrical pioneer.

The world's first trolley bus system was installed by Siemens along the Kurfurstendamm, the main thoroughfare of central Berlin in 1882. He called it the *Electromote*.

The first US rail company to electrify was the Baltimore and Ohio in 1895.

The world's first mainline electric trains began operating in Italy in 1902.

Diesel

It proved impossible to make gearboxes big enough for pure diesel trains. A better solution was to arrange a diesel motor to provide power to an electric generator, which would then drive the wheels. The first diesel-electric locomotives were introduced on German main-line services in 1932.

Diesel-electric trains were introduced in the USA for passenger services in 1935 and for freight in 1939.

Diesel-electric trains were introduced in the UK in 1955.

Air Driven (Atmospheric Railway)

In 1844, Isambard Kingdom Brunel (1806–1859) built a pneumatic (compressed air powered) railway for the South Devon Railway Company. The system consisted of two rails, exactly like other railways, but with a compressed air tube in between the rails, linked to the carriages. Compressed air was pumped in at one end, to propel the carriages forward.

The project was short-lived. The waxed leather which Brunel used to seal the tube had to be lubricated with whale oil in winter to prevent it freezing. This provided a tasty meal for rats, which ate the leather causing continuous air leakages and consequent loss of pressure. Without an alternative means of sealing the tube, the system failed.

Magnetic Levitation (MAGLEV)

MAGLEV trains are electrically powered and when in motion they float approximately 10 millimetres (⅓ inch) above the rail, thus avoiding the need for wheels. Friction is cut down, allowing far higher speeds.

Working together in 1900, American scientist Robert Goddard (1882–1945), known worldwide as the father of rocketry (*see also* Space p. 235), together with the French-born but naturalised American Emile Bachelet (1863–1946), came up with the concept of the 'frictionless railway', by utilising the power of electro-magnetic suspension.

The world's first MAGLEV train began operating in the UK in 1983 as a shuttle between the new terminal at Birmingham Airport and the equally new Birmingham International railway station. The system proved unreliable and needed permanent standby road transport to cater for the continuous breakdowns. It was replaced after a few years with a more conventional monorail link.

US Transcontinental Railroad

On 10 May 1869, at Gold Creek, Montana, USA, the world's first transcontinental railroad was completed. The tracks ran from Omaha to Sacramento, covering 2,825 kilometres (1,756 miles) and were laid in six years. Strictly speaking 'transcontinental' means crossing a continent. No one railway company has ever controlled a route from one coast to the other in the USA, but the route from the Midwest to the Pacific has always been regarded as a 'transcontinental'.

At the narrowest point of the continent of the Americas, in the Isthmus of Panama, the Panama Railway was completed in 1855 after five years' construction work. At only 77 kilometres (48 miles) long, it ran from Atlantic to Pacific Oceans.

Monorail

The first monorail railway was opened in 1957 within UENO Zoo in Tokyo. There were only two stations, one at each end of the track, which ran a length of 0.3 kilometres. The train ran on rubber tyres, and carried a million passengers in its first year.

ROAD (ANCIENT)

Primitive man adopted previously formed animal tracks into roads to help him trade with others. The first evidence of these pathways has been found near Jericho, and they have been dated at around 6000 BC.

The earliest stone road, dated at 4000 BC, has been unearthed near Ur in modern Iraq.

The earliest known timber road was discovered preserved in a swamp near Glastonbury, England. Experts think could be from before 2000 BC.

The first modern roads as we know them were built by the Romans. The first major Roman road was the *Via Appia* (Appian Way). Started in 312 BC by Appius Claudius Claecus (*c.*340–273 BC), the *Via Appia* stretched for more than 600 kilometres (373 miles) across what is now Italy, connecting Rome to Naples on the west coast and Brindisi on the east.

Roman roads in Britain were begun immediately after the conquest in AD 43. Most were built in straight lines, although even Roman engineers had to deviate for major obstacles.

The first toll road in England was built in 1267. Tollgates were introduced in 1663 but abolished in 1893.

The first one-way street in London was introduced in 1617 to regulate the 'disorder and rude behaviour of carmen, draymen and others' using carts. Seventeen alleys around Thames Street and Pudding Lane were made into one-way streets. No more one-way streets were created in London until the system was introduced in Albemarle Street in 1800.

The first one-way street outside London was not created until the age of the motor car in 1923 in Birmingham. It lasted only two weeks due to local objections. It fell to Nottingham in 1924 to have the first permanent one-way street outside London.

The first people to use tar (or asphalt) as a road-surfacing material were the ancient Babylonians in 625 BC.

Modern tarred roads – roads with a surface of asphalt – began with the surfacing of the Champs-Elysee in Paris in 1824 with natural asphalt blocks.

Edward de Smedt, a Belgian engineer working in New York, developed the high-density processed asphalt we see on today's roads. The first trial sheet was laid on William Street, Newark, New Jersey, in 1870, but the first full use of de Smedt's asphalt was in Battery Park and on Fifth Avenue in New York in 1872.

Horse

The horse was first domesticated around 4000 BC and was used as a means of pulling carts from 1500 BC. Men did not master the art of riding horses until 1000 BC. After that, the horse remained the principal means of passenger and freight road transport until well into the twentieth century.

Stirrups were invented in western China in AD 375.

Wheel

The earliest evidence of a wheel being used as part of a vehicle is in a Sumerian pictograph dated 3500 BC, which shows a sledge on wheels. The wheels were made from shaped planks of wood to create a disc. It is thought that the original idea must have come from the use of logs as rollers.

The spoked wheel appeared in 2000 BC first fixed to chariots.

Carts

In use in Sumeria in 3500 BC, carts were an extension of the newly invented wheel, and normally drawn either by a single ox, or sometimes by a man. The horse was not combined with the cart until around 1500 BC.

Chariots

In 3000 BC the Sumerians of Mesopotamia invented chariots, and used them originally for funeral processions, but later for racing and hunting. The earliest versions were pulled by oxen, which made them too slow and cumbersome. Later models used horses.

Later, chariots were used in warfare, although it is doubtful they were actually used as fighting vehicles, more as transport. A war chariot was normally manned by a charioteer, who drove, and a spearman, who had to jump off the chariot to use his spear once the chariot had arrived close enough to the action.

Egyptians were using chariots by 1435 BC and within another 100 years the use of chariots had spread to southern Europe and Crete.

In pre-Roman times, the Celts had improved the fixed-axle design by developing the pivoting front axle to make turning easier. They had also designed an advanced form of harness for the horses, which made control of the chariot much easier.

In the nineteenth century, in both England and the USA, the word 'chariot' was used to describe a form of two-wheeled, horse-drawn carriage, which had been created by cutting off the front half of a four-wheeler.

Charabanc

The charabanc (literally, a wagon with benches) originated in nineteenth-century France. The word charabanc was adopted in twentieth-century

England to refer to a motor coach. Typically charabanc was shortened, in the vernacular, to 'sharra'.

Road (Modern)

Tyres (US: Tires)

In 1839, Charles Goodyear (1800–1860), a bankrupt American metal engineer, invented the vulcanisation of rubber, which is the chemical combination of rubber with sulphur at high temperatures. After processing, the rubber shows greatly improved tensile strength and resistance to abrasion and swelling. The vulcanisation process was essential for the development of the modern tyres that needed to sustain the high mileage and high speeds of motor cars.

The first pneumatic (air-filled) tyre was developed and patented by Robert Thomson (1822–73) of Scotland in 1845. The tyre was made of leather. Thomson called it the 'aerial wheel' and fitted it to a brougham. (A lightweight two-wheeled horse-drawn carriage, with no roof over the driver, named after the designer Lord Brougham, and is pronounced 'broom'.) Thomson's pneumatic leather tyres ran for more than 1,610 kilometres (1,000 miles) with no problems, but his solid rubber tyres proved more popular.

The use of air-filled tyres was abandoned for 41 years until February 1886, when John Boyd Dunlop (1840–1921), a Belfast veterinary surgeon, completed his development of an improved pneumatic tyre made from rubber. Effectively, Dunlop had reinvented the pneumatic tyre.

Dunlop had a keen interest in matters of safety and comfort, particularly where his son was concerned. He feared that bumping along on the hard roads on solid tyres would render his son sterile, and so began a series of experiments that would result in the pneumatic rubber tyre.

Dunlop patented the pneumatic tyre for use on bicycles in 1888, after a legal battle against Thomson's successor in title to the patent. The Dunlop Rubber Company became a massive worldwide business, with the Dunlop patent at its heart.

The first use of pneumatic tyres on motor cars was by Michelin & Cie of France in 1896. The car was produced by Peugeot and named *L'éclair*.

AUTOMOBILES

The original automobile was a *fardier à vapeur* (a steam-driven vehicle) built in Paris by Nicolas-Joseph Cugnot (1725–1804) in 1769. He was also the first person ever involved in an automobile accident when he crashed a later model into a brick wall in 1771.

Motor Cars and Internal Combustion Engines

The motor car could be called the most exciting, and at the same time most useful product in history. The car has liberated millions, who could previously travel only by horse or rail, and it has become a status symbol displaying, to a large extent, the owner's personality.

Over the last century, the production and ownership of cars has helped to catapult the world's economy to a previously unimaginable size. The continually increasing need for private and business motor transport has stimulated the demand for ever-greater quantities of steel, rubber, plastic, chemicals and glass. There have been matching increases in demand for oil, both as a fuel and a lubricant, and also for the finance to support the expanded demand. An array of support services has grown to match the growth of the oil, motor and finance industries.

The rapid expansion of cities in the twentieth century has at least partly resulted from the increased use of motor cars, as people have migrated out to commuter distance from their places of work. This increased traffic has led, despite the perennial complaints, to improved roads.

Although mechanically propelled vehicles, principally to be driven by steam power, were described by ancient Chinese writers, the motor car as we know it (a vehicle with an internal combustion engine) was not developed until the late nineteenth century.

The earliest experiments with internal combustion engines were carried out in 1680 by Christiaan Huygens (1629–93), a Dutch physicist and astronomer. Huygens also discovered Titan, one of Saturn's moons.

The theory of the two-stroke internal combustion engine was developed in 1824, by French mathemetician Sadi Carnot (1796–1832). As Carnot died in an outbreak of cholera, no practical work was done.

The first successful internal combustion engine capable of operating continuously was developed in 1860 by Jean-Joseph Etienne Lenoir (1822–1900) of France. The fuel Lenoir used was coal gas and he used his engine to power a boat he had built (*see also* Questionable Origins p. 205, Samuel Morey 1826 patent).

The world's first gas engine factory was set up in 1864 by Nicolaus August Otto (1832–91) and Eugene Langen (1833–95), a wealthy sugar producer. In 1867 they exhibited their prototype engine at the World Exposition in Paris winning a gold medal. They produced the first four-stroke internal combustion engine in 1876. Otto was never involved in the motor industry, as his engine was destined only for use in factories, but the foundations he laid led to the development of the four-stroke motor-car engine.

The first two-stroke petrol engine was developed in 1878 by Sir Dugald Clerk (1854–1932). He patented it in 1881.

A three-wheeled single cylinder motor car was created in 1885 by Karl Benz (1844–1929). He sold it to a French manufacturer in 1887.

The world's first motorbike was built in 1885 by Gottlieb Daimler (1834–1900).

The first four-wheeled motor vehicle was produced in 1886 by Daimler, working with Wilhelm Maybach (1846–1929), his design partner. The vehicle was actually a modified carriage powered by a four-stroke engine.

The first rotary engine was developed in 1924 by Felix Wankel (1902–1988) and the Wankel rotary engine was awarded a patent in 1929. All

previous engines had used pistons rather than a rotor. Nowadays, the Wankel engine is used mainly by the Japanese car company Mazda. Wankel could not drive and was never issued with a driving licence.

Diesel and Diesel Engines

Rudolf Diesel (1858–1913) invented the diesel engine in 1893 and patented it in 1898. The idea behind the diesel engine is that fuel is ignited, not by sparking, but by compression, thereby eliminating the need for an ignition system. The first diesel engine had a 3-metre-long (10-feet) cylinder and was used to pump water.

Diesel was a believer in social engineering. He had a strong ethical desire to improve the lot of the common man and combat the negative effects of major commercial interests. In the case of his newly designed engines, Diesel felt they could be built by average engineers, which would give them a chance to compete with big business.

The Automatic Gearbox

Lazlo Biro (1899–1985) invented the automatic gearbox. Biro sold the rights to the gearbox to General Motors in 1924 for US$200 per month for four years, plus a share of the income of every gearbox produced. The drawings were buried at the bottom of a filing drawer until Biro's deal had expired and no fees were ever paid (*see also* Person to Person p. 35).

Some Great Marques

Britain

Rolls-Royce In 1904 the Hon. Charles Stewart Rolls (1877–1910) and Henry Royce (1863–1933) formed a company for the production of motor cars. In 1906 they launched their first car, the legendary Silver Ghost. The aim that Rolls and Royce had set themselves was to produce the very best car possible, and their advertising line, with very un-British lack of modesty, was 'The Best Car in the World'. Despite dozens of different designs and many changes of ownership, the Rolls-Royce reputation remains secure to this day.

The Hon. Charles Rolls was issued with British Flying Licence number 2 in 1910 and became the first man to fly non-stop across the English

Channel both ways. He was killed when his aircraft broke up in mid-air later that year, falling to the ground from only 6 metres (20 feet). On the death of Henry Royce, the 'RR' lettering on the Rolls-Royce badge was changed permanently from red to black.

Bentley In 1919, the brothers W.O. and H.M. Bentley produced their first car, which was fitted with a three-litre engine. The 12 glory years of Bentley coincided with the Roaring Twenties and were filled with a whirl of racing successes and financial problems. The car and the era went together, with the Bentley marque being at the heart of the lifestyle of the young bloods of England.

In the 1927 Le Mans 24-hour race, all three Bentleys were involved in one of the strangest accidents in motorracing history. Two were damaged so much that they could not finish, and the third although badly damaged managed to carry on and win. At the victory celebration dinner at the Savoy Hotel in London, the car was brought into the dining room, in its fully battered state, as the guest of honour.

In 1931, the assets of the Bentley company were acquired by Rolls-Royce. After that, Bentley cars came to be seen as more sporting versions of various Rolls-Royce models, an early version of badge engineering.

Aston Martin Cornishman Lionel Martin (1878–1945) and Robert Bamford, the founders of Aston Martin, formed their first company Bamford & Martin Limited in 1913 to sell Singer cars.

Lionel Martin, who was a renowned hill climb specialist, won the Aston hill climb in a modified Singer car. The Aston hill climb was a nationally publicised race, which took place every year at Aston Clinton in Buckinghamshire. With this success behind them, Martin and Bamford decided to build their own car, and the first Aston Martin car was registered in 1915. It was named Coal Scuttle.

The second car was not built until 1920, and the company was forced to call in the receivers in 1925. After that, the company had a series of different owners, until it finally became part of the Ford Motor Company in 1994.

Jaguar William Walmsley (b. 1891) founded the Swallow Sidecar Company in 1921 to produce sidecars for motorcycles. He was joined in 1922 by

William (later Sir William) Lyons (1901–85). Walmsley retired in 1928 and Lyons decided to enter the motor industry. Swallow's first motor car, the SS1, was produced in 1932, and the company changed its name to SS Cars.

After the Second World War, when the SS emblem proved too reminiscent of the Nazi shock troops of the same name, the company again changed its name, this time to Jaguar. The incomparable E-Type Jaguar was launched in 1961 and Jaguar Cars was acquired by Ford in 1989–90.

Lotus Cars was set up by Colin Chapman (1928–82) in Hornsea, East Anglia, in 1952. The company entered Formula 1 racing in 1958 and won the Constructors World Championship in 1963, with Jim Clark (1936–68) at the wheel. Clark died in a Lotus car when a tyre failed on a bend.

Morgan The Morgan Motor Company was set up in 1910 by H.F.S. Morgan, and remains in the hands of the Morgan family. Morgan is famous for its earliest cars, which were three-wheelers. Restricting the number of wheels to three meant that the cars avoided punitive car tax, as they were classed as 'cyclecars'.

The company's most compelling advantage over other marques in the same class is that they can truly claim to be handmade.

Vauxhall The company began life in 1857 as the Vauxhall Iron Works, producing pumps. The first car, a five-horsepower model with a tiller for steering, was produced in 1903. The company's name was changed to Vauxhall Motors in 1907 and it was bought by General Motors of the USA in 1925.

The Land Rover was launched by the Rover Car Company at the Amsterdam Motor Show in 1948, as the British version of the US-made Jeep. Maurice Wilks, the designer, built the prototype Land Rover on a Jeep chassis. Jeep is short for GP, the US Army's abbreviation for general-purpose vehicle.

The Austin Seven was the brainchild of Herbert Austin. It was unveiled in 1922 and continued in production until 1939. It was the most famous car produced by the Austin Motor Company, which was formed in 1905 by Herbert (later Lord) Austin (1866–1941). The board of the Austin Motor Company (always known to its workforce as 'The Austin') would not agree to finance development, so Austin paid for the whole thing from his own pocket.

Morris Motors was founded in Oxford in 1912 by bicycle maker William Morris (later Lord Nuffield) (1877–1963), with the financial backing of the Earl of Macclesfield. The first Morris car, the famous Bullnose, was produced in 1913, unfortunately too late for the Motor Show of that year. Undeterred by the fact that his car was not yet on the production line, Morris took drawings to the show and walked away with orders for 400 cars.

The Morris Minor was developed in secret during 1946 and 1947 in an isolated corner of the Morris factory without the full knowledge of the company's owner Lord Nuffield. The car was unveiled at the London Motor Show in 1948, but not before Nuffield had scathingly said it looked like 'a poached egg'. The Morris Minor remained in production until 1971, selling well over 1,000,000 vehicles.

The Mini The pioneering car with a transverse engine and front-wheel drive was launched by the British Motor Corporation in 1959. It became the best-selling car in Europe, winner of the Monte Carlo Rally in 1964, 1965 and 1967, and remained in production until 2000.

The Mini was the great design triumph of Alec (later Sir Alec) Issigonis (1906–88). Issigonis, a naturalised British subject, was born in Smyrna, which at the time was a Greek port, but now known as Izmir in Turkey. He was famously dismissive of comfort and luxury in cars, feeling that comfortable seats and radios were unnecessary.

Italy

Ferrari In 1920, Enzo Ferrari (1898–1988) began his career driving racing cars for Alpha Romeo. In 1929, when Alpha Romeo dropped racing to concentrate on commercial car production, he took over the racing team and renamed it Ferrari.

Ferrari's first road cars were built in 1947. The Ferrari prancing horse motif, that has become such a potent symbol of powerful and exciting cars the world over, was donated to Enzo by Countess Paolina Biancoli.

Maserati In 1907 the seven Maserati brothers started building racing cars, and built their first production car in 1922.

FIAT stands for Societa Anonima Fabbrica Italiana di Automobili Torino (Turin Automobile Manufacturing Company.) The company was formed in 1899, and among its founder members was Giovanni Agnelli (1866–1945), whose family remains in charge to this day.

FIAT's first factory was opened in 1900, and the first car, the three and a half horsepower Torino, was launched in 1902. In 1979, FIAT acquired control of Ferrari, together with Lancia. Alfa Romeo was added to the list of FIAT brands in 1985 and Maserati in 1993.

Bugatti Ettore Bugatti (1882–1947) began designing cars in 1899. He set up on his own in Strasbourg, launching his first car, the 1300 c.c. 'Type 13' in 1907. The Bugatti Bebe of 1920 was produced in France by Peugeot to a Bugatti design.

After the great racing successes of Bugatti cars in the 1930s the brand failed after the outbreak of the Second World War. Volkswagen of Germany now owns the name and has resurrected the brand with the Veyron 16.4, which is rumoured to have a top speed of 253 miles per hour. The Veyron is not only the world's fastest production car, but costs an eye-watering US$1,200,000.

Sweden

SAAB was formed in 1937 as Svenska Aeroplan Aktibolaget, a manufacturer of high-performance aircraft. The first SAAB car, the 92, which was produced in 1949, had a two-stroke, two-cylinder engine, producing only 25 horse power. Of the 16 engineers who built the first SAAB car, only one had a driving licence.

Volvo began as a spin-off from the SKF ball-bearing company. Indeed, the brand name Volvo (Latin for 'I roll') was originally supposed to be for a new ball-bearing product. The company produced its first car in 1927. Ford Motor Company acquired Volvo in 1998–9.

USA

Ford On Christmas Eve 1893, Henry Ford I (1863–1947), at the age of 30, fired up his first self-made engine. It was sitting on the draining board in the kitchen of the lodgings he had taken in Detroit. With his wife Clara dripping gasoline into the fuel intake and the spark for the sparkplug being generated from the household electricity supply, Ford's engine ran after the second attempt, and the seeds of the Ford Motor Company had been sown. In its heyday during the 1920s to 1970s, Ford would become the world's second largest motor manufacturer.

In June 1896, Ford's first vehicle, a quadricycle with a domestic door-bell in place of a horn, was completed. Henry sold it in 1898.

I will build a motor car for the great multitude. It will be so low in price that no man making a good salary will be unable to own one – and enjoy with his family the blessing of hours of pleasure in God's great open spaces.
Henry Ford

In 1908, the Ford Motor Company announced the launch of the famous Model T. Two years later, more than 18,000 were produced in the year, and in 1911 the figure increased to 78,000. By the time it went out of production in May 1927, almost 16,000,000 Model Ts had been produced world-wide. It remained the world's biggest-selling motor car until it was overtaken in 1972 by the Volkswagen Beetle.

What's good for General Motors is good for America.
Charles Wilson (CEO of General Motors)

General Motors was incorporated in 1908 by William C. (Billy) Durant (1861–1947) previously a horse-drawn carriage maker and an inveterate gambler. In a series of breathtakingly quick acquisitions, Durant merged Oldsmobile, Buick and Cadillac together with dozens of other lesser car brands, and added Champion Spark Plugs to form what was to become the world's largest business.

Durant lost and won back control of General Motors, only to lose it again. He was hit hard in the 1929 Stock Exchange crash and filed for bankruptcy in 1936. In 1940 he opened a bowling alley in Flint, Michigan.

Oldsmobile was set up as the first car factory in the USA in 1899 by Ransom E. Olds (1864–1950) an accountant from Michigan, although he had produced his first handmade car in 1897. Their Curved Dash brand became the USA's first mass-produced car in 1901. Engines were supplied by Dodge Bros, who would go on to produce their own range of vehicles. In 1940, the Oldsmobile became the first car to be fitted with automatic transmission. The last car produced under the Oldsmobile brand left the factory in 2004 after a history of over 100 years, with more than 35,000,000 vehicles produced.

Buick The first car was built under the Buick label in 1900–01. David Buick (1854–1929) had begun building gasoline engines in 1899 and by 1908 the Buick brand had overtaken Ford and Cadillac to become the largest producer of cars in the USA. Buick employed Louis Chevrolet as a driver for his racing team.

The Cadillac Motor Car Company was formed from the remnants of the Henry Ford Company, which Ford had left to start the Ford Motor Company in 1902. A new name was required, and the new owners chose Cadillac after the French explorer who had founded Detroit in the eighteenth century. The first Cadillac car was revealed at the New York Auto Show in 1902, where it took 2,000 firm orders.

Chrysler Walter P. Chrysler (1875–1940), who had been works manager for Buick, bought the Maxwell Motor Co. in 1923 and renamed it the Chrysler Corporation in 1925. The first Chrysler car, which could achieve 70 miles per hour, sold 43,000 units in 1925 at a price of US$1,645.

Chrysler, which had built a reputation for advanced features, was the first company to offer a car with headlamps included in the price, and in 1939, the first with a steering-column gear change. The world's first gas turbine road car was revealed by Chrysler in 1951, but only 50 were produced.

In 1998 Chrysler merged with Daimler to create the world's second largest automobile maker.

Germany

Volkswagen Dr Ferdinand Porsche (1875–1951), who had worked for both Auto-Union and Daimler, managed to make the concept of a 'people's car for Europe' a reality in 1934.

In 1932, Adolf Hitler (1889–1945) produced a sketch and broad specifications (two adults plus three children at 62 miles per hour), from which Porsche produced his final 1934 design and prototypes. The Nazi party named the new car the Volkswagen and promised to mass-produce it for the German workers.

The car remained in full production until the 1980s, and became known worldwide as the VW Beetle, although its official title was Type 1. In 1972 the Beetle overtook the Ford Model T as the highest-selling car of all time when car number 15,007,034 left the production line.

An unsung British hero of the revival of Volkswagen after the Second World War is Major Ivan Hirst (1916–2000) who, after being ordered to take control of the bombed-out Volkswagen factory, persuaded the British military to order 20,000 cars. By 1946, 1,000 cars per month were being delivered.

Porsche In 1949, the first car to be sold under the Porsche brand was launched as the 356, being the 356th design to come off the drawing board.

Mercedes Karl Benz (1844–1929) launched the Benz Patent Motor Car in 1886. Benz's new car was the first attempt by any manufacturer to produce a new design concept, rather than merely converting a horse-drawn carriage by adding an engine.

In 1899, Emil Jellinek (1853–1918), a major customer of Benz, entered a Benz Phoenix racing car in a race meeting in Nice. The team named itself Mercedes, after Jellinek's favourite daughter, and the name stuck. The first car produced under the Mercedes brand was a 35 horse power racing car, which was manufactured in 1901 and proved to be unbeatable. The trading name Mercedes was registered in 1902.

In June 1903, Jellinek changed his own name to Jellinek-Mercedes, commenting that it was probably the first time a father had taken his daughter's name.

Audi In 1910 August Horch (1868–1951) set up Audi Automobilwerke GmbH after a series of disputes with previous business partners over the use of his own name as a trademark. Horch had previously produced motor cars, starting in 1899 under the Horch brand, but had fallen out with his partners, leaving the company in 1909. The first Audi branded car was a 2612 cc model.

In 1932, Audi, together with DKW, Wanderer and the original Horch company, were merged to form Auto Union. The four rings in the Audi trademark signify the four founding companies of Auto Union.

BMW (Bayerische Motoren Werke AG) was founded by Karl Friedrich Rapp in 1913 as an aircraft engine manufacturer, known originally as Bayerische Flugzeug Werke. After the end of the First World War, when it was forbidden for German companies to produce aircraft parts, the company began producing brakes for railway engines, and then in 1923 produced its first motorcycle, the R32.

The company's first car was produced in 1928. BMW had actually bought a company producing the British Austin 7 under licence, and rebranded it from the Dixi, to become the BMW 3/15. BMW now produces Rolls-Royce cars.

France

Citroën André-Gustave Citroën (1878–1935) formed his first company, André Citroën & Cie, in 1905 at the age of 27, and until the end of the First World War produced armaments in a factory on the outskirts of Paris.

In 1919, Citroën produced his first car, the Type A. In the last six months of that year, 2,500 cars were shipped out of the factory. In 1920, more than 20,000 cars were produced.

The Citroën 2CV was launched at the Paris Motor Show of 1948. The acronym '2CV' was an abbreviation of the car's name, the *deux chevaux*, which simply means 'two horse power'.

Renault In 1898, at the age of only 21, Louis Renault (1877–1944) converted a De Dion Bouton motor tricycle into a four-wheeled motor car. This hybrid vehicle became the first Renault car, and was marketed as the Renault Type A Voiturette. By driving his Type A up the steep Rue Lepic, in Montmartre, Paris, Renault gained national publicity, and his first 12 orders were secured as a result of this exploit.

In the same year he patented the direct drive system, which superseded the standard chain and cogs system then in use. The new system would be the cornerstone of Renault's great financial success. Louis went on to create the Renault car company, one of the world's great motor companies, but he was arrested in 1944 for collaboration with the Germans during the Second World War. Renault died in prison in October that year, and there were rumours that he had been murdered.

Peugeot The Peugeot family, which produced 'penny-farthing' bicycles in their factory in Paris, began producing steam-driven three-wheelers in 1889. In 1891, Peugeot produced its first petrol-driven motor car, powered by a Daimler engine. Five were sold that year, 29 in 1892, rising to 72 in 1895 and 300 in 1899.

In 1974 Peugeot acquired Citroën and the remains of the European Chrysler plants in Britain and France to create PSA Peugeot Citroën.

MISCELLANEOUS

Road Deaths

On 17 August 1896, Bridget Driscoll, a 44-year-old mother of two, entered the history books as the first person ever killed as the result of a motor accident. Bridget was crossing the grounds of Crystal Palace to watch a dancing display and was struck by a 'speeding' car driven by Arthur Edsell. The car's speed was estimated at 4 miles per hour. At the inquest, which took six hours, the coroner said 'This must never happen again.'

The first driver ever killed in a car accident was Henry Lindfield in 1898. Lindfield crashed into a tree in Purley in Sussex and died from his injuries later the same day in Croydon Hospital.

Steam Engines

The first steam engine was not produced by James Watt, nor Thomas Newcomen, but was invented in the first century AD by Hero of Alexandria who created an aeolipile.

The aeolipile uses the propulsion of escaping steam to create rotary motion in a stationary object. It was in fact a miniature steam turbine, which Hero describes in his book *Pneumatica*. Neither Hero nor anyone else could think of a practical purpose for it, so the product that could have revolutionised the world was used merely as a toy. It would be another 1,600 years before the Industrial Revolution harnessed the power of steam for practical use.

Hero also invented hydraulically operated automatic doors.

Traffic Lights

The world's first traffic lights were installed before the motor car was invented. They were installed in 1868 at the intersection of George Street and Bridge Street, close to the Houses of Parliament in London. Horse-drawn traffic was controlled by a hand-operated lever, which turned the lights round on a swivelling post.

The world's first automatic traffic lights were installed in Princess Square, Wolverhampton, in November 1927. Wolverhampton was unusual in having a slightly different sequence of lights to the rest of the UK until the 1970s. There was no intermediate stage between red and green (normally red and amber together). The lights went straight from red to green, and strangers had to be quick off the mark to avoid locals 'giving them the horn'.

Wolverhampton Council reckoned it eliminated the 'amber gambler' and was therefore safer than the national sequence. The Department of Transport forced Wolverhampton Council to change to the national standard sequence.

Parking Meters

Carlton Cole Magee invented the parking meter in 1932. The first parking meter, which was supplied by the Magee-Hale Park-O-Meter Company, was installed in Oklahoma City in 1935.

Taxi

Horse-drawn vehicles for hire, known as hackney carriages, have been on the streets of London and Paris since the early seventeenth century.

The taxi (also known as a cab) is named after the taximeter, which was invented in Germany in 1891 by engineer Wilhelm Bruhn to record distance and time so that arguments over fares would be avoided.

The first petrol-driven taxi to be equipped with a Bruhn taximeter was the Daimler Victoria, which was introduced in Stuttgart in 1897. Bruhn was promptly thrown in the river by local cab drivers, who did not want their fares regulated by machine. (A form of taximeter was used in ancient Rome. It was a device fixed to the axle of a cart that released small wooden balls to denote the distance travelled.)

The first motorised London taxi was the Bersey of 1897. It was battery-driven and nicknamed the Hummingbird as a result of the sound it made. Paris followed Stuttgart with petrol-driven taxis in 1899, London in 1903 and New York in 1907.

The word cab originates from 'cabriolet', a form of horse-drawn vehicle.

Bus

The first steam-driven public transport buses appeared in Nantes, France, in 1826, and were introduced in London and New York in 1829.

In 1895 the Netphenor Company of Germany converted a Benz truck into **the world's first petrol-driven bus**, for carrying eight passengers.

London is famous for its double-decker buses, particularly the Routemaster, which was first exhibited at the Commercial Motor Show in 1954, and entered service with London Transport on 8 February 1956. Routemasters were the last public transport vehicles specifically designed for use on the narrow streets of London, and, apart from operating on two remaining 'heritage' routes in the city, were finally withdrawn from service on 5 December 2005.

Oil Pipelines

The cost of transporting oil from the oil fields to refineries and onwards to the consumer has always been one of the major costs of oil. Often the cost of transportation has been greater than the cost of drilling and pumping oil out of the ground. Pipelines were developed to enable oil to be transported more cheaply than overland.

When the first oil well in the USA was drilled in 1859 by railway conductor 'Colonel' Edwin Drake (1819–80) in Titusville, Pennsylvania, the cost of rail freight for oil was prohibitive. The US Teamsters Union held a monopoly of overland transport and continuously increased labour rates as the demand for oil increased. Freight rates had to be increased by the carriers to recoup the extra costs. Pipelines cut overland transportation costs to a tiny fraction of the original price, and, at the same time, bypassed the union problems.

The first pipeline was built in 1865 out of wood and was just over nine miles long. It carried crude oil from the well at Pithole, Pennsylvania, to the railhead. It went on to break the monopoly of the US Teamsters Union.

The first long-distance oil pipeline was built in 1879 by Tidewater Corporation to compete with John D. Rockefeller's (1839–1937) Standard Oil.

One of the most famous pipelines was opened on 12 August 1944. It was the brainchild of Winston Churchill, and was known as PLUTO (Pipeline Under the Ocean). PLUTO delivered fuel from Shanklin on the Isle of Wight, under the English Channel, to France, to provide fuel for the Allied fighting vehicles.

The Trans-Alaska Pipeline System (TAPS) was opened in 1977 to carry, at full capacity, 2,000,000 barrels of oil per day the 1,300 kilometres (800 miles) from Prudhoe Bay to Valdez.

WAR

COVERING: Poison Gas and Stink Bombs, Ancient Projectiles and Launchers, Rockets, Gunpowder and Guns, War at Sea, Tanks, Radar, Air Combat, Nuclear Weapons, War Crimes, Awards, Some Wars in History, Espionage, Terrorism, Miscellaneous.

Jaw jaw is better than war war.
WINSTON CHURCHILL

POISON GAS AND STINK BOMBS

The Hague Convention of 1899 banned use of specially designed shells for the dissemination of poison gas. Even earlier, the Brussels Declaration forbade the use of poison weapons, although it is not clear if this refers to gas.

Poison Gas

It is a common misconception that the German mustard gas attacks of the First World War signalled the first use of lethal gas as a weapon of war. More than 400 years earlier, Leonardo da Vinci (1452–1519) had devised a form of shell for Ludovico Sforza, the Duke of Milan (1452–1508) to use in defence of his city. The shell, containing powdered arsenic and powdered sulphur, would explode on landing to create a poison gas cloud. It is not known if the shells were ever deployed.

Even earlier, the first recorded use of poison gas was in the Peloponnesian War 2,400 years ago, when the Spartans used arsenic smoke during the sieges at Plataea in 429 BC and Delium in 424 BC.

The first-full scale use of poison gas in a modern war was the German use of chlorine gas on 15 April 1915 during the Second Battle of Ypres.

The French had used tear gas earlier in the conflict, but in a limited deployment.

Porton Down

The British Bacteriological Warfare establishment at Porton Down was opened in 1915 as an experimental station for the Royal Engineers. The main task was to conduct research into the effects of mustard gas, phosgene and chlorine and to design and produce adequate protection for troops and civilians in the form of effective masks. The station began as two small huts, and by the end of the First World War in 1918 there were almost 1,200 personnel.

Stink Bombs

In 80 BC the Romans used toxic smoke, a filthy combination of urine, rotten eggs and beer, in a battle against the Charakitanes in Spain. As well as smelling foul, the smoke caused pulmonary problems and blindness, leading to the defeat of the Charakitanes within two days.

Only in the twentieth century were stink bombs used as a form of practical joke.

ANCIENT PROJECTILES AND LAUNCHERS

Bow and Arrow

Prehistoric bows and arrows have been found in every part of the inhabited world with the exception of Australia.

The earliest evidence of bows is in Tunisia where a 50,000-year-old bow has been discovered.

The English–Welsh longbow played a key role in English military dominance in the Middle Ages. It was used extensively in the Battle of Agincourt, which famously took place on St Crispin's Day 1415, between the English led by Henry V (1387–1422), and the French led by Charles VI (1368–1422) (also known as Charles the Mad). The victory at Agincourt, which was part of the Hundred Years War, enabled Henry to claim the throne of France.

The V-sign used as an insult originated on the battlefield of Agincourt. English bowmen gave the sign to their French opponents to show that their index and middle fingers were intact, after the French had started the punishment of cutting those fingers from captured enemy bowmen.

The first use of the longbow in a significant battle was at the Battle of Crecy on 26 August 1346. Using bodkin arrows, which had squared metal spikes for arrow tips, the English archers were able to pierce the body armour of the advancing French knights, and as many as 1,200 were killed in this way.

Crossbow

The earliest record of crossbows used in war is at the Battle of Ma-Ling in China in 341 BC.

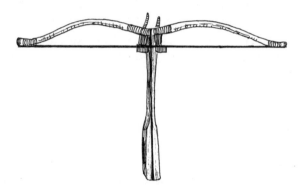

Catapulta

The ancient Romans used the *catapulta* to fire arrows and darts at enemy armies. It resembled a large horizontal bow, about 2 metres (6 feet) from tip to tip, and standing shoulder height to a centurion. The arrows varied from approximately 50 centimetres (18 inches) to more than 1 metre (3 feet) in length.

Even earlier, the ancient Greeks had a form of *catapulta* from 375 BC called the *oxybeles*, which translates literally as the 'bolt shooter'. Even earlier, in 400 BC they had the *gastrophetes* (belly bow) which was braced against the abdomen.

Ballista

The term *ballista* includes all forms of catapult-type weapons and was used by Philip II of Macedon. The Romans also used the *ballista* as one of their principal siege weapons. It was a larger machine, which hurled heavy stones into enemy strongholds. Both the *catapulta* and *ballista* used the power of the sudden release of tension on the throwing arm. Tension in the ballista was created with the use of cords made from wound horsehair, animal gut or sinews.

Trebuchet

It is thought that a similar machine to the *trebuchet* was first developed in China around 400 BC and by around AD 500 had been introduced into Europe.

The medieval variant of the *ballista* and *catapulta* was the *trebuchet*, which acted somewhat like a huge slingshot. It used heavy counterweights on the throwing arm to create the throwing power. The missile was carried in a net suspended with rope from the end of the throwing arm. The additional slingshot effect created extra throwing power. The trebuchet was mainly used as a siege weapon to break through enemy walls and used a large rock or metal ball for ammunition.

ROCKETS

An early form of rocket was seen in a toy developed by Archytas in ancient Greece in about 400 BC. Archytas suspended a wooden pigeon on a wire, and arranged for escaping steam from its tail to propel the bird round in a circle, to the utter amazement of his audiences.

The first use of rockets in a theatre of war was at the Battle of Kai-Keng in AD 1232, between the Chinese and Mongol invaders. The Chinese called their rockets 'fire arrows' and launched them in an attempt to have a psychological effect against the opposition troops. The rockets were simple paper and shellack tubes filled with gunpowder, open at one end. When ignited, the explosive effect of the gunpowder's rapid burning caused the rocket to be propelled forward with great speed. The Mongols eventually prevailed over the Chinese, but were impressed with the effect of fire being delivered by air, and rapidly began to develop their own rockets.

The first rocket attack in Europe was made by the Mongols in 1241 at the Battle of Legnica in Poland, the furthest west the Mongols fought. Very little is known of the course of the battle except that the Polish leader, Hendryk II, Duke of Silesia was killed, and that the Mongols withdrew.

V-1 (FZG 76) rockets were test launched in 1942 and first launched offensively by the Germans on 12 June 1944 against England. Although the V-1 is refrerred to as a rocket, it was propelled by an air-breathing pulse jet.

V-2 (Vergeltungswaffe 2 – Reprisal Weapon 2) was the world's first ballistic rocket. (A ballistic missile is one that follows a prescribed course that cannot be significantly altered once the fuel is spent, and whose flight is governed by the laws of ballistics.)

Testing of the V-2 began at Peenemunde, the German rocket test centre, in March 1942 with a spectacular explosion on the launch pad. Testing continued with equally disastrous results until the first partial success in October 1942. Mass production of the V-2 began in 1943 in an underground works near Nordhausen in Germany.

The first successful V-2 offensive launch was on 8 September 1944 against Paris. The final tally of V-2 rockets launched against England was more than 1,400.

The V-2 rocket has a unique characteristic in the history of arms. More deaths were caused by its production, than by its military use.

Gunpowder and Guns

Gunpowder

It is thought that gunpowder was invented in China in the eleventh century AD. The English scientist and Franciscan friar Roger Bacon (1214–94) is also credited with its invention; the formula was discovered in his papers after his death.

The first large-scale facility for gunpowder production was set up in England in 1865 by the Grueber family, who were Huguenot refugees from France. Most of the production was sold to the monarch.

In a tragic twist of fate, Grueber's son was killed as a result of an explosion in the factory. He was out boating on a nearby lake when the explosion happened. Falling debris landed on the boat and killed him.

Human urine was a vital ingredient of the best gunpowder, and in 1626 a statute was imposed by King Charles I, which compelled the storage and collection of urine from households every three months. Failure to supply urine risked severe punishment.

It was wrongly thought that only male human urine would be suitable as an ingredient for the best gunpowder. Nevertheless, during the American Civil War, the Nitre and Mining Bureau appealed for 'The Ladies of Selma to preserve all their chamber ley collected about their premises for the purpose of making Nitre.' Nitre was another name for saltpeter (potassium nitrate), a component of gunpowder. 'Ley' was urine. This request inspired a number of waggish rhymes such as:

We think the girls do work enough, in making love and kissing,
But now you've put the pretty dears, to patriotic pissing.

Guns

Handguns

The first handheld gun was the cumbersome, slow-firing matchlock that appeared in 1450. To fire the ammunition, a length of matchcord was used to ignite powder in a flash pan (the expression 'flash in the pan' came from this), which in turn ignited powder in the barrel. This then propelled a lead ball in the general direction of the target.

The system had a significant number of flaws, not least of which was the need to keep an open spark close to the powder. This allowed the enemy to pinpoint the soldier at night, and the high number of accidental discharges proved more dangerous than facing the enemy.

The wheel-lock of 1517 was an improvement on the matchlock, and then came the wonderfully named snaphaunce of 1570, an early version of the flintlock.

The flintlock was introduced in 1617. It incorporated the first reliable mechanism for firing a gun, and became the weapon of choice for 200 years, until self-contained, or cartridge, ammunition was developed. The main design advance of the flintlock involved the use of flint, an extremely hard rock, to strike a spark. A small piece of flint was held in a spring-loaded striker (also called the cock – hence 'cocking a gun'). Pulling the trigger released the cock, which struck the flint against a steel striking plate, known as the frizzen. The resultant spark ignited gunpowder loaded in the barrel which propelled a lead ball, or, sometimes, round shot. The flintlock had an effective killing distance up to 90 metres (100 yards).

The revolver was developed by Connecticut-born Samuel Colt (1814–62). Legend has it that Colt, who was working as a deck hand on a ship, observed the way the capstan worked to lift the anchor, and formed the idea of a self-loading firearm.

The unique feature of Colt's design was that six rounds of ammunition were held ready in a cylindrical revolving magazine, each round to be fired through a single barrel. Previous attempts at automatic loading had involved the use of revolving barrels and a single loading mechanism. The Colt design saved both cost and weight, and was far more reliable. Colt patented his idea in England and France in 1835 and in the USA in 1836.

The production line and interchangeable parts were developed by Colt with the help of Eli Whitney (1765–1825) in order to produce the vast number of revolvers needed by the US Army in the 1845–48 war with Mexico.

The first silencer for revolvers was invented by Hiram Maxim. He called it the 'suppressor' and was granted a patent in 1909.

The first gun specifically designed to be fired from the shoulder was the Spanish harquebus (also known as the arquebus or hackbut), which was designed in 1450. This forerunner of the modern rifle was effective up to 200 metres (660 feet).

Cannon

Crude cannon were first used on a European battlefield in 1327 by Edward III of England (1312–77) in his military actions against the Scots.

Machine Guns

James Puckle (1667–1724), a London lawyer, patented a tripod-mounted machine gun with a revolving ammunition cylinder in 1718. It fed rounds of ammunition into the gun's single chamber, and was capable of firing nine shots without reloading. The weapon failed as a result of its unreliable flintlock firing system. Puckle tried and failed to raise funds to mass-produce his guns. One newspaper neatly observed, 'Those are only wounded who hold shares therein.'

The first successful machine gun was the hand-cranked Gatling gun that was developed during the American Civil War by Dr Richard Gatling (1818–1903), and first used in 1861. The Gatling gun used cartridges that contained the primer, propellant and bullet. It could fire 200 rounds per minute.

The first truly automatic machine gun was developed by Hiram Maxim (1840–1916) in 1884. Maxim patented his machine gun, which harnessed the recoil force from the firing of each bullet to work the bolt, expel the spent cartridge and load the next bullet. The Maxim gun could fire 500 rounds per minute. Maxim was born in the USA and emigrated to England in 1881. He became a naturalised British citizen in 1900 and was knighted by Queen Victoria in 1901.

Grenades

Invented in the fifteenth century in France grenades were so named after the early models' resemblance to pomegranates. The French word for pomegranate is *grenade*.

Soldiers who were specially trained to throw grenades were called grenadiers.

The grenade went out of fashion and was almost unused during the nineteenth century, but its use was revived during the Russo-Japanese War of 1902 and the First World War.

The grenades used during the early months of the First World War were as dangerous to the soldier throwing them as to the enemy, because the handler could catch the rear of the trench during the throw causing the grenade to fall back and explode in the trench.

The first safe grenade was the British Mills Bomb, named after William Mills (1856–1932) of Birmingham, who developed it. The Mills Bomb was first used on the front line in the First World War in May 1915. It looked more like a pineapple than a pomegranate. Over 70,000,000 Mills Bombs were issued to soldiers up till 1970.

Shrapnel

Sir Henry Shrapnel (1761–1842) was appointed Inspector of Artillery in 1804, and promptly invented the shrapnel shell. The artillery shell-case contained fragments of metal and was designed so that upon striking its target it exploded, scattering lethal red-hot metal over a wide area. The idea was to wound and disable, as much as to kill.

WAR AT SEA

Submarines, Torpedoes and Depth Charges

Far from being a modern concept, undersea warfare originated centuries ago when the dominance of the surface warship was challenged from below the waves.

Submarines

The principles of the submarine were first accurately described in 1578 by William Bourne (1535–82), an English mathematician and innkeeper. His design was for an underwater rowing boat, covered in waterproof leather, but not one was ever built.

The first submarine to be built and hold successful trials was by Cornelius Drebbel (1572–1633). He was born in Holland but lived in England from 1604. Between 1620 and 1624 he built the first submarine and held successful trials in the Thames. Drebbel's vessel was propelled by 12 oarsmen, and there is a possibility that James I (VI of Scotland), who was Drebbel's patron, took a short ride in it, becoming the world's first monarch to travel underwater.

The invention of goatskin ballast tanks in 1747 overcame the problem of controlling descent to significant depths.

The first submarine to be used in war was the *Turtle*. In 1776 David Bushnell (1742–1824), a student at Yale University, designed the *Turtle*, which was built by the US Navy to his specification, using a screw propeller. Sergeant Ezra Lee sailed it close to a British battleship in New York harbour, planning to attach explosives to the hull by drilling into it. The hull of the British ship was too tough and the attempt failed, but this was the first time a submarine had been used in war.

The first submarine to deliver and detonate a torpedo successfully was the Confederate CSS *H.L. Hunley*, in 1864, during the American Civil War. The torpedo, which had been attached to the bow of the *Hunley*, sank its target, the USS *Housatonic*. The *Hunley* also sank in the same action, with the loss of all on board.

In 2000, the *Hunley* was raised from the seabed, and is now in the process of restoration.

Torpedoes

The torpedo is named after the torpedo fish, which disables its victims with an electrical discharge.

The modern self-propelled torpedo was developed by Robert Whitehead (1823–1905), a British designer working for the Austrian Navy. By 1866 he had produced a successful working prototype, with an explosive charge in the nose.

The modern torpedo guidance system was invented in 1942 by Hollywood beauty Hedy Lamarr (1914–2000). She patented the invention, which was based on frequency switching, but the patent ran out before it was taken up by the military.

The same system is used today in mobile phone technology (*see also* Communication p. 41 and Sex on Screen p. 233).

Depth Charges

The main weapon used by surface vessels against submarines are depth charges. They are in effect waterproof bombs dropped into the sea and set to explode at a pre-determined depth. Depth charges were developed by the British Navy in their war against the German U-boats during the First World War, and were first used in 1915.

TANKS

The modern tank was developed in 1914 by Sir Ernest Swinton, DSO (1868–1951), who was an official British war correspondent on the Western Front during the First World War. Swinton was alarmed at the high casualty rate of front-line soldiers, who were being cut down in their thousands by machine-gun fire. Taking his inspiration from a Holt's tractor, which was a heavy caterpillar-tracked vehicle, Swinton wrote a strong memo to the Secretary of the War Council in London, urging him to develop a protected means of transport.

The British Landship Committee was set up by the government and agreed to adapt tractors for military use. The resultant vehicles, known as tanks, were used for the first time on 15 August 1916 in the First Battle of the Somme.

Leonardo da Vinci, whose work pre-empted the designs of many later inventions, designed a self-propelled tank nearly 500 years earlier.

RADIO DIRECTION AND RANGING (RADAR)

(*See also* Inventions p. 165.)

The use of radar was first developed by the German physicist Heinrich Hertz (1857–1894) in 1887. Hertz conducted a series of experiments with radio in his laboratory, and found that, while the radio waves would pass through certain materials, other materials reflected the waves, creating a sort of echo.

Radar's practical use for the detection of ships and aircraft that were otherwise invisible to the naked eye was refined during the Second World War. Late in the war, British fighter aircraft were equipped with portable radar sets, which enabled them to locate the enemy well before they were seen themselves. It was fed back to the British that German High Command were becoming increasingly frustrated that their aircraft were being shot down in ever larger numbers at night.

Seizing the opportunity to spread disinformation, British counter-intelligence leaked a story that their pilots were eating a diet high in carrots to improve their eyesight in the dark. This story put the Germans off the scent of mobile radar for nearly a year.

AIR COMBAT

Airplanes are interesting toys, but of no military value.
FERDINAND FOCH (1851–1929)
French Marshal – Allied Commander-in-Chief, First World War

The world's first fighter aircraft was the Vickers EFB1 (short for Experimental Fighting Biplane), nicknamed the Destroyer, which first flew in 1912. The EFB1 was exhibited in 1913 at the Olympia Air Show and went into service with the Royal Flying Corps in 1914 as the Vickers Gunbus. The Destroyer was armed with a Maxim .303-inch-calibre machine gun on a swivel mount, and saw its first action on Christmas Day 1914 when it intercepted and shot down a German monoplane.

The first aerial 'dogfight' took place on 5 October 1914 when a French Voisin 3, armed with a Hotchkiss 8mm-calibre machine gun, shot down a German Aviatik B1.

The world's first bomber aircraft was the German airship Zeppelin, named after its pioneer Count Ferdinand Graf von Zeppelin (1838–1917). The Zeppelin began its role as a bomber in August 1914, when it bombed military targets in Liege in Belgium.

The first time civilians were bombed was on 19 January 1915 when a Zeppelin bombed Great Yarmouth. Four people were killed and 16 injured. It was also the first time the British mainland had been bombed from the air.

London was bombed for the first time on 31 May 1915, also by a Zeppelin.

The first time a bomb was dropped by aircraft was in 1911 when an Italian pilot dropped four hand grenades on Turkish targets in Libya. However, the aircraft was on reconnaissance and not strictly recognised as a bomber.

The first aircraft launched from a ship was on 4 November 1910. To test the effectiveness of ship-launched aircraft, Eugene Ely (1886–1911), a civilian pilot who had learned to fly only earlier that year, was launched off a platform on the USS *Birmingham*.

The first successful landing of an aircraft on a ship was also by Ely when he managed to land safely on the quarter-deck of the battleship, USS *Pennsylvania*, on 18 January 1911. The arresting gear on the *Pennsylvania*, designed to stop the aircraft shooting off the far end of the deck, was constructed of wire attached to heavy sandbags.

Spitfire

The Supermarine Spitfire became the icon of British resistance to the Nazi airborne invasion of the Second World War. It was designed by Reginald Mitchell (1895–1937) in response to the growth of Germany's Luftwaffe, and the first prototype, the F37/34, flew in March 1936. The Spitfire entered Royal Air Force service in 1938, and by the outbreak of war in 1939, the RAF had 2,160 on order.

The first vertical take-off and landing (VTOL) aircraft with fixed wings, rather than a rotor, was the AV8A Harrier jump jet. It first flew on 31 August 1966 and entered service with the RAF on 1 April 1969.

Stealth

It has been found that certain shapes show up more easily on radar screens. Stealth technology employs radical changes to the designs of both airframes and engines that enable aircraft to fly missions into highly defended target areas with no loss of capability, and yet avoid being detected by radar.

The first aircraft to employ stealth capability was the US F-117A Nighthawk, originally codenamed Senior Trend, which had its first test flight in 1981. The F-117A is produced by Lockheed Aeronautical Systems Co., and the first combat-ready aircraft was delivered to the US Air Force in August 1982. US Air Combat Command's 4450th Tactical Group, the only F-117A unit, achieved operational capability in October 1983. The F-117A remained classified until 1988, and was first revealed to the public in 1990.

Aircraft Carrier

The first vessel specifically designed for use as an aircraft carrier was HMS *Argus*, which was launched in 1917 and used at the end of the First World War.

The *Argus*'s keel had originally been laid down as an Italian cruise liner, which would have been named the *Count Rosso* if it had been launched under the Italian flag, but, before construction was completed, the Royal Navy commandeered the ship and had it installed with a flush or flat-top deck to serve as a take-off and landing area. The flush deck became the standard configuration for future aircraft carriers.

Kamikaze

Ritual suicide once formed part of the Japanese Samurai Code for the atonement of sins and failure, and was regarded as an honourable act. During the Second World War, volunteer Japanese pilots known as kamikazes committed to fly their planes on suicide missions, directly into enemy ships. In a formal preparatory ritual, the pilots were bolted into their specially built aircraft. The pilots regarded their deaths as the most honourable way of serving their emperor and their country, believing, as they did, that they were the natural successors to the ancient Samurai.

The first kamikaze attack took place in October 1944 on the US aircraft carrier *St Lo*, which was sunk after 26 kamikaze aircraft were detailed to attack.

Kamikaze translates as 'divine wind', a reference to the typhoon that drove Kublai Khan's invading fleet away from the shores of Japan in 1281. The underwater remains of Khan's fleet have recently been discovered by archaeologists.

NUCLEAR WEAPONS

The energy produced by the breaking down of the atom is a very poor kind of thing. Anyone who expects a source of power from the transformation of these atoms is talking moonshine.

LORD RUTHERFORD (1871–1937)

Atomic fission was discovered in 1938 at the Kaiser Wilhelm Institute in Berlin by German chemist Otto Hahn (1879–1960) in co-operation with Dr Fritz Strassman (1902–80), a radio chemist.

The first detonation of an atomic bomb, known as the Trinity Test, took place on 16 July 1945 in the desert of New Mexico. The test was a spectacular success, and eyewitnesses from 20 miles (32 kilometres) away reported feeling the heat of the explosion.

The first atomic bomb detonated in war was dropped on Hiroshima on the mainland of Japan on 6 August 1945. Ninety per cent of the city was destroyed. Out of a population of around 250,000 people, about 45,000 died on the first day, with a further 19,000 dying in the next four months.

Previously, on 25 July 1945, US President Harry Truman (1884–1972) issued the bombing order to General Carl 'Tooey' Spaatz (1891–1974), Commander of US Strategic Air Forces in the Pacific, which would result in the bombing of Hiroshima. Truman noted in his diary that he had ordered the bomb to be dropped on a 'purely military target'.

The Soviet Union developed its first atom bomb in 1949 following the betrayal of US nuclear secrets by the spy Klaus Fuchs (1911–88) to the Soviet Union.

Fuchs was born in Germany, and fled to England in the 1930s when the Gestapo began to round up communists. He worked on the British atomic bomb research project before being transferred to the USA to work on the Manhattan Project, which led to the development of the atomic bomb. After his arrest for spying in 1949, and his trial in 1950, Fuchs was sentenced to 14 years in prison, of which he served nine. On his release, Fuchs illegally relocated to East Germany, one of the Soviet vassal states, where he began lecturing in physics.

The world's first hydrogen bomb was detonated by the USA on 1 November 1952. The explosion of the device, which was codenamed 'Mike', caused the island of Elugelab in the Pacific to disappear, leaving a crater 1.6 kilometres (1 mile) wide and 48 metres (160 feet) deep. In the process 80,000,000 tonnes of earth were lifted into the air. The characteristic mushroom cloud rose to 17,400 metres (57,000 feet) in 90 seconds, and eventually spread to a width of 1,600 kilometres (1,000 miles). The results so terrified Norris Bradbury (1909–97), the director of Los Alamos, the US National Laboratory, that he considered keeping the magnitude of the detonation secret.

The bomb was the eventual result of a meeting in 1949 between President Truman and Edward Teller (1908–2003), known as the father of the hydrogen bomb, who pressed for an urgent study to be undertaken for the development of a super bomb. The plan was to build a thermonuclear device, which ultimately came to be known as the hydrogen bomb. Truman authorised a crash development programme, which was immediately opposed by many others, including Robert Oppenheimer (1904–67), who had led the team which developed the first atom bomb in 1945.

The first true hydrogen (fusion) bomb tested by the Soviets was detonated on 22 November 1955. Within the Soviet Union it was named Sakharov's 'Third Idea', having been designed by the famous scientist, and later dissident, Andre Sakharov (1921–89).

The UK tested its first hydrogen bomb on 8 November 1957, dropping a 1.8 megaton thermonuclear device off Christmas Island. The aircraft carrying the bomb was a Valiant Bomber XD 824, piloted by Barney Millett. After being released from the bomber, the device fell for 52 seconds before being detonated 2,000 metres (6,600 feet) above ground.

The first submarine-launched nuclear missile known as Polaris was deployed by the US Navy. It was test-launched on 20 July 1960, the first ever underwater rocket launch.

The US President John F. Kennedy (1917–63) came to an agreement with Prime Minister Harold Macmillan (1894–1986) to supply Britain with Polaris nuclear missiles. The Polaris Sales Agreement was signed in 1963, and Polaris missiles were installed on British submarines by the Royal Navy in 1970.

WAR CRIMES

The first War Crimes Tribunal was set up in Nuremberg in 1945 for the prosecution of Nazi war criminals after the end of the Second World War. The trials lasted until 1949. Several hundred prisoners were detained on suspicion of war crimes, and in the first trial, which indicted the 24 most important of the accused, 12 death sentences were handed down, and executed. Three of the accused in that trial were acquitted.

Concentration Camps

One of the most reviled aspects of the Nazi regime during the Second World War was its use of concentration camps. Six million Jewish prisoners and up to 4,000,000 others are known to have died in these camps in appalling circumstances at the hands of the Nazis.

The Japanese also built concentration camps throughout Indo-China and Manchuria, and prisoners were badly mistreated and exploited for slave labour. Adding to the misery, medical experiments were carried out on prisoners in German and Japanese camps, but neither the Germans nor the Japanese were the first to make use of such camps.

The first use of concentration camps was during the Third Cuban War of Independence (1895–98), which pitted the local populace against their Spanish occupiers. In an act of desperation to stop attacks by insurgents from the countryside, the Spanish Governor of Cuba, Valeriano Weyler (1838–1930), organised a mass relocation of the non-combatant rural population into specified areas within cities. He called these areas reconcentration camps, but failed to provide adequate medical treatment or sufficient food. Hundreds of thousands died, and the legacy of bitter resentment is felt to this day.

During the Boer War of 1899–1902 in South Africa, the British Army built 109 concentration camps to hold Boer women and children, and other prisoners. The camps had been built during fighting between the British, and the disaffected Dutch and German settlers in the Transvaal. Forty-five of the camps were for white people and 64 for black people. The initial plan in London had stressed the need for humane treatment of the prisoners, but in reality the treatment was brutal. Poor food rations, inadequate hygiene and lack of proper medical facilities led to outbreaks of typhoid and dysentery. Nearly 28,000 Boer prisoners died, of whom 22,000 were under 16 years old. At least another 14,000 black prisoners died.

Awards

Victoria Cross

The Victoria Cross is the highest honour awarded to British servicemen in the face of the enemy. It was instituted on 21 January 1856 during the Crimean War, and each medal is cast in bronze from parts of captured cannon taken at Sebastopol.

The first award of a Victoria Cross went to 20-year-old Irishman Charles Davis Lucas (1834–1914) two years after the Battle of Bomarsund in the Baltic. On 21 July 1854, Lucas was serving as a mate on board HMS *Hecla*, when a live shell landed on the deck with its fuse still hissing. Showing immense presence of mind and courage, he ran forward and threw the shell overboard, where it exploded before hitting the water. Lucas's action saved the lives of shipmates and prevented injury to many more. Having risen through the ranks, he retired a Rear Admiral.

Only one VC has been awarded on the evidence provided solely by the enemy. On 11 August 1943, New Zealander Flight Officer Lloyd Allen Trigg (1914–43) sank German U-boat U468 despite catastrophic damage to his own aircraft. When Klemens Schamong, the captain of the submarine, and one of only seven survivors, was rescued by the Royal Navy, he recommended Trigg for a bravery award. Trigg, along with his whole crew, died in the action.

SOME WARS IN HISTORY – ORIGINS

Roman Conquests

The Romans did not set out with a plan to subdue the world and introduce Roman culture into its conquered territories; each conquest seemed to lead to the next until the Roman Empire spanned most of Europe and large swathes of Africa and Asia.

In 509 BC, Rome temporarily came under the control of the Etruscans, who came from north of Rome. The expulsion of the last Roman king, the violent Tarquinius Superbus, by the Etruscan king Porsenna, signalled the beginning of the Roman Republic. Porsenna left Rome before he could assume the monarchy, and at the end of the fifth century BC Rome began to take territory from the Etruscans. Rome's first major war of expansion lasted between 437 and 426 BC, and ended in victory over the town of Fidenae. The important Etruscan city of Veii was taken in 396 BC. By 275 BC, Rome controlled the whole of the Italian peninsula and then embarked on the domination of most of the known world.

Alexander the Great's Conquests

After he had succeeded his father, Philip II of Macedon, Alexander the Great began his conquests in 336 BC. His driving ambition was to expand the Macedonian Empire, conquering Persian-dominated Asia Minor, Syria, Egypt, Persia itself, and reaching as far as India.

Norman Conquest of England

The Norman Conquest of England originated from William of Normandy's claim to the throne of England. In 1066 he defeated Harold Godwinson at the Battle of Hastings and he became known as William the Conqueror (1028–87) and King of England.

The Crusades

The First Crusade took place in 1097 to protect the Holy Land from the Muslims, and Jerusalem was captured in 1099.

The Hundred Years War

These were conflicts involving attempts by the English kings to claim the French crown and dominate France. They started around 1337 in the reign of Edward III and ended about 1453 in the reign of Henry VI, when the vast majority of the captured territory in France had been recovered by the French crown. However, Calais was not recovered until 1558.

The Thirty Years' War

What is known as the Defenestration of Prague in 1618 marked the beginning of the Thirty Years' War. It was a protest by Bohemian Protestants against a violation of their religious rights and led to a revolt against the Hapsburg Emperor Ferdinand II. The war, which was mainly fought in central Europe, spread to involve most of the countries of Europe and was fought generally on religious lines between Protestants and Catholics. It ended with the Treaty of Westphalia in 1648.

The English Civil War

In 1642 the English Civil War was precipitated by the attempt by King Charles I to arrest five members of Parliament. The attempt failed, following which the Royalists, who supported Charles I and the Parliamentarians, prepared for war.

There had been a long-running background of conflict between the two sides with Charles insisting on his right to rule, especially to collect taxes, without interference, whereas Parliament wanted a reduction of Charles's power. Charles insisted on preserving his powers and, in 1649, after losing the war, he was tried and beheaded. Oliver Cromwell (1599–1658) forcibly dissolved Parliament, and was installed as Lord Protector in 1653.

The American War of Independence

When a British force was sent to Concord to destroy American rebel stores, in 1775, the American War of Independence began. The Battles of Lexington and Concord were the opening skirmishes in the war that lasted until 1783 resulting in the independence of the 13 American colonies, which eventually became the USA.

The war was preceded by years of strife between the colonies and Britain. One of the most famous events in history, the Boston Tea Party of 1773, sparked the events that led to the war. Britain was extracting tax from the colonists, without allowing them any voting rights. The watchword became, 'No taxation without representation.' On the night of 16 December 1773, hundreds of cases full of tea were emptied into Boston harbour (*see also* Tea p. 128).

The Crimean War

In 1853 a dispute arose between Russia, who demanded the right to protect Orthodox Christians in the Ottoman Empire, and the Ottoman sultan. There was also a dispute between Russia and France over the privileges of Orthodox and Catholic churches in the holy places in Palestine. An alliance between France, the Ottoman Empire and Britain was formed to fight Russia, mainly on the Crimean Peninsular. The war lasted until 1856.

The American Civil War

It is generally supposed that the American Civil War started in 1861 over the abolition of slavery, but debate still rages over the undisputed reason for this complicated war. Twenty-three states, known as the Union, were opposed by 11 Southern states, known as the Confederacy.

The 11 states had seceded from the Union during the early stage of Lincoln's presidency, but were decisively returned into the Union after the bloody war, which began with the Confederate attack on Fort Sumter in 1861. About 3 per cent of the population were casualties in the war that lasted until 1865.

Boer War

Actually there were two Boer Wars. The first, which is more properly known as the Transvaal War, took place in 1880–81, and was a victory for the Boers, who kept their disputed territory. The British government signed a peace treaty which allowed the Transvaal to be self-governed.

The Second, and better-known, Boer War, also known as the South African War, began in 1899. The British were again in dispute with Dutch and German settlers, this time over the Orange Free State and the Transvaal territory in South Africa, following the discovery of major gold deposits around Johannesburg. The immediate cause of the war was an ultimatum made by the Boer leader, Paul Kruger, against British re-inforcement of a garrison. Convinced that war was inevitable the Boers invaded Natal Province and Cape Colony in late 1899.

Following the defeat of the Boers, in 1902, both the Transvaal and the Orange Free State became part of the British Empire.

First World War

On 28 June 1914 Archduke Franz Ferdinand of Austria (1863–1914) was shot dead in Sarajevo by Serbian student Gavrilo Princip (1894–1918). This event precipitated the First World War, creating a domino effect, which triggered the implementation of international treaties following Austria's invasion of Serbia and Germany's invasion of Belgium. The treaties brought Britain, Russia and France into the conflict.

Second World War

Germany invaded Czechoslovakia in March 1939 and Poland on 1 September 1939. This second invasion led to Britain and France declaring war on Germany two days later, and established 3 September 1939 as the start of the Second World War.

Some historians have argued that the invasion of China by Japan in July 1937 was the actual start, although this is not generally accepted.

Chinese Civil War

In 1927, Generalissimo Chiang Kai-shek (1887–1975), the leader of the Chinese Nationalist Party purged Communists from the alliance which had been set up between the Nationalists and the Chinese Communist Party. Spanning the Agrarian Revolution of 1927–37, the fabled Long March of 1934–35, the power struggle of 1945–47, the final struggles from 1945–50, the Chinese Civil War established Communist control of main-land China in 1950. Mao Zedong (1893–1976) assumed the Chinese lead-ership, and Chiang Kai-shek fled to Taiwan.

Korean War

The first attack of the Korean War came on 25 June 1950, when the Com-munist North Koreans, with Soviet backing, launched a massive attack on South Korea, across what was known as the 38th Parallel. The 38th

Parallel was a line drawn across the map of Korea in 1945, to establish the North–South boundary.

After this attack the United Nations called on all its members to halt this aggression and the USA sent troops to defend South Korea. The conflict became a proxy war between the USA and its allies, and the communist bloc, including China.

The Korean War established the precedent of the USA defending territories under attack from communism, and after more than 3,000,000 people had died, an armistice was agreed on 27 July 1953.

Vietnam War

Similar in many ways to the Korean War, the Vietnam War was provoked by the efforts of the USA and the South Vietnamese to stop the spread of communism from North Vietnam.

The French had tried to re-establish control over Vietnam in 1945, having lost control during the Second World War. With Vietnamese troops (Viet Minh) under the command of Ho Chi Minh, the French were badly defeated. The 1954 Battle of Dien Bien Phu was decisive in French withdrawal. The USA entered the conflict by providing economic aid in 1956 and the last US personnel were withdrawn in 1975.

Falklands War

In the middle of a devastating economic crisis in Argentina, with massive civil unrest and public criticism of the ruling military junta, President General Leopoldo Galtieri (1926–2003) tried to establish sovereignty over the Falkland Islands, or Malvinas as they are called by the Argentines. His main objective was to divert attention from the problems at home.

The first offensive action of the war was the invasion of the small island of South Georgia by 50 Argentine fishermen on 19 March 1982. The invaders proceeded to raise the Argentine flag and a full-scale occupation of the Falkland Islands took place on 2 April 1982. British forces recaptured the capital, Stanley, on 14 June 1982 and by 20 June hostilities came to an end with the retaking of the South Sandwich Islands.

First Gulf War

Although Kuwait had been a British protectorate following the end of the First World War and an independent country since 1961, the territory had been claimed by various Iraqi rulers, particularly after the discovery of oil there in 1938.

The immediate lead-up to this conflict came from Iraqi accusations that Kuwait was illegally directionally drilling for oil across the Iraq–Kuwait border. On 2 August 1990, Iraqi forces occupied Kuwait. The USA led a coalition of forces numbering over 600,000 troops which achieved a decisive victory with little loss of life on the coalition side. The war ended on 28 February 1991, with Saddam Hussein still in power in Iraq.

Second Gulf War

The aftermath of the First Gulf War was the continuation of tensions between the USA, some of its Western allies and Iraq. Following the bombing on the World Trade Center on 11 September 2001 and the invasion of Afghanistan in October 2001, the invasion of Iraq was justified on the basis of the Saddam Hussein regime's stockpiling weapons of mass destruction. The opening skirmish came on 20 March 2003. Baghdad fell on 9 April 2003.

ESPIONAGE

Blake's Law Dictionary defines espionage as 'The practice of gathering, transmitting or deliberately losing secret information related to the national defence.'

The earliest documented reference to espionage was around 1300 BC in Sun Tzu's classic book *The Art of War*. In this he lists the five types of spy needed by an army commander:

- Local spies – hired from the countryside.

- Inside spies – subverted government officials.

- Double agents – captured enemy spies who have been 'turned'.

- Doomed spies – deceived professionals who take army orders to the enemy.

- Surviving spies – who return with reports.

The ancient Egyptians (*c.*3000–343 BC) also used a well-established network of spies for gathering intelligence on potential enemies both within the state and outside.

Britain

MI6 was founded in 1909 by Sir George Mansfield Smith-Cumming (1859–1923) as the overseas arm of the Secret Intelligence Service. He began the practice of signing his letters and memos in green ink with the letter 'C'. This practice was adopted by all subsequent holders of the office of Director of SIS, hence they were all referred to as 'C'. This was also the idea behind James Bond's chief being known as 'M'.

MI5 was founded in 1909 as the intelligence agency responsible for internal security and domestic counter-intelligence. It was originally designated the Directorate of Military Operations Section 5 (MO5). The first Director General was Sir Vernon George Waldegrave Kell (1873–1942), who doubled as foreign correspondent of the *Daily Telegraph*.

The first female Director General of MI5 was Stella Rimington (now Dame) (b. 1935) who served between 1992 and 1996.

USA

The Central Intelligence Agency (CIA) The US government's principal intelligence and counter-intelligence agency was created in 1947 by President Truman as the successor to the Office of Strategic Studies (OSS). The OSS had been the chief intelligence-gathering arm of the US government during the Second World War and was disbanded in 1945

The Federal Bureau of Investigation (FBI) was established as the Bureau of Investigation in 1908 by Attorney General Charles Bonaparte (1851–1921). The name was changed to the FBI in 1935. Most of its existence has been spent in federal law enforcement investigating the activities of political activists, most especially during the period of the Cold War from the 1940s through to the 1970s.

Soviet Union

The **KGB** (Committee for State Security) is the best known of the old Soviet state security services. It was formed in 1954, as successor to the infamous NKVD, and operating through many offices has exercised pervasive influence on the people of the former Soviet Union and those countries and organisations with whom the Soviet Union had any contact. With the dissolution of the Soviet Union in 1991 it came under the control of the Russian government with greatly reduced powers and influence.

The NKVD, headed by Yavrenty Beria (1899–1953), was the forerunner of the KGB and was itself a descendant of the Cheka, which was set up in 1917 by Polish-born Felix Dzerzhinsky (1877–1926), one of the founding fathers of the Russian Revolution.

Germany

The Gestapo (Geheime Staatspolizei) was established in 1933, taking over the role of the Prussian Secret Police. Hermann Goering (1893–1946) took charge from 1934, expanding the Gestapo's role over the whole of Germany with the exception of Bavaria, which came under Heinrich Himmler (1900–45) and his SS troops. Later that year Goering handed over control of the Gestapo to Himmler.

Code-breakers and Code-breaking

Far from the supposedly glamorous end of spying, sit the code-breakers, the men and women whose job it is to decrypt enemy messages.

The first treatise on code-breaking, *On Deciphering Cryptographic Messages,* was written in the ninth century AD by the Arab scientist and mathematician Al Kindi (AD 801–873) who lived in what is present-day Yemen.

Perhaps the most celebrated code-breakers were the team at Bletchley Park during the Second World War, who were led by Alan Turing (*see also* Computers p. 158). They succeeded in breaking the seemingly unbreakable German Enigma code using the famous Bombe computers, the first time electronics had been used in code-breaking.

The USA's code-breaking operation within the State Department –

MI8 – was closed down in 1929 on the orders of Secretary of State Henry Stimson (1867–1950), with the words 'gentlemen do not read each other's mail'.

British Female Spies

The first known British female spy was Ann Bates, a Philadelphia schoolteacher, who spied for the British and penetrated George Washington's inner circle. During the years 1778 to 1780, Bates disguised herself as a peddler and walked almost unchallenged through the American lines, checking gun emplacements, numbers of troops and types of weaponry. After the American War of Independence, Bates sailed to England. She was abandoned by her husband, but succeeded in obtaining a pension for her work.

Spy Planes

The first spy plane was the 1917 De Havilland DH4, equipped with a rigid-mounted camera, which was fixed to the fuselage for vertical photography. Vibration proved a drawback until the revolutionary K-3 camera, which was developed in 1920 by the American inventor and entrepreneur Sherman Fairchild (1896–1971). Fairchild was later to found the Fairchild Semiconductor, which made major contributions to the advancement of computers.

Fictional Spies

James Bond was the brainchild of Ian Fleming (1908–64) and was introduced in *Casino Royale*, published in 1953.

George Smiley first appeared in *Tinker Tailor Soldier Spy*, a novel by John Le Carré (b. 1931), which was first published in 1974. Smiley appeared in two other Le Carré books, *The Honourable Schoolboy*, in which he was not the main character, and *Smiley's People*.

TERRORISM

Those who make peaceful revolution impossible, make violent revolution inevitable.
US PRESIDENT JOHN F. KENNEDY (1917–63)

In the *Oxford Dictionary of English*, terrorism is defined as 'The unofficial or unauthorised use of violence and intimidation in the pursuit of political aims.'

The word terrorism first came into use during the French Revolution of 1789–99, when 'The Terror', which lasted from June 1793 through July 1794, was at its height. 'The Terror' was effectively state terrorism, when the ruling Jacobin faction led by Robespierre ruthlessly executed anyone thought to be a threat to the regime.

The Zealots

The earliest example of terrorism appears to be the campaign waged by the Zealots, a Jewish political movement, against the Roman occupiers of Israel during the first century AD. Zealots were known as 'dagger men' as they frequented public places with daggers concealed beneath cloaks. Without warning, they would strike down people known to support Rome.

The Zealots conducted an unrelenting anti-Roman campaign in the eastern Mediterranean region during the Jewish Revolt of AD 66–70, managing to capture Jerusalem at one point. Masada, a mountain fortress in southern Israel, was the site of the Zealots' last stand in AD 70 after Jerusalem had been lost. The Romans conducted a two-year campaign, and when it was inevitable that Masada would be captured, the Zealots committed mass suicide, with only seven women and children surviving.

The Jewish historian Josephus (*c.*AD 37–*c.*100) tells of their murderous activities, and they were criticised in the Talmud.

Irish Republican Army

Many regard the 1916 'Proclamation of the Republic' during the Easter Rising, as the founding document of the Irish Republican Army (IRA). There had been a history of armed uprisings against British rule well before the Proclamation, with the most notable ones taking place in 1798, 1803, 1848 and 1867. (The Irish Republican Brotherhood, supported by American money, carried out the 1867 attacks.)

The Ulster Volunteer Force (UVF) was formed in 1913, and in 1914 was allowed by the British to import arms, unhindered. Until the Easter Rising of 1916, the UVF had been regarded as little more than 'toy soldiers', according to IRA leader Ernie O'Malley, speaking in 1923, but by 1917 the UVF had managed to achieve strong support throughout Ireland, and were regarded as a viable fighting force.

The UVF changed its name to the IRA in 1919, and began its guerrilla campaign. Bombings of military and civilian targets became the tactic of choice. These tactics, employed effectively by such legendary divisions as Tom Barry's Flying Column in Cork, became textbook examples of this type of armed struggle, and became the inspiration for other similar organisations throughout the world.

Tom Barry regarded the Crown Forces of 1920 as the real terrorists.

Al-Qaeda

To most people in the West, al-Qaeda is seen as a byword for terrorism, a single, highly centralised structure, with Osama bin Laden as its shadowy mastermind and leader. However, it is now widely believed that al-Qaeda does not exist in this form, and is in fact merely a convenient label applied to the general groupings of Islamic militants. The literal meaning of al-Qaeda can be a base or a foundation. Alternatively it can mean a rule or a maxim.

Islamic militancy in its present form sprang from the Soviet occupation of Afghanistan in 1980, and the rise of the mujahedin resistance fighters. The stated aims of the militant Islamic groups, commonly referred to as al-Qaeda, are to overthrow secular Arab regimes and to reinstate the Caliphate across the Arab world. Indiscriminate suicide bombing of civilians is the tactic of choice.

Harakat al-Muqawamah al-Islamiyyah (Hamas)

An Islamist paramilitary organisation based in Palestine, Hamas has evolved through a number of stages; the main two of which are the founding of the Muslim Brotherhood in the Gaza Strip between 1967 and 1976, and the formation of Hamas as the combatant arm of the Muslim Brotherhood in 1982.

The stated aims of Hamas are to eliminate the state of Israel, and to create an Islamic theocratic state on the land currently in the possession of Israel, including the West Bank and Gaza Strip. Suicide bombings have been the main tactic of choice, including the use of female suicide bombers.

In February 2006, Hamas won an overwhelming poll success, and was elected the ruling party of the Palestinians.

Brigate Rosse

Renato Curcio (b. 1945) founded the Brigate Rosse (Red Brigades), an extreme Italian Marxist/Leninist group, in 1969 while he was still a university student. The stated aim was to create a revolutionary state through armed struggle, and their subsidary objective was to take Italy out of the Western Alliance.

In November 1970 Brigate Rosse announced their existence with fire-bombings in Milan. Another preferred tactic is assassination of government ministers and business leaders, and in 1978 they captured the Prime Minister of Italy, Aldo Moro (1916–78), and murdered him.

By the end of the 1980s, following the imprisonment of many of its leaders, the organisation was greatly weakened, and remains almost ineffective.

The Shining Path

Abimael Guzman (b. 1934), a university philosophy professor, founded the Shining Path in the late 1960s, as an offshoot of the Communist Party of Peru. Shining Path's stated aim is to replace Peruvian bourgeois institutions with a communist peasant revolutionary regime. Guzman was captured and jailed in 1992, since when Shining Path has not been active.

Between 1973 and 1975, Shining Path gained control of student councils, and adopted a Maoist 'criticism and self-criticism' doctrine, which led to students denouncing their peers as being insufficiently revolutionary. Their savagery against union leaders and peasants has led to widespread condemnation.

Euzkadi Ta Azkatasuna

Young nationalists seeking independence for the Basque region from Spain founded Euzkadi Ta Azkatasuna (ETA) in 1959.

ETA is an armed organisation, which considers the unique Basque language – Euskara – to be a national defining characteristic. It aims, by violent means, such as assassination and murder, to create a Basque state, separate from Spain. The earliest death is reported to have been a baby killed in a June 1960 bombing attack.

Shootings and bombings are the tactics of choice, and despite much lower levels of activity since the 1997 murder of a 29-year-old local councillor, more than 800 people have been killed by ETA since its formation. However, it is now thought that ETA no longer believes it can achieve its aims by violent means.

Aum Shinrikyo (renamed Aleph)

On 20 March 1995, sarin gas was released on the Tokyo subway, resulting in the deaths of twelve people.

The attack was by far the most widely reported action of Aum Shinrikyo, a controversial neo-religious group led by Shoko Asahara (1955–present). Aum claim to be guided by Buddhist and Hindu doctrines.

Shoko has been sentenced to death by hanging.

Japanese Red Army (JRA)

Fusako Shigenobu (1945–present) founded the JRA in 1971 as a breakaway group from the Japanese Communist League. The stated aims of the JRA were to overthrow the Japanese government and monarchy, and to start a world revolution. During her travels around Europe and the Middle East, Fusako forged strong links with the PFLP (Popular Front for the Liberation of Palestine), who gave help with training, finance and weapons.

Fusako was arrested in Osaka in 2000 and sentenced to twenty years in prison.

Khmer Rouge

Khmer Rouge was formed at the 1959 Congress of the Peoples Revolutionary Party of Cambodia, but kept its name secret until 1967.

Under the leadership of Brother number 1, Pol Pot (born Saloth Sar) (1925–98), Khmer Rouge launched national insurgency and a guerrilla war across Cambodia in 1968. They managed to gain control of the country in 1975, and continued to rule until 1979. Estimates of the deaths which are directly attributed to Khmer Rouge during this period vary between 1.7 million and 3.3 million.

Pol Pot 'officially' dissolved the organisation in 1996, but a few of the surviving leadership await trial for crimes against humanity.

MISCELLANEOUS

Bulletproof Vest

The first US patent for a bulletproof vest was issued in 1919, but body armour was not introduced into general police use until 1931, when the vest's effectiveness was demonstrated to the Washington Police Department.

The so-called bulletproof vest was not successful against high velocity bullets until Kevlar was introduced in 1971. Kevlar is a lightweight, high-strength synthetic polymer fibre, which was the first to offer the level of protection needed for stopping bullets. It was developed in 1965 in the laboratories of DuPont of America by Stephanie Kwolek (b. 1923).

Peace Treaty

The earliest known peace treaty was concluded in 1269 BC between the Egyptian pharaoh Rameses II and King Hattusilis of the Hittites, following the Battle of Kadesh, in modern day Syria, in 1275 BC. The battle was inconclusive although Rameses claimed it as a great triumph.

The language of the treaty is Akkadian, and it is written in cuneiform script on clay tablets, fragments of which still exist. The greater threat to both countries by invaders known as the 'Sea Peoples' encouraged the signing of the Treaty of Kadesh, which covered non-aggression, and mutual protection in the event of invasion of one country by an enemy.

Zoos

Modern zoos are places of education, conservation and research. In the Western world they are subject to the scrutiny of animal welfare organisations, and staffed by dedicated, professional animal experts, and are generally open to the public. Zoos were not always this way: they began as places of entertainment for the privileged few.

The first known example of birds held in captivity is in 4500 BC, in Arpachiya (modern-day Iraq). Pigeons were kept captive in large numbers for exhibition.

The earliest examples of animals held in captivity took place simultaneously in India and Egypt around 2500 BC. The Mohenjo-Daro civilisation of India kept elephants for both work and exhibition, and the ancient Egyptians kept a variety of exotic animals, including lion, mongoose and baboon, which were generally preserved for the amusement of royalty.

Two great zoos were constructed in ancient China In 1150 BC, the Empress Tanki had a 'house of deer' built of marble, and in around 1000 BC, the Emperor Wen Wang established what he called the Garden of Intelligence, for the housing of rare animals. The grounds of the Garden of Intelligence extended to 1,500 acres.

King Solomon (reigned 962–922 BC), who is widely regarded as the greatest of the ancient kings of Israel, not only established a massive harem, but also a zoo in about 930 BC.

The first serious study of animals began in the zoos of ancient Greece, between 700 and 200 BC. In 340 BC after detailed research in the zoos, the Greek philosopher Aristotle (384–322 BC) wrote his book *The History of Animals*. Aristotle's most famous pupil, Alexander the Great (356–323 BC), arranged for the capture of strange and exotic animals on his military campaigns, which he had shipped back to Greece for study.

The Greek philosophers Epicurus (341–270 BC) and Anaximander (*c.*610–*c.*546 BC) both thought of ideas about evolution. These were not fully developed until Charles Darwin's work in the nineteenth century.

The first to stage large-scale fights between animals and later between animals and gladiators were the ancient Romans. The animals had initially been kept for observation and display, but were quickly used for public entertainment, including the spearing of animals by the audience.

The first English collection of animals was made in the twelfth century by Henry I (AD 1069–1135), who maintained a zoo in Woodstock, Oxford. Henry established collections of big cats such as lion and leopard, together with camels and birds of prey such as owls.

It is thought that modern zookeeping began in 1752 with the opening of the zoo at the Tiergarten Schonbrun in Vienna. The Empress Maria Theresia (1717–80) and her husband Franz Stephan (1708–65), who later became Holy Roman Emperor Francis I, commissioned the design and construction of the zoo at their summer palace at Schonbrun. The zoo was opened to the public in 1778, but only to 'decently dressed persons', and only on Sundays.

The term zoo was first used in 1826 after the foundation of the Zoological Society of London. The principal founders were Sir Stamford Raffles (1781–1826), who also founded Singapore in 1819, and the physicist Sir Humphry Davy (1778–1829) who, among many other things, invented the miners' safety lamp, which bears his name. The stated objective of the Zoological Society was 'the advancement of zoology and animal physiology, and the introduction of new and curious subjects of the animal kingdom'.

The Zoological Society also led the way in publishing the first scientific journal on the study of animals, and its publication the *Journal of Zoology* has been continuously published since 1830. A Royal Charter was granted to the Zoological Society by George IV (1762–1830) on 29 March 1829.

London Zoo opened its collection to the public in 1847 although it had originally begun to collect the animals for scientific research in 1828. Sited on the north side of Regent's Park, London Zoo claimed to be the world's first scientific zoo (ignoring Aristotle's work in the fourth century BC). The full title of the collection of animals was the Zoological Gardens, but this was soon shortened to 'The Zoo' by the visiting public, and the word 'zoo' passed into common use.

The first zoo in the USA was New York's Central Park Zoo, which opened in 1864. In the four years leading up to the authorisation of the zoo by the State Legislature, the growing collection of animals was put together through donations from members of the public. A black bear cub and 72 white swans were among the donations.

Although grizzly bears, captured by the famous bear hunter James 'Grizzly' Adams (1812–60), had been kept for exhibition in a San Francisco basement as early as 1856, the San Francisco Zoo, known as Woodward's Gardens, was not opened until 1866.

The revolutionary breakthrough in zoological studies came on 24 November 1859 with the publication of *On the Origin of Species by Means of Natural Selection*, written by Charles Darwin (1809–82). In his book Darwin puts forward his now generally accepted theory of evolution, in which traits arising in species are passed from generation to generation.

The original paper on the evolution of species was presented to the Linnean Society of London on 1 July 1858. The paper was a joint presentation between Darwin and Alfred Russel Wallace (1823–1913). Darwin had spent many years formulating his theory, and Wallace had written his own paper, exactly mirroring Darwin's theory, while working in Malaya. In all innocence he sent his findings to Darwin for advice, and it looked for a while as if he had beaten Darwin to the announcement of the theory of evolution. In the end Wallace was persuaded by Darwin's friends to share the honours and the two became lifelong friends.

Although the theory of evolution, or natural selection, is referred to as Darwinian theory, Charles Darwin was not the first to propose the idea in modern times. His own grandfather, Erasmus Darwin (1731–1802), wrote:

Would it be too bold to imagine that in the great length of time since the earth began … would it be too bold to imagine that all warm-blooded animals have arisen from one living filament … possessing the faculty of continuing to improve by its own inherent activity, and delivering these improvements by generation, world without end?

Earlier, several French botanists had proposed the basis of organic evolution. In 1815, one of their number, Jean-Baptiste Lamarck (1744–1829), had even produced an evolutionary diagram charting the progress of humanity from a single cell to man. He proposed the theory that organisms possess an 'inner feeling' towards perfecting their species, thus preparing the way for evolution theory. However, none of the French theorists presented persuasive evidence of the process.

Epilogue

In compiling the *Book of Origins*, much has been left by the wayside. I excuse myself that even the *Encyclopaedia Britannica* misses some things out, although to be fair – not much. Let's hope what is in this book provides an insight into the origins of some important things, and that it helps, if only in a pub quiz.

A good book has no ending.
R.D. Cumming

The author and editors have made painstaking efforts to ensure the information in *The Book of Origins* is accurate, and in accordance with the latest information available. The most revered textbooks have been systematically scoured, and the World Wide Web has been 'Googled' in the quest for accuracy and precision. However, it is acknowledged that some of the facts within this book are the subject of debate.

We would be pleased to hear from readers who wish to add to the knowledge within this book. The author and publishers will be happy to include any corrections or fresh information in the next edition.

Please send all comments or suggestions to Trevor Homer either by email to info@piatkus.co.uk or by post, c/o Portrait Books, 5 Windmill Street, London, WIT 2JA.

INDEX